Understanding
Emerging Markets

Understanding Emerging Markets

CHINA AND INDIA

Peter Enderwick

Routledge
Taylor & Francis Group
New York London

Routledge
Taylor & Francis Group
270 Madison Avenue
New York, NY 10016

Routledge
Taylor & Francis Group
2 Park Square
Milton Park, Abingdon
Oxon OX14 4RN

© 2007 by Peter Enderwick
Routledge is an imprint of Taylor & Francis Group, an Informa business

Printed in the United States of America on acid-free paper
10 9 8 7 6 5 4 3 2 1

International Standard Book Number-10: 0-415-37085-X (Softcover) 0-415-37084-1 (Hardcover)
International Standard Book Number-13: 978-0-415-37085-1 (Softcover) 978-0-415-37084-4 (Hardcover)

Library of Congress Cataloging-in-Publication Data

Enderwick, Peter.
  Understanding emerging markets : China and India / Peter Enderwick.
    p. cm.
  Includes bibliographical references.
  ISBN-13: 978-0-415-37084-4
  ISBN-13: 978-0-415-37085-1
    1. China--Economic policy--2000- 2. India--Economic policy--1991- 3. International trade. 4. International economic relations. 5. International business enterprises. I. Title.

HC427.95.E53 2007
330.951--dc22   2006029144

Visit the Taylor & Francis Web site at
http://www.taylorandfrancis.com

and the Routledge Web site at
http://www.routledge.com

Contents

Acknowledgments

I would like to express my appreciation to Professor Des Graydon, Dean, and Jenny Bygrave, Deputy Dean, AUT Business School, for providing me with the time, space, and resources to complete this book. Associate Professor David Taylor supplied a constant stream of useful articles and discussion pieces on China and India that were extremely valuable. Finally, excellent research assistance was provided during 2005 by Pai-Ling Huang for which I am most grateful.

Auckland
October 2006

1

INTRODUCTION

Introduction

This book addresses one of the key economic trends of the early twenty-first century—the spectacular economic resurgence of large emerging economies, in particular the economies of China and India. While economic development has a long history, the pace and scale of development within these two countries is unprecedented and will have far-reaching implications for anyone interested in business. Already, local stores are packed with goods manufactured in China, university classes are shared with international students from China and India, and few have not heard about the threat to jobs as services are *outsourced* to lower-cost economies such as India. It is no exaggeration to say that these economies and the business models they encourage are changing the structure and operation of the world economy. In many ways this is a positive development—China has brought lower prices and greater choice, India adds tremendously to the world's stock of intellectual capital, and both countries offer huge new market opportunities. On the other hand, there will be problems adjusting to the rise of these countries. Production will shift, jobs may be lost, demand for commodities and energy resources will result in higher prices, and levels of pollution are likely to rise.

For those interested in the world economy, the present time is one of unprecedented change and importance. Recent estimates (*Economist* 2006a) suggest that for the first time in almost 200 years, emerging economies have begun to regain the importance they enjoyed for most of the last two millennia. Measures of gross domestic product (GDP) based on purchasing-power parity suggest that emerging economies now produce slightly more than half of world output, and that in the past five years their growth has accounted for more than one-half the increase in global GDP. Furthermore, in 2004 and 2005 the thirty-two largest emerging economies all enjoyed positive growth—a sign, perhaps, of their increasing robustness (*Economist* 2006a; *Economist* 2006h).

Emerging economies' share of world exports has grown from 20 percent in 1970 to 42 percent in 2005 (*Economist* 2006h). Their increased integration and trade success means that they now account for two-thirds of the world's foreign-exchange reserves. In terms of international trade, they offer huge opportunities for producers in wealthy countries. Half of American, European, and Japanese exports now go to emerging economies, and this trade is growing twice as fast as trade among wealthy countries. In large part, this is a result of the considerable dynamism within these countries and their very high growth rates. At the same time, economic growth within wealthy countries is increasingly constrained by low population growth rates and an aging workforce.

While we may debate the relative merits and drawbacks of the rise of China and India, we can all probably agree on four things. First, the rise of these economies has had, and will continue to have, a tremendous impact on our lives as consumers and producers. Second, barring a major crisis, high rates of economic growth will continue in these countries, and their relative economic importance will increase. Third, we have no moral right to deny the opportunity of economic growth to the more than two billion people living within these and other developing countries. While the rise of China and India may appear to threaten lifestyles within the already wealthy countries, we have no moral basis for excluding other aspirant nations. Fourth, the driving force behind the growth of emerging economies is globalization and the increased integration of these countries within the global economic system. This means that we are all likely to be impacted by their economic success and to enjoy opportunities to share in this success. For all these reasons, it is essential that anyone with an interest in business have an understanding of the economic, political, and strategic implications of the rise of these countries. This is the aim of this book. It offers what I hope is a topical, practical, and holistic interpretation of the economic resurgence of China and India.

Rationale for the Book

The plethora of books and articles addressing the economic renaissance of China and India and its likely impact on the world economy means that some justification for a further addition to this literature is required. There are two sets of justifications. The first recognizes the limitations of current studies. While many of these are excellent single-country studies, their focus is necessarily selective. It is the concurrent renaissance of China and India, together representing more than two billion people or 40 percent of the world's population, which is such a unique and far-reaching development. This unprecedented scale of economic development has profound implications for the international business environment. Furthermore, considering these emerging markets separately is unhelpful: the reality is that in many areas—the attraction of manufacturing and services, or the pursuit of energy resources for example—China and India work closely together.

A second justification is that this book attempts to go beyond existing treatments and develop a number of new insights. One distinguishing feature is the emphasis on the dynamism of big emerging markets and, how they have developed and are likely to evolve in the future. A second innovative feature is the broadening of the discussion beyond simply the immediate business concerns in emerging markets to include consideration of the political and strategic implications of the rapid growth of these large economies. Third, this book also considers the emerging cooperative relations between China and India and what they might mean for business competition.

Structure of the Book

The eight chapters that follow analyze the rise of China and India. Chapter 2 provides a discussion of the significance of both countries for the world economy. Reversing 300 years of economic marginalization, China and India are expected to reemerge as major economic powers over the next few decades. Their development is already having measurable effects on world markets and relative prices. Chapter 3 broadens the discussion to consider the challenges of doing business in large emerging markets. Unlike most of the developed economies, emerging markets are characterized by sizable risks, market failures, widespread corruption, and the disadvantages of foreignness. At the same time, these economies are developing rapidly, and Chapter 4 attempts to model the evolutionary process as well as highlight some of the obstacles that must be overcome in China and India if growth is to be maintained. Chapter 5 starts from the perspective that examining either China or India in isolation may be erroneous, and that their primary importance stems from their overlapping economic renaissance. While they complement each other, they also actively compete and collaborate in other areas. The relationships between the two are complex and dynamic. Chapter 6 recognizes the reality that China and India have implications for more than just the international economy. Strategic, political, and military impacts are also apparent and are changing the nature of global relations. The lessons of all this are summarized in Chapter 7, which highlights what must be done by both business and policy makers as they seek to adjust to the rapid economic rise of more than two billion producers and consumers. The final chapter offers some closing thoughts.

The balance of this chapter discusses what is meant by the term *large emerging markets* (LEMs) and the key characteristics of these markets, followed by a discussion of the opportunities that LEMs offer international business.

What Is a Large Emerging Market?

To understand what we mean by a large emerging market we must first define the concept of an emerging market. Initially the term *emerging market* was applied to the former Soviet satellite states that were emerging from a *planned* to a *market* economy. More recently its use has been generalized to replace the term *developing country* in describing economies at relatively low income levels (Cavusgil et al. 2002; Montiel 2002). Emerging markets share many of the characteristics that used to define developing countries. They typically have large agricultural sectors; marked disparities between the rural and urban or modern and traditional sectors; low productivity; poor infrastructure; and unfavorable outcomes in health, education, and nutrition. Using this interpretation there are more than 150 emerging economies accounting for almost 85 percent of the world's population.

However, not all poor countries can accurately be termed emerging economies. *Economist* magazine monitors a group of some 25 emerging countries. A defining criterion is that these economies are experiencing positive momentum with concomitant change and development. The World Bank defines an emerging economy as one that has an average per capita income of less than $9,000 and is experiencing rapid growth and economic transformation. A large emerging economy is simply one that has a sizable population. The most commonly identified large emerging economies are the so-called BRICs—Brazil, Russia, India, and China.

Characteristics of Emerging Economies

It is possible to identify a number of characteristics that are widely shared by emerging economies.

Economic Characteristics

In economic terms, emerging markets enjoy some of the fastest growth rates in the world. However, this growth is often variable with marked fluctuations. This was shown most clearly with the 1997 Asian economic crisis, which dramatically slowed growth rates in the region for around two years. While China has enjoyed high and relatively stable growth over the past two decades, Indian growth rates over the same period have shown significant fluctuations. Between 1985 and 1987 the GDP growth rate was around 4 percent (the so-called *Hindu rate*); this peaked at 10 percent through 1989 before falling below 2 percent in the crisis year of 1991. The liberalization triggered by this crisis saw average growth of around 6 percent in subsequent years.

A further complication is that rapid growth is often accompanied by high levels of inflation, which in turn can prompt government to curb growth. The fear of price bubbles, typically in property or stock markets, exacerbates growth fluctuations. China experienced a sharp rise in the inflation rate in 1996 and 1997, and fear of a resurgence of inflation triggered a sharp monetary squeeze in the second quarter of 2004, which is credited with bringing the underlying rate of inflation back down.

Furthermore, the benefits of growth in emerging economies are not enjoyed universally. Growth is often accompanied by a widening of income disparities. In many countries the most significant disparity is between the traditional (generally agricultural) and modern (industrial) sectors. In the case of China, there are huge disparities between the rapidly developing coastal cities and the more remote inland areas. Similarly, recent growth in India has been heavily concentrated in just four of its fourteen major states (Commonwealth of Australia 2001).

One economic characteristic shared by both China and India is their reliance on remittances from nationals working overseas. Not surprisingly, given their considerable diasporas, India and China are the two leading recipients, both receiving more than US$20 billion in 2005. For India this represented 3.1 percent of GDP; for China this represented a more modest 1.3 percent (World Bank 2005).

Technological Characteristics

A second characteristic of emerging markets is their limited investments in technological development and their dependency on the advanced economies for technology (Singh 2006). While R&D (research and development) spending in China and India has increased in recent years, these levels are far below those of the advanced economies. In 2002 R&D spending as a percentage of GDP was 1.23 percent in India, 1.29 percent in China, and 2.7 percent in the United States. In absolute terms in the same year, the United States spent US$252 billion on R&D; China's spending at $60 billion was less than one-quarter of this amount, while India spent just $19 billion. Because of the considerable cost differences between these countries, it is illustrative to also consider standardized measures such as R&D workers per million of the population. The United States with 4,048 had seven times as many R&D workers than China and twenty-six times more than India.

Technological outcome measures, such as high-tech products as a percentage of all manufactured exports or patents granted, also show how China and India lag behind the developed countries. High-tech products comprised 32 percent of all U.S.-manufactured exports in 2002, 20 percent for China, and just 6 percent for India. In addition, most of China's high-technology exports are produced by foreign-funded firms (Dauderstadt and Stetten 2005; Gilboy 2004; Goodman and Segal 1997). In terms of patents granted by the United States Patent and Trademark Office in 2002, China's figure of 266 was just 0.27 percent of the U.S. level, while India's was a mere 0.18 percent. A more general index, the UNCTAD (United Nations Conference on Trade and Development) Innovation Capability Index, which combines various technological and human capital measures, ranks China at 74 and India at 83 of a total of 117 countries in 2001 (UNCTAD 2005).

In the case of China, this reliance is apparent from its massive imports of high-technology products, often from the United States; its dependence on inward investment for technology transfer; and the dominant role that foreign-funded firms play in the export of high-tech products from China. China's decision in the 1990s to permit wholly owned foreign investments rather than requiring joint ventures as it had previously has probably limited this source of technology transfer. China's expenditure on technology is heavily biased toward foreign manufacturing equipment, which typically accounts for around 80 percent of technology imports compared with knowledge in the form of licensing, know-how, or consulting. China is also weak in terms of its technological infrastructure, such as collaborative linkages, market knowledge, and domestic technology supply chains (Gilboy 2004).

Technological conditions in China and India are improving rapidly. Both countries recognize the importance of developing capability in higher-value activities (*Economist* 2006e; Rodrik 2006; Shenkar 2005). Both are successfully attracting R&D investments from major multinational enterprises (UNCTAD 2005). Major multinationals, including Microsoft, Motorola, GE, and Intel, all have R&D facilities in India; many others are also in China. At the same time, Chinese and Indian companies are increasing their R&D spending. The Chinese telecommunications and networking company Huawei spends 10 percent of turnover on R&D. The same is true of the Indian pharmaceutical producers Dr. Reddy's and Ranbaxy. Firms from these emerging economies are also internationalizing their operations in an attempt to get access to technological resources. Huawei now has research centers in India, Sweden, the United States, and Russia. The Chinese computer manufacturer Lenovo acquired IBM's personal computing division in part to gain access to its technological capability. Complementing these initiatives at the firm level, both the Chinese and Indian governments are seeking to improve the technological climates within their countries. India has recently strengthened its intellectual property laws. By the end of 2002, China had established 53 technology parks and 49 economic and technology development zones. We will consider the technology capability of both countries in more detail in Chapters 4 and 5.

Sociocultural Characteristics

The sociocultural conditions in many emerging markets present formidable challenges. Many emerging markets are characterized by considerable ethnic and cultural fragmentation (Luo 2002), with some, such as Indonesia or the former Yugoslavia, to the point of destruction. China and India are relatively well placed in this regard. China comprises 92 percent Han Chinese, the largest ethnic group in the world. The small ethnic minority population is found mainly in the border areas. Ethnically, India is predominantly Indo-Aryan, accounting for more than 70 percent of the population. In terms of religious composition, 82 percent of Indians are Hindu and 12 percent are Muslim. Generally, these groups coexist successfully.

Both countries have experienced continued urbanization, although levels are lower than in many other emerging economies. More than 60 percent of China's population is still in the rural sector. However, income differentials and attractive employment opportunities mean that the urban drift will continue. China has 666 cities; 34 of these have populations in excess of one million. India is experiencing similar pressures with its urban population accounting for just over 30 percent of the total. One-third of the urban population lives in metropolitan cities, those with populations of at least one million. India has 40 such cities. Because of low agricultural productivity, India's urban population accounts for 60 percent of national income. Both countries will experience further internal migration, reducing upward pressure on wages.

Political Characteristics

It is widely argued that a universal characteristic of emerging economies is political risk. This results from a number of factors. One is political instability—the uncertainty surrounding the continuation of a particular regime. While this is not a significant concern in China with the domination of the Communist Party, or in India with its vibrant democracy, it is commonplace in other emerging economies. Many emerging markets are also characterized by ethnic conflict and instability. According to the Human Security Centre (2005), India was the second most conflict-prone country (number of conflicts multiplied by duration) in the postwar period. This was largely the result of its long-term involvement in Kashmir.

A second source of political risk occurs where there is widespread protectionism and government intervention. High tariff levels, assistance for infant industries, and ideological views that support government ownership and control of strategic industries create significant risks for international business. While China has traditionally pursued state ownership, this support is declining in the face of reform and significant growth of the private sector. India presents a far more confusing picture with high levels of trade protection, extensive restrictions on foreign ownership, and conflicting signals from national and state-level governments. The experience of Enron's uncompleted Dabhol energy project, which the company claims incurred total losses of $5 billion, is illustrative. Enron claimed that the project was rendered no longer viable when the Maharashtra state government reneged on a contract to buy the electricity produced.

Economic reform represents a third type of political risk commonplace in emerging markets. While liberalization and privatization create new opportunities for international investors, those who move early face high risks as operating conditions may be unclear and subject to unpredictable change. These risks are compounded where other institutional reforms, such as judicial processes and intellectual property protection, fail to keep pace with reforms.

Nature of Business Systems

Business systems in emerging markets are likely to differ considerably from those found in the mature market economies of the West and Japan. The major difference is that many emerging economies, particularly those in Asia, are best described as relationship based rather than market based. This means that business relationships have a strong personal content—friendship or kinship based—creating difficulties for outsiders seeking to break into the market. This type of system is termed *guanxi* in China, for example. Relational business systems are often challenging for those accustomed to the greater certainty of a rule-based system.

Relationship-based economies are also vulnerable to the problem of corruption. Indeed, many of the most corrupt business systems are found in emerging economies. Both India and China are rated as highly corrupt by Transparency International (2005). Corruption adds to the costs of doing business (Gray and Kaufmann 1998). It raises both transaction costs and uncertainty. It is unfair in the sense that it is a regressive tax that imposes a considerable burden on smaller firms. Corruption also distorts resource allocation. By raising transaction costs, corruption reduces the amount of investment, both domestic and foreign. It can also distort sectoral resource allocation, favoring large projects (where potential bribes are likely to be greater), and encourage greater levels of technology intensity than would be warranted by factor costs and conditions. More generally, corruption encourages behavioral shifts favoring rent-seeking as opposed to wealth-creating activities.

The markets of emerging economies also display some notable characteristics. Many are best characterized as *sellers markets* because of the considerable restrictions on imported products and inward investment, as well as the concentration of inefficient production in the hands of state or private monopolies. The result is often pent-up demand, which is rarely satisfied by low-quality products at seemingly expensive prices. Marketing sophistication is generally low, and limited market research information discourages investments in differentiation. Few local firms are able to utilize product, process, or organizational innovations and therefore offer little technological competition. These conditions offer both challenges and opportunities to international businesses and are explored more fully in subsequent chapters.

Opportunities in Emerging Markets

For international businesses, emerging markets offer a wealth of opportunities. Their size, high rates of growth, and diverse cost and operating conditions mean that they feature strongly in the strategic planning of many multinational firms. An overview of the structure of the Chinese and Indian economies is provided in Table 1.1. We can identify three principal types of opportunities offered by large emerging markets like China and India. They are attractive markets for goods and services, low-cost sources of supply, and locations for learning about competition and new business practices.

Markets

The first opportunity provided by emerging economies is as new markets. It is only comparatively recently that countries such as China, Russia, and India have opened themselves to international trade and investment. In many cases these emerging markets are relatively large and are experiencing high growth rates. As a result, there has been strong growth in both investment and consumption. Rapid growth brings strong demand for commodities as significant investment in plant, equipment, and infrastructure occurs.

This has created a boom and high world prices for exporters of commodities such as cement, steel, and energy. As per capita incomes rise, many millions of households acquire consumer goods such as automobiles, white-wear goods, and electronic products. Emerging

Table 1.1   An Overview of China and India

	CHINA	INDIA
Population (millions)	1281	1048
Population growth rate (%)	0.87	1.51
Political system	Communist, centralized	Parliamentary democracy, increasingly decentralized
Key economic driving sector	Manufacturing	Services
Economic policy focus	Outward	Inward
Involvement in the global economy	High	Low but rising
Attitude toward trade and FDI (foreign direct investment)	Positive and consistent since 1978	Ambiguous, inconsistent since 1947
Recent economic liberalization commenced	1978	1991
Size of diaspora (millions)	55	20
Major internal challenges faced	Demands for democracy Political change Income disparities	Terrorism Infrastructure needs Economic change Income disparities
Geopolitical risks faced	Taiwan South China Seas	Kashmir Pakistan
Press freedom (country ranking 2005)	159th	106th
Value of retail sales 2003 ($ billion)	550	250
Consumption data 2003		
Cement: Total market volume (million tons)	816	108
Per capita consumption ('00 kgs)	6	1
Steel: Total market volume (million tons)	255	32
Per capita consumption (kgs)	197	30
Cars: Total market volume (000's)	14,550	6,900
Per 1,000 people	11	7
TVs: Total market volume (millions)	391	103
Per 1,000 people	301	97
Telephone lines: Total market volume (millions)	545	65
Per 1,000 people	420	62

Source: Ahya and Xie 2004.

markets are particularly attractive because ownership levels of these products are generally low; the potential for future growth is immense. Furthermore, consumers in these markets are not as loyal as in the advanced countries, and it is possible to both grow a market and capture significant market share. For all these reasons, the major international consumer goods producers and retailers have flocked to emerging markets.

Attempts have been made to quantify the size, growth, and attractiveness of emerging markets. One such attempt by Michigan State University CIBER (Center for International Business Education and Research) (Cavusgill 1997) ranks the major emerging markets on several dimensions, including size and growth rate, business conditions, and risk. Market size, as measured by population and energy consumption, clearly favors China and India. Similarly, both countries score well in terms of market growth rates. They compare less favorably with other emerging economies on measures of purchasing power and importance of consumption. Both score badly in terms of the ease of doing business as measured by commercial infrastructure, market openness, and country risk. Overall, in 2005, both China and India were ranked within the top ten most attractive emerging markets (GlobalEdge 2005).

Success in emerging markets generally involves more than simply introducing products that were developed for advanced countries. Differences in income levels and consumer behavior mean that attractive market segments may necessitate lower prices, quality, or engineering specifications. Good examples of these qualitative differences and the need to rethink market segments and strategies are provided in the following boxes. In the case of the Indian car market, sales trends seem to suggest the benefits of focusing on smaller vehicles. This market development has important implications for potential investors. First, it favors Japanese and European producers, who have considerable expertise with cars of this size. Second, it shows that the Indian market is quite unlike that of China, where institutional buyers (government and business) have favored larger more expensive vehicles. Third, this example highlights the need to rethink traditional business models, which in the car industry have not associated small vehicles with profitability and certainly have never indicated that cars can be produced profitability for less than US$2,500.

Box 1.1 The Indian Car Market: Where Small Is Definitely Better

While car sales in India are growing rapidly, the strongest growth is in the small car segment. Of the 800,000 cars sold in 2005, 600,000 (75 percent) were small cars with an engine capacity of less than 1,300 cc. This type of car appeals to the majority of Indian consumers because of relatively low incomes, increasingly con-gested roads, a government tax policy that favors small cars, and the expertise of Indian-based producers of such vehicles. Indeed, India is rapidly becoming a global base for small car production.

Expertise in small car production is strong in Japan, where about 1.5 million small cars are sold each year, as well as in Europe, with around one-half million per year. Not surprisingly, manu-facturers from these parts of the world, rather than the United States, dominate the Indian market. Suzuki, the majority partner in India's Maruti Udyog, is Japan's leading producer of small vehi-cles and is now investing huge sums in its Indian capacity. Of the five new models that Maruti expects to launch over the next five years, at least three are expected to be small cars. Hyundai, which has been Maruti's strongest competitor, produces only its small car, the Santro, in India. It also exports from India. Hyundai expects India's small-sized car market to grow to 960,000 units by 2010 from 600,000 in 2005, driven by economic growth of 7 to 8 percent and the stronger purchasing power of India's burgeon-ing middle class. European producers, such as Renault (who have a tie-in with Mahindra and Mahindra), Volkswagen, Fiat, and Skoda, all of whom have expertise in the production of small cars, are showing considerable interest in India. Local producer Tata is talking about a new car costing less than US$2,500 for the local market.

India has a number of factors favoring the development of a global hub in small cars. Costs of production, particularly labor, mean that small car manufacturing can be profitable in India. Several international firms accept that they can build in India for one-third the cost in the United States. The Indian car-components sector is well developed with many innovative, high-quality suppliers.

Source: Suveen K. Sinha, Rediff.com, January 13, 2006.

Box 1.2 Danfoss: Overengineered for the Market?

Danfoss is a large Danish industrial controls company that has been cautious in tackling the Chinese market. During the mid-

1990s the company moved some of its manufacturing of valves, compressors, and motion controls to China to take advantage of low labor costs. Some of the output was sold to Chinese companies, while some was exported.

However, Danfoss has recognized that its strategy in China needs to be rethought. It started by replicating European production lines and in the early years used the same suppliers. More recently some local subsuppliers have been contracted. In 2004 the company took a close look at its Chinese operations. It discovered that while it was meeting the top end and some of the middle of the market, its product lines ignored the low end. And the low end was large—large enough to give the company a 15 to 20 percent market share if it could successfully penetrate the bottom end.

To do this, Danfoss had to create new products. Existing products were seen as too well engineered for this part of the market. Developing new products also meant substantial operational and organizational change, in fact, the adoption of a new management model. Products had to be made with local components and manufactured with less capital-intensive techniques. They had to be distributed within some 40 urban areas across the country, and this required a significant boost in staff. New products had to be designed from scratch, and European engineers were not thought to have the appropriate mind-set. In response, Danfoss acquired a number of Chinese companies and began to tap into their products, R&D, and distribution systems. They also established their own R&D centers within China focusing on the major market segments for refrigeration, air conditioning, and heating.

Neither product replication nor adaptation was enough. For Danfoss, success in China required a major revision of existing business models.

Source: W. E. Hoover Jr. 2006.

For Danfoss in Box 1.2, a failure to fundamentally rethink their business model in China caused them to overlook the largest part of the market. Tapping into this segment meant major structural change to overcome the inertia and mind-set of a Eurocentric strategy. However, overcoming these constraints does open up immense market opportunities.

Low-Cost Production

The second major attraction of emerging markets is as a source of productive resources—human, natural, and technological—that can be combined to lower production costs. The very large emerging markets of China and India offer a wide variety of resources, including natural resources such as coal, iron ore, and agricultural land and people ranging from the most to the least skilled. Because of a plentiful supply, human resources are also far cheaper in these markets than in the advanced economies. Labor costs at a West German car plant are around fifty times higher than at a comparable plant in China. Wage levels for software engineers in the United States are five to six times those of their equivalents in Bangalore. Technological capability, while still restricted to pockets of expertise in India and China, is increasingly attracting research and development investment. Major multinationals are investing to take advantage of India's expertise in IT (information technology) and pharmaceuticals, as well as China's engineering capabilities. Of course, many talented Chinese and Indian nationals leave each year to study or work overseas.

The opportunities for accessing resources are even greater within regional economies such as Greater China. In this case, through investment or offshore sourcing, an overseas producer can access the design and manufacturing expertise of Taiwan; the low-cost manufacturing facilities on the mainland; and the financial, logistics, and design capabilities of Hong Kong. The synergistic interaction among these activities makes the Greater China region particularly attractive.

While the labor cost savings offered by markets such as China and India are considerable, overall savings may be much lower when other costs such as shipping, tariffs, and currency fluctuations are factored in. There may also be hidden costs associated with offshore sourcing, including problems with information security, high defect rates, concerns over ensuring business continuity, and the negative publicity that offshoring can bring. Offshoring consultants suggest that a wage gap of 300 to 400 percent is necessary to make a move offshore worthwhile. Indeed, evidence on the financial benefits of offshore sourcing is mixed. The large number of firms that have relocated work overseas would suggest that there are sizable benefits. Delta Airlines, for example, expects to save $15 million per year by shifting its reservation services to India and the Philippines. But at the same time, a number of well-known companies including Dell, Ford, Powergen, and Group 1 software have brought processes back home. Survey evidence also reveals a mixed picture. Several studies have reported savings with average estimates of 11.4 to 14 percent (Ethiraj et al. 2004; Weber 2005), while other research highlights the possibility of higher costs (Bona 2004). Regardless, the strong competition faced in many industries means that the pursuit of lower-cost resources and production locations will continue.

Learning Opportunities

The third attraction of emerging markets results from the opportunities they provide for learning. Their diverse and, for many Western-based businesses, novel business systems create unique opportunities to understand the behavior of consumers, competitors, suppliers, and government officials. With their massive markets and unique supply conditions, China and India offer huge opportunities for companies to pioneer new strategic approaches and business models. This is important because of the massive profits that can result from operating in a market where there are few competitors— so-called *Blue Ocean strategy* (Kim and Mauborgne 2005). Such markets are generally created through the development of a new business model, as illustrated in the cases of Google, e-Bay, and Cirque de Soleil.

Consumer behavior in emerging markets is likely to differ quite significantly from that in wealthier markets. There may be less brand loyalty, more experimentation in product use, considerable ignorance of market offerings, and a much greater focus on value for money. In many cases, products must be tailored to match particular market needs. Cummins launched a range of small diesel engines in India, targeted at farmers, shops, and commercial establishments, which suffer frequent power outages. Tailored to the needs of the Indian market, these generators were low in cost, fuel efficient, and very reliable. Generators supplied to farmers feature comprehensive dust covers and filters to enable operation under the harshest conditions. Car companies in China have developed features that are of particular interest to local buyers. For example, the Hyundai Elantra sold in China has a strengthened chassis and wider tires to cope with the rough roads and includes a hands-free kit for the large number of mobile phone users. The Hyundai Santro, the company's small car offering in India, has a reduced engine output to increase fuel efficiency. Hyundai also strives to keep down the prices of spare parts to suit Indian market conditions.

The centrality of relationships in many emerging economies highlights the importance to investors of successful relations with government officials. The value of local knowledge and contacts also encourages the use of joint venture modes of entry. Historically, such ventures have been of particular importance in China but are becoming increasingly widespread in India. Achieving success in such relationships provides valuable lessons for any international business.

As indicated above, operating in emerging economies gives access to new sources of supply and supply cost structures. This can result in a lower cost of components or complementary business services. For example, having the Cummins R&D center in Pune, India, gives it access to a sufficiently large number of low-cost software engineers, allowing it to simulate modeling and testing of engines on a scale that was never possible using high-cost North American research staff. This has substantially reduced subsequent prototyping costs (*BusinessWeek* 2005a). A number of global producers, such as General Motors, now use suppliers in China and India to lower their costs of production as part of a global strategy. Wal-Mart's dependence on numerous Chinese suppliers has enabled them to pass on substantially lower prices to their U.S. customers.

A unique learning experience is provided by the rapid evolution of emerging markets. Investors attracted from the mature industry structures of the developed economies face decisions regarding the timing of entry and the development of strategic positioning, which they may not have faced at home for many years. Entry timing—whether to enter before or after competitors—can be critical to success in many emerging markets. Similarly, the rapid growth of these markets means that strategies must be revised on a regular basis. The car industry in China, which is experiencing rapid growth in demand for smaller vehicles as more private buyers enter the market, has moved to the disadvantage of early entrants such as Volkswagen, which established itself as a producer of large vehicles targeted at government and corporate buyers. Similarly, the most profitable segment of the market for beer in China is now at the top end, requiring foreign brewers to have, or to acquire, a premium brand.

One of the key lessons that international investors in China have learned is that competition is relentless and profit margins are difficult to maintain (Bremner 2005; *Business Week* 2005m). This is illustrated by the experience of Volkswagen. In August 2005 the company announced that it was slashing prices on more than a dozen models in an attempt to regain market share. The reductions of up to 13.7 percent put the price of a basic model Santana at 79,800 yuan ($9,800). This represents a 10,000 yuan discount. With output soaring and capacity increasing, Volkswagen and other auto producers have been obliged to continually cut prices. Although costs have been trimmed through local sourcing of parts, profit margins have withered. In 1990, Santana's sold for about $27,000. Facing fierce competition from global competitors such as General Motors, and local producers such as Chery Automobile, Volkswagen has seen its market share fall from over 50 percent in the 1990s to a present level of 18 percent.

Doing business in emerging markets also increases the likelihood of facing new, and sometimes different, competitors. Many indigenous firms may be national in their focus. In India the larger firms are likely to be family owned and may form part of a large conglomerate. They may enjoy considerable protection from both national and local government officials and cumbersome industrial policies. Within China, state ownership also brings government protection and preferential access to resources. Part of the opposition to CNOOC's (China National Offshore Oil Corporation) attempt to buy a U.S. oil company was the result of a belief that the Chinese state oil company had access to virtually unlimited government-guaranteed, low-cost finance. State ownership is used to build national champions in China. Favored firms have access to cheap land and credit and to lucrative government contracts. Where desirable they are selected as partners for foreign investors, providing them access to leading technology and management skills. The Legend Group, which is the majority owner of Lenovo, is two-thirds owned by the Chinese Academy of Sciences, giving Legend preferential access to the country's 60,000 leading scientists. To international businesses from Western market economies, the presence of such less-than-arm's-length relationships may be seen as an unfair competitive advantage.

In the extreme case, success in an emerging market may necessitate major product adaptations or even the adoption of a completely new business model. These changes may result from the problem of product counterfeiting, which is extremely widespread in markets such as China. Counterfeits are found in industries as diverse as vehicle parts and pharmaceuticals. In some cases, product adaptations can reduce the problem. Because of widespread faking of its Budweiser brand in China, often involving the refilling of old bottles, Anheuser-Busch began to use an expensive and rare imported foil. The company also introduced temperature-sensitive labels that turned red when cold. This significantly raised the cost and difficulty of counterfeiting. Nokia has started to produce cell phone batteries with holographic images and 20-digit identification codes that can be verified online. Yamaha, while licensing five plants in China to make its motorcycles, discovered another 45 that also produced bikes branded as Yamaha. This prompted them to rethink their design and manufacturing processes in China and to more than halve sales prices. This has forced counterfeiters to also lower prices and presumably margins (*Business-Week* 2005b).

Where problems of counterfeiting are seemingly insurmountable, new business models may be necessary. For example, the market for electronic games in China is quite different from those in Japan and the United States. Pervasive counterfeiting of software discourages manufacturers such as Sony and Microsoft from selling consoles in China. Rather, the 26 million players participate in online gaming where software can be protected on corporate servers. Furthermore, consumers can access these games with simply a PC and Internet access. For lower-income consumers, the advantage of not having to buy a specific console is considerable. This new business model has been pioneered by Chinese companies such as Shanda and online games by South Korean firms, who are the world leaders.

The Chinese pop music industry provides an even more extreme case where artists make most of their earnings not from the sale of recordings but from concerts, endorsement deals, and appearing in commercials. CD recordings are seen primarily as a promotional tool. More generally, the ability of Chinese and Indian manufacturers to push down costs and prices to levels previously unthinkable by Western manufacturers is forcing all firms to look at how products are designed, produced, and distributed in emerging markets. However, some emerging markets may not yet be ready for the innovative business models that have provided competitive success in advanced economies. Dell's pioneering direct sales approach in PCs has seen it achieve a world market share of more than 17 percent. However, in the high-growth emerging markets of India and China, its share is less than one-quarter of this. The problem is the low level of Internet access in these countries. As a result, PC buyers favor retail outlets and computer specialists to the benefit of firms such as HCL Technologies, HP, and IBM (whose PC division is now Chinese owned) who have invested in traditional distribution channels (*BusinessWeek* 2005c). The marketing innovations made by Hindustan Lever in India (see Box 1.3) have enabled the company to grow both the overall market and its own market share.

Box 1.3 Marketing Innovation: Hindustan Lever, Ltd.

Hindustan Lever, the Indian subsidiary of Unilever, recognizes the importance to its future success of rural consumers. The company has spent more than 20 years building a distribution system that gets its products into almost every town and village in India. It is now using that system to access a new market segment—the very poorest rural residents. This is a consumer group that wants value above all else. It is also a group that traditionally has had very little disposable income and even less brand loyalty.

Lever recognizes that tapping into this sizable segment requires more than just lowering prices; real creativity is necessary. The company has been forced to rethink its product development, sales, and marketing strategies. In terms of selling, to reach millions of rural consumers the company has had to move to a direct selling model, using entrepreneurial women to resell its products. This is a significant departure from its traditional stratified distribution channels and highly trained sales reps. Marketing of its personal products emphasizes folklore through music, performance, and drama. The message is one of understanding the need and value of hygiene, not simply brand switching. Product development for this segment has turned out to be more expensive than for higher-income groups. This may be surprising for those who believe that developing products for lower-income consumers simply involves a watering down of standards and quality.

The market for shampoo in India provides a fascinating case study of what must be done to capture poorer consumers. While India is home to 16 percent of the world's population, it accounts for 28 percent of the world's hair because of the long locks that Indian women maintain throughout their lives. While self-indulgence is discouraged among Indian women, there is pride in hair grooming. However, for Hindustan Lever, one challenge was overcoming the traditional practice of using soap for hair and body wash. Product developers spent a year developing a low-cost soap that would be suitable for both the body and the hair. An existing beauty brand, Breeze, was extended to Breeze 2-in-1. To target women who were not even willing to try shampoo because they believed it was too harsh for the hair, the company undertook a creative advertising campaign and marketed a Lux shampoo in sachet size. The results have been pleasing. One-third of India's 60.6 million pounds of shampoo sales in 2000 came from sachets in rural India, and Lever has 70 percent of those rural sales.

Source: R. Balu, June 2001.

Why the Focus on China and India?

Of the two major emerging countries, China is clearly the most significant by virtue of both its earlier start on the development path and its higher growth rates. For this reason it receives greater prominence in this book. This is justified by the statistical picture. Of the four largest emerging economies, the so-called BRICs—Brazil, Russia, India, and China—China is by far the largest, larger in fact than the other three combined. China's GDP is more than twice that of India, and its contribution to world economic growth over the past five years has been more than three times that of India. China's dominance is also apparent from external economic relations. China's trade is six times larger than India's; indeed, in 2003 China's *increase* in trade exceeded the value of India's total trade. A similar picture emerges with regard to foreign direct investment (FDI), where China's stock of such investment is thirteen times that of India. China has also been fortunate in the timing of it growth surge. Historically, this has occurred at a time when China's traditional rivals—Russia and Japan—have been weak. For all these reasons, China is undoubtedly the most important emerging economy and is treated as such in our discussions.

A number of reasons have been suggested in explaining India's underdevelopment when compared with China. One explanation is simply that India suffers from a later start in pursuing development. While China began to open its economy in 1978, it was not until 1991 that India commenced serious economic reforms (see Table 1.1). Second, the differences in political systems between the two countries are also used to explain the differences in economic growth and development. China, with its highly centralized and authoritarian political system, is better able to direct resources and to move quickly in terms of policy implementation. India, in contrast, finds its economic policy process hampered by its political democracy. Democracy per se is not the problem; it is the highly fragmented nature of the political system that creates problems. The Indian government at the turn of the millennium comprised 42 political parties, 17 of which had only one seat. The present coalition comprises more than 20 parties. The tendency toward moderation and the difficulties of achieving consensus has impeded further policy reform. A third factor is thought to result from the highly protectionist and insular industrial policy regime that operates in India. This has resulted in severe restrictions on foreign investment and even firm size in selected industries.

In contrast, China has opened key development sectors such as electronics, telecommunications equipment, and automobile manufacturing to foreign investors. The outcome has been much higher rates of growth, competitiveness, and beneficial spillovers. Fourth, much higher savings rates as well as huge inflows of direct investment have enabled China to make extensive and sophisticated infrastructure investments. This is despite the fact that China appears to use capital less efficiently than India (*Economist* 2005a). On almost any measure Indian infrastructure lags well behind China. China has ten times as much paved roadway as India, power costs are 40 percent lower, and telephone penetration rates are six times higher in China (*Economist* 2005a). This raises the costs of doing business in India and may discourage business investment when managing supplier relations and distribution become more difficult.

Conclusions

This chapter has provided an introduction to our discussion on the rise of China and India. An overview of large emerging markets highlights their distinctive characteristics as well as the considerable business opportunities they bring. They provide untapped markets, sources of low-cost and unique factors, and opportunities for the development of new business models. Of the four large emerging economies—the BRICs—China and India are by far the most important and the focus of subsequent chapters.

Implications for Management

1. Into the foreseeable future, rapid growth in some of the world's most populous countries will create unprecedented opportunities.
2. However, such markets also bring huge managerial and strategic challenges.
3. Large emerging economies offer more than just new markets; they can be a low-cost production location or provide resources

and learning opportunities for the creation of new forms of competitive advantage.

4. Of all the large emerging markets, including Brazil, Russia, and Indonesia, China and India appear to be the most attractive.

5. Modification of products and services for these markets may not be sufficient; product or business model innovation are often prerequisites for success.

Discussion Questions

1. Identify the types of firms and industries that are likely to see China or India as primarily:
   a. a market for selling products and services;
   b. a source for low-cost production;
   c. a source for creating competitive advantage.
2. Do the challenges of operating in emerging markets outweigh the benefits? What would you say to convince a Western personal computer maker thinking of entering the Chinese market?

2

THE SIGNIFICANCE OF CHINA AND INDIA

Introduction

Interest in the growth and development of China and India is at an unprecedented level. This interest ranges from admiration through fear to downright hostility (Enright et al. 2005; Prestowitz 2005a; Sull 2005). The rise of China and India is triggering a matching range of national responses from upgrading to maintain competitiveness to selective protectionism. Perhaps surprisingly, much of the concern is not recent. More than 100 years ago, commentators were raising the spectra of Chinese competition and its threat to Western economies (Thery 1901). The problem with this and similar more recent views is the failure to recognize that the rise of economies such as China and India has positive as well as negative impacts. This suggests that preventing trade, investment, or outsourcing in these countries is not in the best interests of anyone. Far more important is the need to understand the likely impacts—both positive and negative—as well as their distributional effects and, where desirable, how to devise appropriate policies to minimize the detrimental impacts.

The spread of globalization to emerging economies has caused a massive shift in relative prices—particularly those of labor, capital, commodities, and products. The most apparent of these concern commodities and labor. High oil prices, which have coincided with the rise of China and India, are one manifestation. Emerging economies now account for 47 percent of global oil consumption. Their demand has meant consumption has matched output despite a 14 percent increase in supply between 1997 and 2005 (National Intelligence

Council 2004). The result has been a very strong oil price over the last three years. With regard to labor, the integration of China, India, and the former Soviet bloc into the world economy has doubled the size of the global labor force. Not surprisingly, this has had a detrimental effect on poorly skilled workers in the wealthy countries, many of who now compete with a much less expensive workforce in emerging economies. The result has been stagnant or declining real wages for the least skilled, particularly within the least regulated labor markets such as the United States. At the same time, the new opportunities and more efficient global deployment of capital has pushed up returns to businesses and investors.

Data highlighting the growing importance of the large emerging markets are supported by survey evidence on the intentions of international executives. This reveals the growing significance of China and India in particular in international operations. Also noteworthy is the attraction of these markets as sources of new customers and resources and not simply lower cost production locations (PricewaterhouseCoopers 2006).

A Return to Domination?

China and India playing an important role in the world economy is not something new.

Before the Industrial Revolution brought the economic rise of England and continental Europe, today's emerging economies dominated world output. Indeed, estimates suggest that for almost two millennia (until 1820) they accounted for around 80 percent of global production (Maddison 2001). However, throughout most of the twentieth century their share was only 40 percent. Within the group of emerging economies, China and India have historically been the most important. For most of recorded history, China has been the world's largest economy. Two hundred and fifty years ago, Asia (primarily China and India) accounted for more than half the world's gross domestic product. European and, later, American industrialization saw a dramatic change of fortunes. By the end of the twentieth century the United

States and Europe accounted for two-thirds of global GDP while Asia accounted for only 20 percent (*Economist* 2006a; Mandel 2004).

Competition between China and India also illustrates radical changes in fortunes. Maddison's figures show that while China's and India's per capita real incomes were approximately equal in 1870, India enjoyed significantly faster growth until the start of the First World War. Both experienced a decline in per capita incomes in the interwar period, with China experiencing the sharpest decline. By 1950, India's per capita income was about 40 percent higher than China's. Since 1980, China's very high growth rates have propelled it past India, resulting in an average per capita GDP level twice that of India (see Table 2.1).

China and India: Similarities and Contrasts

The simultaneous emergence of China and India as high-growth economies suggests that these two countries might be quite similar in many ways, and these similarities might help explain why these particular countries have grown so strongly, in contrast to the many other emerging economies. Certainly, there are many similarities. Both countries are demographic giants—the only two countries with populations in excess of one billion. Both have long and venerable histories, and both have experienced a sharp decline in economic power and influence over the past three centuries. Both have been subjugated by Western colonial powers. Their march to national independence has, in both cases, been led by forceful and charismatic leaders—Nehru in India and Mao in China. In line with thinking at the time, both leaders advocated relative economic and cultural protectionism, with key industries under state control. This condemned their economies to decades of slow growth and at times crisis and decline. More recently, both China and India have begun to reverse these policies, increasingly integrating themselves into the global economy. And in both countries economic resurgence is being driven by the creation of relatively low-skilled jobs.

Both countries possess multiple strengths, not just economic power. They both enjoy considerable political, diplomatic and mili-

Table 2.1   China and India: Economic Structure and Trade

	CHINA	INDIA
Nominal GDP 2003 ($bn)	1410	575
Per capita GDP 2003 ($)	1087	545
GDP per capita growth 1991–2003 (annual average % rate)	9.9	4.2
Composition of GDP 2003 (%)		
Agriculture	14.6	22.2
Industry	52.3	26.8
Services	33.1	51.0
Informal economy as a % of income 2004	13.1	23.1
Savings as a % of GDP 2002	42	24
Gross fixed capital formation as % of GDP	40	22
Level of FDI 2002 ($bn)	53.0	4.7
FDI as a % of GDP 2002	4.1	0.8
Remittances from overseas nationals 2004 ($bn)	21.0	21.7
Remittances as a % of GDP 2004	1.3	3.1
Exports as a % of GDP 2002	25.7	10.3
Imports as a % of GDP 2002	23.3	12.8
Export growth, annual average		
1980s	11.1	6.9
1990s	16.9	9.9
Share of world merchandise trade		
1948	0.9	2.2
1983	1.3	0.5
2003	5.9	0.7
Exports of goods per capita 2003 ($)	260	55
Share of world services exports		
1980s	0.6	0.7
1990s	1.4	0.6
2003	2.5	1.4
Services as a % of total exports	12	33
Main export destinations (% share of total exports)		
Asian countries (excluding Japan)	32.1	24.7
United States	21.1	20.8
Japan	13.6	3.6
European Union	16.4	21.7

Table 2.1   China and India: Economic Structure and Trade (continued)

Main import origins (% share of total imports)		
Asian countries (excluding Japan)	37.7	18.9
United States	18.0	3.0
Japan	12.9	20.4
European Union	8.2	7.2
Share of all exports accounted for by foreign affiliates (%)	50	—
Share in high-tech industries	90	—
Share of all imports	52	—
Manufacturing exports as a % of GDP 2004	30	8
Average tariff (%)	18.2	32.5

Sources: Data from Ahya and Xie 2004; *Economist* 2005a; .

tary influence. Both also have powerful diasporas, particularly in other parts of Asia. China has some 55 million and India 20 million overseas nationals. These individuals have played quite different roles in facilitating development (Bolt 1996; Cohen 1997; Panagariya 2001). Overseas Chinese from Taiwan, Hong Kong, and Singapore have been active in bringing capital, technology, and buyer links to the mainland, particularly in the form of direct investment. This has greatly facilitated Chinese economic growth. Indians living overseas have not played a similar role, in part because many of them have followed professional rather than business careers. Those in business tend to focus on small-scale, location-specific activities, such as restaurants and retail outlets. Their main contribution has been in the form of remittances to relatives and friends in India. At the same time, China and India face similar economic challenges. The governments of both countries are concerned about unemployment, regional disparities, and persistent poverty in the rural sector.

While sharing these similarities, it is the contrasts between the two countries that are most striking. Their economic structures are markedly different. China is the manufacturing workshop of the world; India, in contrast, excels in services. Thus, one country has emphasized hardware, the other software. This difference in development path is reflected in recent economic growth. Between 1990 and 2003, industry accounted for more than half of the GDP increase experienced by China, while services accounted for 62 percent of the GDP increase experienced by India over the same period. Indian industry experienced very modest growth during the 1990s, and its share of GDP has remained more or less stagnant at around 27 percent (Roach 2004). China produces two-thirds of all photocopiers, microwave ovens, DVD players, and shoes; over one-half of all digital cameras; and around two-fifths of personal computers. India, by contrast, is strong in software, IT consulting, call centers, and chip design. It is increasingly competitive in financial analysis, industrial engineering, analytics, and drug research.

The two countries also have complementary capabilities. China excels in infrastructure, such as buildings, roads, power distribution, and telecommunications networks—areas where India is weak. On the other hand, India enjoys a vibrant democracy, an independent media, and rapid rates of information dissemination. These are all areas where China could learn a great deal.

It should be apparent that India is pursuing a very different and pioneering development model—one built on services. This is in marked contrast to the more traditional manufacturing-led path pursued by China. There are two main reasons for India's choice of development path. First, the service sector is less constrained by India's weaknesses—a low level of savings, limited inward foreign direct investment, bureaucratic regulation, and inefficient infrastructure. Second, India's strengths in education, particularly tertiary-level technical skills, widespread usage of the English language, and information technology competency, all facilitate the development of internationally traded services. Technical developments and the opening of once-protected service industries means that this model may provide an increasingly viable base for national development. It is not only low-skilled service tasks such as call centers, remote data entry, and data processing that are internationally tradable; increasingly professional services, business processes, and most recently research and development work are being relocated (UNCTAD [United Nations Conference on Trade and Development] 2005).

These complementarities between China and India have led, in recent years, to a surge of interest in bilateral business relations. This has been facilitated by political initiatives that have created closer relations between the two countries following the low point resulting from the Sino–Indian War of 1962. Progress on a long-running border dispute over Kashmir, China's support for India becoming a permanent member of the UN Security Council, and the possibility of a bilateral free trade agreement has boosted economic relations. The two governments have also identified the desirability of combining Indian software with Chinese hardware technology to dominate the global information technology industry (Prestowitz 2005b). Trade between the two countries has grown from US$300 million a decade ago to US$10 billion in 2004 (Greenspan 2004). India supplies IT services, raw materials, and semifinished goods, as well as shipping services to China. China has begun to serve Indian consumers by exporting electrical machinery, home appliances, consumer electronics, and mechanical goods. These complementarities are discussed more fully in Chapter 5.

Size Versus Growth

Interest in the emerging economies of Asia is more about their growth rates and potential than it is about absolute size. China accounted for less than 5 percent of world GDP in 2004, compared with 32 percent in the United States and 13 percent in Japan (*Economist* 2006a).

One of the most influential sources regarding the growing significance of China and India has been the Goldman Sachs report (Wilson and Purushothaman 2003) that examines future growth trends of emerging economies. Simply extrapolating recent growth rates and assuming that current policies are maintained results in the conclusion that India's economy will be larger than Japan's by 2032, and that China will overtake the United States by 2041. This means that the three largest economies by 2050 would be China, the United States, and India. Despite very high growth rates, per capita income levels in China and India will still be well below those of the United States and other wealthy economies, but in terms of economic size, China and India will be among the giants. Because of its much higher birth rate, India is likely to enjoy the strongest growth, particularly beyond 2020. This could enable a thirty-five-fold increase in per capita income in India between now and 2050. Of course, predictions of this type are highly sensitive to underlying assumptions. The key assumptions relate to the continuation of sound macroeconomic policies, the development of stable political institutions, investment in education, and a commitment to economic openness. As Table 1.1 identifies, some of these assumptions are highly questionable for India where there have been sharp reversals in policy, problems in raising the quality of education, and slow progress in liberalization and deregulation. The management implications of these projections are far-reaching. They suggest that in the future the largest economies may no longer be the richest countries, and to capitalize on these opportunities, marketing effort will need to focus further down the wealth pyramid (Prahalad 2005).

Global Engine of Growth

Size and growth rates in China and India have made them a key growth pole in the world economy, contributing significantly to global growth. While both countries are blamed for the loss of manufacturing and service sector jobs in the developed countries, they are also a key source of growth. China's high growth rate saw imports rise faster than exports in 2003. U.S. exports to China increased by more than 20 percent in 2003, more than ten times faster than trade with the rest of the world. China accounted for more than 70 percent of Japan's export growth over the same period, adding 0.7 percent to GDP growth. Consumers worldwide have enjoyed falling prices as a result of increased sourcing from China (*Economist* 2003a). One estimate suggested that China contributed a full 1 percent to world growth of 2.7 percent in 2002 (*Asia Today International* 2003).

At the regional level, China is having a far more significant impact than India. China's imports have had a major impact on neighboring economies, particularly Indonesia, South Korea, and Japan. Chinese investments in Australian energy have been important in maintaining that country's high growth in recent years. India, despite being the largest and fastest growing economy in South Asia, has had less of a regional impact. To a large extent, this reflects the difficult relations between India and Pakistan. Where India has implemented a trade agreement, such as in the case of Sri Lanka, business has increased markedly.

The most impressive example of regional development is Greater China—the result of the growing economic integration of mainland China, Hong Kong, and Taiwan. There are a number of manifestations of this growing integration: (1) there are an estimated 500,000 Taiwanese living in China, (2) China has become Taiwan's leading trade partner, and (3) Taiwanese firms control about 70 percent of China's output of IT products. More generally, Greater China's share of total world exports has reached 9.6 percent, exceeding Japan.

The development of Greater China is being driven by both the market reforms pursued by China and the complementary resources, such as capital, manufacturing expertise, business services, and access to overseas markets, provided by Taiwan and Hong Kong. The result is the establishment of a massive manufacturing base replete with component suppliers. In 2000, more than 80 percent of components used in Taiwanese-owned factories in south China came from Taiwan; by 2002, more than half were sourced locally (*BusinessWeek* 2002a). China's principal growth impacts are likely to be on other Asian developing countries as opposed to the developed countries. It runs a trade deficit with much of Asia, and its top import markets in 2003 were Japan, Taiwan, and South Korea. Similarly, its most important import categories were electrical machinery, office and other machinery, and telecommunications equipment. If it is capturing jobs, most are likely to be at the expense of developing countries such as Mexico.

China as a Threat?

At the same time, China is a competitive threat to a number of other regional economies. China brings a combined threat in that its growth rate has pushed up the prices of commodities, adding to production costs, while at the same time its huge cost advantage has brought lower prices and sharpened competition. The threat to Asian economies that have followed the dominant regional model of government-directed, export-oriented manufacturing is obvious. This is the same path that China has pursued with such success. China not only dominates labor-intensive manufacturing of textiles, shoes, and toys but is also rapidly gaining market share in computer components, telecommunications equipment, and other electronics. Of its exports in 2003, office machinery, telecommunications equipment, and electrical equipment were worth more than three times the value of apparel exports. The injection of foreign capital and know-how is raising competitiveness in more sophisticated products, including automobiles, machine tools, and petrochemicals. This rapid upgrading is possible because it is supported by the activities of foreign investors in China. Similarity in product categories imported and exported suggests that China is a processing center, with much of this undertaken by multinational firms. In 2000, foreign-funded firms absorbed 52 percent of all Chinese imports (Lardy 2002).

The extent of China's competitive threat varies among economies. One estimate suggests that China and Japan compete directly for around 20 percent of goods exported to the United States. For Malaysia and the Philippines, the corresponding figure is closer to 65 percent, and for Thailand and Indonesia it is almost 70 percent (Kwan 2004). However, the fact that countries such as South Korea, Malaysia, and Thailand have trade surpluses with China suggests that the market attraction effect may outweigh the competitive effect. This view is supported by analyses of manufactured export performance, which suggest that Chinese imports from neighboring Asian economies have outweighed any export displacement effects (Ahearne et al. 2003; Shafaeddin 2004). However, this may be changing as China becomes increasingly competitive in medium-technology industries (Lall and Albaladejo 2004). China's upgrading is occurring at a faster pace than many rivals realize. The government is supporting local firms, which are attempting to develop new, superior technologies that could form the basis for new global standards. This is occurring in telecommunications, enhanced DVD players, and software. The thinking behind this strategy is based on the size of the Chinese market and the likelihood that standards accepted there could then be transferred to other markets around the world (*BusinessWeek* 2003a).

Concerns have also been expressed about the ability of China to attract a disproportionate share of FDI in the Asian region. In 2004, south, east, and Southeast Asia received 59 percent of all FDI attracted to developing countries, with China and the Special Administrative

Region of Hong Kong attracting 69 percent of the regional total. While this may appear to indicate a dominant position, empirical analysis suggests that China has a complementary effect on regional FDI; that is, as China attracts FDI, so do neighboring economies (Wu and Keong 2003). This may be the result of the development of integrated regional production systems, particularly in industries such as electronics (Zhou and Lall 2005).

China, acutely aware of the concerns created by its rise, is eager to build strong relationships with neighboring countries. For a number of reasons, Central Asia is an increasingly important target. The energy resources that countries such as Kazakhstan and Turkmenistan offer are one reason. A second motive is the desire to ensure that this region is prosperous and stable. Instability is likely to be rapidly transmitted to China through Xinjiang, its westernmost province. Third, strong cooperative relationships with this region would offer China support as the rest of the world struggles to accommodate China's growing power and influence (Bransten 2004). China's interest in both Africa and Central Asia highlights the opportunism of Chinese thinking: in both cases there existed a vacuum in terms of involvement by other major powers. In the case of Central Asia, the Soviet influence has declined markedly in the last decade. With regard to Africa, an apparent lack of interest has created an attractive opening for China. Involvement in these areas also highlights the broadening conception of globalization that China appears to hold, a conception that now encompasses political and security concerns and not just simply economic issues (Deng and Moore 2004).

Impacts on World Markets

The high growth rates enjoyed by China and India are impacting consumer, commodity, and capital markets.

Consumer Markets

Economic growth is likely to bring larger, wealthier, and more sophisticated markets. China's high rate of economic growth has seen over an eightfold increase in its economic power between 1978 and 2002; at the same time individual purchasing power has grown by more than six and one-half times. Of particular significance is the number of consumers who constitute a middle class—a group with sufficient discretionary income, around $3,000 per capita, to purchase consumer durables such as washing machines, televisions, motorcycles, and cars. In China and India, the number of people with such income levels is expected to double over the next three years. Indeed, if current growth rates are maintained and the distribution of income is not changed dramatically, by 2020 China will have 100 million households with income levels equivalent to those currently enjoyed in Western Europe (*Economist* 2004a). China is already the world's largest market for refrigerators and mobile phones, with more than 200 million subscribers. Over the period from 2000 through 2003, China accounted for one-third of the total increase in world import volumes and about one-half of the total export growth of other East Asian economies. However, as Box 2.1 illustrates, the growth and development of major markets is not independent of government policy. Where policy is restrictive and inconsistent, market development is likely to be impaired.

Box 2.1 Government Policy and Market Development in Mobile Phones

While China and India have similarly sized populations of around one billion consumers each, their markets have not developed at the same rate. In the case of mobile phones, China has around 200 million subscribers, while India, after seven years of service, has just 10 million users. A number of factors appear to explain this difference. One is location. The domination of China's eastern coastal region in terms of business and income growth meant that its mobile providers could enjoy huge economies of scale, which facilitated lower prices and further market growth. The Indian market is much more fragmented. Second, cultural differences have seen the mobile phone emerge as a fashion item in China. Indeed, local firms offer sharkskin and diamond-encrusted handsets. Third, and perhaps the most significant factor, has been differences in the ways the two markets are regulated.

India chose a licensing policy that divided the country into 22 regions, each with two licenses to operate mobile networks. Bidding in multiple regions was restricted. This aimed to promote competition but led to a fragmented market with a baffling array of operators, none of which achieved economies of scale. The limited availability of spectrum also hurt service quality.

China fostered competition by creating a second state-owned operator, China Unicom, to compete with the incumbent, China Mobile. Regulations favored the new player. China Unicom was, for example, allowed to undercut China Mobile by 10 percent in 1999. Prices fell, helping the market grow. Chinese providers also had access to spectrum.

In India, meanwhile, mobile operators found themselves embroiled in a series of legal wrangles with the government. The resulting uncertainty prompted many foreign operators to withdraw from the market altogether in the late 1990s. The Indian mobile operators then participated in a wave of consolidation, from which three dominant groups emerged: Bharti, Hutchison, and IDEA (a joint venture between Birlas, AT&T, and Tatas).

A more recent government intervention has enabled entry into the mobile business by fixed-line telecom firms offering *limited mobility* wireless services, with wireless coverage limited to a certain area. Mobile operators have bitterly opposed limited-mobility services, as they feel that the government's rules for the two services are different. As fixed-line firms have paid a lower license fee than mobile firms, they may be able to lure away consumers with cheaper services. Mobile operators have to pay access charges for every call made from a mobile to a fixed-line network; the fixed-line operators do not.

The result of this intervention is that the uncertainty remains, the battle between the fixed and mobile firms is far from over, and the contrast with China in market size and business outlook remains as striking as ever.

Source: *Economist* 2003d, 65.

One consumer item likely to exhibit high growth rates is car ownership (see Box 2.2). Car ownership in both China and India is expected to treble over the next decade, with take-off occurring in the Chinese market before that in India. It is not only high growth rates that these countries exhibit; in 20 years the Chinese market for cars is likely to exceed that of the United States, with India becoming the second largest market some 15 years later. Recent evidence suggests that the take-off has already occurred in China. Vehicle sales in 2005, including imported vehicles, were 5.8 million, making China the world's second largest market after the United States and marginally larger than Japan.

Box 2.2 Can China Become a Global Player in the Car Industry?

With sales of 5.8 million vehicles in 2005, China, the world's second largest vehicle market, appears to have entered the age of mass car consumption. From a small base of about 10 million vehicles, growth has been exponential, increasing 56 percent in the year 2002–2003 and 75 percent the following year. Market penetration at 7 or 8 vehicles per 1,000 people is well below the global average of 120 and the U.S. level of 600. Sales growth has been fueled by a number of factors. One involves significant recent expansion of the highway network. By the end of 2004, China had 34,000 kilometers of motorways, more than double the 2000 level. China's total road network is now the world's third longest at 1.8 million kilometers, with almost half of it less than 15 years old. By 2020, it is expected to double again.

Second, China has been able to rapidly add to capacity through the attraction of foreign investment, generally in the form of joint ventures.

Third, demand for vehicles has been stimulated by policy decisions and modernization. A restriction on the use of motorcycles in the largest cities has omitted a stage of transportation development that countries such as Thailand and Taiwan are still experiencing. WTO (World Trade Organization) membership brought increased imports and a sharp decline in domestic prices. Foreign joint ventures have also introduced new cheap models that appeal to the growing middle class. Changes in work and commuting patterns have also encouraged car ownership. With fewer workers living in accommodations provided by (and close to) state-owned enterprises, more car journeys are undertaken.

Fourth, a car culture has been encouraged through the creation of a car production cluster around Shanghai that includes component suppliers, a world-class racetrack and museum, as well as the attraction of Formula 1 racing.

In addition to the attraction of the domestic market, China is also beginning to export vehicles. In 2005, China became a net exporter for the first time, with an export surplus of 7,000 vehicles destined mainly for markets in Asia, Africa, and the Middle East. About one-quarter of these vehicles were produced by Chinese manufacturers Chery and Geely. Chery has indicated a commitment to developing new models specifically for the United States. It has an ambitious plan to sell 250,000 vehicles in the United States in 2007. To build models especially for the U.S. market, Chery has hired AVI (an Austrian company) to develop the engines and two Italian design companies that have experience with Lamborghini and Maserati. It is also arranging a distribution agreement with a company that has previous experience with Yugo and Subaru in the American market. Brilliance China, BMW's joint venture partner, plans to introduce a model into the German market in the near future. Of the foreign vehicle manufacturers, only Honda has indicated a clear commitment to export from China.

Chinese vehicle manufacturers face a number of challenges if they are to succeed in Western markets. They have limited design capabilities, problems of assuring quality, restricted access to financing, and no secure domestic market such as is enjoyed by South Korean producers. But Chinese car makers are nothing if not ambitious.

Sources: *Economist* 2005j; *Financial Times* 2005.

Commodity Markets

The most obvious manifestation of this growth effect has been in the market for oil. Rapid industrialization of China, and higher growth in India, have been central in driving up the growth in demand for energy and particularly oil to more than 2.5 percent annually. China was responsible for one-third of the increase in global oil consumption in 2003. The result has been strong upward price pressure. China's share of oil demand is expected to more than double to around 16.5 percent by 2025, while India's inefficient use of oil resources makes it likely that its global share will eventually approach that of China (Wilson et al. 2004). Growth has also fueled demand for other commodities. China accounts for about 30 percent of the world's coal consumption and 25 percent of steel products. The demand for imports has been so high that China has pushed up regional cargo shipping rates.

Capital Markets

To date, the impact of China and India on global capital markets has been limited. However, economic growth and development brings a need for deeper and more efficient capital markets, so they may be expected to grow strongly. China and India combined hold less than 5 percent of the world's financial assets, and predictions suggest that this might reach 8 percent by 2020, depending on the pace and extent of their capital market development (Wilson et al. 2004). This would still leave world financial markets dominated by the United States and Europe.

However, commitments that form part of WTO membership and the growing need for professional financial expertise mean that China is rapidly opening its financial markets to foreign banks and fund managers. This will create huge opportunities for foreign investors. Investment banks will be indispensable in driving privatization and consolidation among state-owned firms. Domestic savings, much of it languishing in bank accounts, are around $1 trillion, of which only $16 billion is in mutual funds.

Exchange Rates and Trade Balances

The United States in particular has expressed concern with China's fixed exchange rate system and the existence of a huge U.S. trade deficit. This concern has fueled protectionist sentiment. China's exports to the United States increased by 1,600 percent between 1990 and 2005, while U.S. exports to China grew by only 415 percent over the same period. In part, this phenomenal growth is the result of major U.S. buyers switching to Chinese suppliers. For example, in 2004 Wal-Mart imported $18 billion worth of goods from China, where 80 percent of Wal-Mart's suppliers are now based (Zakaria 2005). The result of a continuing trade imbalance has been a huge surplus enjoyed by China, which now has foreign reserves in excess of US$800 billion, second only to Japan.

China has faced considerable pressure to devalue its currency, the yuan, which has been pegged to the U.S. dollar. An undervalued Chinese currency provides an advantage in exporting. At the same time, to maintain this value, China must buy huge amounts of U.S. currency. Any depreciation would reduce the demand for U.S. Treasury bonds, putting upward pressure on U.S. interest rates and threatening world prosperity.

There are a number of reasons why China is reluctant to devalue the yuan. One is that any devaluation would effectively reduce the value of its foreign reserves. Second, any slowing of export growth could threaten domestic stability. China needs to create 15 to 20 million new jobs each year just to absorb population growth, workers moving from the agricultural sector, and displaced workers from SOEs (state-owned enterprises). Export industries are a major source of employment growth. A slowdown in exports would be matched by a corresponding drop in imports.

There are alternatives to revaluation. One would be to cut subsidies to exporting firms. A second would be to allow foreign investors to borrow local currency rather than bringing in U.S. dollars. A third policy alternative would be to allow Chinese investors and financial institutions to buy foreign stocks.

Domination of Labor-Intensive Manufacturing

For many countries, a particular concern is the potential competitiveness of Chinese firms in labor-intensive industries such as clothing and textiles. As trade barriers are eliminated in the clothing sector, China appears capable of achieving a dominant market share, often at the expense of other developing-country exporters (*BusinessWeek* 2003b). The elimination of quotas introduced under the 1974 Multi-Fiber Agreement has made the market for textiles virtually free. Predictions suggest that China's share of this US$350 billion global business could rise from its present 20 percent to as much as 60 percent. Much of this increased market share will be achieved at the expense of other developing countries such as Indonesia, Vietnam, Sri Lanka, Bangladesh, and Mauritius. China's advantage is more than simply low labor costs. Indeed, labor costs in the textile industry are lower in countries such as India or Indonesia than they are in China. Rather, China has built a strong competitive advantage based on a number of factors, including higher productivity; economies of scale; access to raw materials and competent suppliers; advanced equipment brought in through investments from Japan, Taiwan, Hong Kong, and South Korea; and access to buyers, designers, and logistics in other parts of Greater China (Lim 2005).

Early evidence suggests that China has certainly enjoyed a rising market share since quotas were eliminated on January 1, 2005. China's share of the U.S. clothing market rose from 12 percent in December 2004 (period of quotas) to 17 percent by mid-2005. The European Union also experienced sharp increases in uncontrolled categories including shoes (*BusinessWeek* 2005d).

Such domination is likely to be good for consumers, who will benefit from lower prices, but will entail job losses in both advanced and developing countries with significant textile industries. The question then arises as to how these countries should respond to China. Protectionist measures, such as those pursued by the European Union and the United States, are at best a short-term response. Textile firms within these countries are likely to leave the industry, relocate to lower-cost locations (including China), or upgrade to more sophisticated products and technologies. If protectionism disadvantages Chinese manufacturers, these jobs are unlikely to be created or retained in advanced countries; rather, they are likely to be taken by other low-cost competitors such as India and Pakistan. Developing countries should perhaps learn from China and seek to develop their industries as India and Pakistan have tried to do. Others are likely to lose a substantial number of jobs.

From this discussion it would be difficult to argue that China's domination of textiles is unequivocally a bad thing for the world economy. First, there are more consumers who benefit from lower prices and increased variety than those whose jobs are eliminated because of China's success. Morgan Stanley suggests that U.S. consumers have saved more than $600 billion in the past decade as a result of having access to lower-cost Chinese products. In simple terms (assuming that displaced textile workers eventually find other jobs), this suggests a significant increase in global economic welfare. Second, many of the jobs eliminated were artificially created or were in locations that long ago lost their competitive advantage. That is, their elimination was likely anyway and perhaps only hastened by the success of China.

Upgrading into High-Tech Products

One of the unique features of China's rise is its domination of labor-intensive manufacturing while it has rapidly moved up the value chain. This unprecedented combination of developments is made possible on the one hand by China's massive supply of poorly skilled labor and on the other hand by the country's ability to attract high-technology investment from overseas. This rapid upgrading is illustrated by the changing composition of China's exports. Machinery and electrical appliances went from 2.8 percent of exports in 1986 to 23.7 percent in 1997. China's share of world output of personal computers increased from 4 percent in 1996 to 21 percent in 2000; for keyboards, the increase over the same period was from 18 to 38 percent (Deloitte Research 2003).

This rapid upgrading has occurred for a number of reasons. The first has been the attraction of high-tech manufacturing plants from countries such as Taiwan, Korea, Japan, and the United States, which have shifted in a search for lower costs as well as new market opportunities. Second, China has an efficient infrastructure, particularly suppliers and logistics, that facilitates high-tech production. Third, China's annual production of graduate engineers (around 450,000) is one of the highest in the world. Their wages are low in comparative terms—

about one-tenth that of an engineer in the Silicon Valley. Fourth, a number of domestic companies are also enjoying success in relatively high-tech markets. Chinese producers now have more than one-quarter of the domestic mobile phone market, the largest in the world. More ambitious producers such as Legend have invested overseas, in this case purchasing the PC business interests of IBM to acquire more advanced technology. Fifth, government policy, and in particular the determination to set global technical standards, has facilitated the growth of high-tech manufacturing (Deloitte Research 2004a).

India is moving in a similar direction and is attempting to move into higher-value manufacturing and services. As well as call centers and remote data processing, the country is now attracting more sophisticated business processes and higher-value services, including design work and research and development. Large Indian service firms such as Wipro, Infosys, and Tata Consultancy are moving into more developed markets in Europe and North America to provide better service to their global clients. In the manufacturing area, India has developed a well-regarded automobile components industry (Box 2.3).

Box 2.3 GM's Cost Cutting Means Increased Purchases from Asian Suppliers

General Motors (GM) is planning to purchase more material in Asia and trim capacity in North America as it struggles to contain the huge financial losses in its basic automotive business. The plan includes increasing its purchases from suppliers in India from roughly $150 million currently to more than $1 billion by the end of 2008, GM spokesman Tom Wickham said in an interview.

The need to cut supply costs has been heightened by a sharp rise in steel and oil prices and steady losses in the company's North American business unit. GM buys roughly $85 billion in automotive components, steel, and other material to feed its automotive operations every year. It hopes to reduce those costs by buying more components from suppliers operating in Eastern Europe, India, China, and other parts of Asia where costs are significantly lower than in North America or Western Europe. A recent study by McKinsey estimated that carmakers could cut their annual bill for auto parts by 25 percent by sourcing more components from China and India.

The Chinese government has identified auto parts as one of the sectors it plans to expand over the next decade. Its goal is to export 10 percent of the world's $120 billion in sales of automobiles and auto parts by 2015. GM's Korean affiliate, GM Daewoo Auto and Technology Co., is expanding its role in developing new products and recruiting suppliers.

Source: J. Szczesny, *AFP (Agence France-Presse)*, August 16, 2005.

Positive Links to Developing Countries?

One of the distinctive elements of the development of the large emerging markets, and China in particular, is their economic interest in some of the poorest countries in the world. Both China and India have made substantial investments in Africa in recent years. China has made investments in more than 40 African countries (*Economist* 2004b). Much of this is prompted by the desire to secure supplies of oil, but Chinese investments increasingly target mineral exploitation, infrastructure, and even simple manufacturing. While Asia has become a significant market for African exports, Africa also finds itself importing huge volumes of manufacturing products from China—products that compete with domestic industry in South Africa. China enjoys two key advantages in developing country markets. One is a willingness of the Chinese government to complement investments with soft loans, as in the case of an oil deal with Angola. Second, Chinese firms are less constrained by domestic government policies, which in the case of the United Kingdom or United States require high levels of transparency or impose business sanctions on questionable regimes.

At the same time, China's rising competitiveness has become a threat to many developing countries. This is certainly the case in the quota-free textiles industry but also impacts on countries such as Mexico, which enjoys preferential access to the large U.S. market. Superior rates of market reform and upgrading have seen China capture market share in the United States and other markets at the expense of Mexican producers (Rosen 2003b). Employment at Mexico's *maquiladora* plants, which produce primarily for export, fell by 20 percent between 2000 and 2003 from a peak of 1.4 million (*BusinessWeek* 2003c). Continual upgrading also means that China constitutes a significant competitive threat to those economies that are at a similar or slightly more advanced level of technological development (Phelps 2004).

Is China More of a Threat Than Japan Was in the 1980s?

China's phenomenal rise, and the concerns raised by it, is not something new for the world economy. In the postwar period, similar concerns were raised by the emergence in the late 1960s of Japan as a major competitor. While China's engagement with the world economy may be at its highest point ever, these levels have been surpassed by others. For example, China's current share of world exports at 5 percent (see Table 2.1) is only half of the 10.1 percent share that Japan enjoyed in 1986. In fact, it is less than Japan's current figure of 6.6 percent. Today, China and India account for a mere 6 percent of global GDP, half that of Japan. China's trade surplus, at almost 3 percent of GDP, is smaller than that of South Korea (3.2 percent) (*Economist* 2003b).

Furthermore, there are some notable differences in the ways in which China is impacting the global economy when compared with Japan. First, China has adopted a far more open approach to development and is more fully integrated into the world economy than Japan. China's ratio of trade to GDP was 50 percent in 2004 compared with Japan's 27 percent (Table 2.1). Similarly, China's imports exceed those of Japan, even though the Japanese economy is three times larger.

Second, China's openness is mirrored in its dependence on inward investment. As Table 2.1 illustrates, FDI as a percentage of GDP in 2002 was 4.1 percent in China; for Japan the figure was a mere 2.1 percent. Foreign affiliates accounted for 57 percent of China's exports in 2004 and an astonishing 85 percent of high-tech exports (Gilboy 2004). Their share of Japanese exports is minimal.

Third, China's penetration of world markets is occurring on a much broader front than did Japan's. As well as clothing and textiles, China has rapidly gained a dominant global market share in products as diverse as luggage, bedroom furniture, and color televisions. China is also unique in its rapid shift into higher-technology products while at the same time maintaining its competitiveness in simple manufacturing products. This is in contrast to the much more focused approach of Japan, whose ascendancy was based primarily on consumer electronics and motor vehicles and an incremental shedding of labor-intensive activities. For this reason, China is a competitive concern for a much wider range of countries and industries.

Fourth, China's ability to drive down prices and threaten the security of other producers around the world is considerably greater than that of Japan ever was. Competitors report price cuts of 60 to 70 percent by Chinese producers, while the Japanese threat was more usually around 20 to 25 percent. *BusinessWeek* (2004a) believes that "The China Price" are the three scariest words that American industry can hear. Price cuts are already affecting the engineering molding business, bedroom furniture, LCD TVs, and telecommunications networking equipment. If China becomes a significant exporter of motor vehicles, similar price cuts could bring a potentially massive disruptive effect in the industry in North America, Europe, and Japan.

Fifth, China's ability to maintain a strong competitive cost advantage is much greater than was Japan's. The massive supply of labor and much weaker labor and environmental regulation mean that increased output can be managed without significant increases in labor and related costs. In Japan's case, sharp wage increases led to automation, upgrading, and overseas relocation of productive capacity. China seems likely to avoid such constraints for the foreseeable future.

Sixth, China shows remarkable speed in moving into and building critical mass within new product areas. The vast number of competing producers and government direction to tackle resource or infrastructure bottlenecks give the country remarkable responsiveness. For example, production of hand power tools was increased by 1,000 percent in just one year.

For all these reasons, China is seen as bringing a different level of economic threat to that experienced with the rise of Japan. China's scale, ability to hold down costs, and simultaneous upgrading and maintenance of labor-intensive activities, as well as its openness to the rest of the world, constitute a new type of challenge.

Is China Driving the World Economy?

The influence of China on the world economy may be much greater than many realize. In examining discrete effects—trade, employment, income distribution, demand for resources—there is a danger that we fail to see the integration of these effects and their systemic impact. The *Economist* (2005b) argues that China now effectively runs the world economy. This, it argues, is a result of China's size, its growth rate, and its openness. Because of its size and very high growth rate, since 2000 China's contribution to global growth has been almost twice that of the other large emerging economies—India, Brazil, and Russia—combined. Furthermore, China's extensive integration into the world economy means that its actions rapidly spread to other economies.

The argument the *Economist* makes is that China's reentry into the world economy has brought massive changes to supply-side conditions, adding hugely to the supply of relatively unskilled labor and productive capacity. This had a threefold effect—increasing the world growth rate; lowering inflation through of the supply of cheaper products; and changing the relative prices of labor, capital, goods, and assets.

Furthermore, these processes are not unrelated. China's massive workforce has lowered returns to labor, particularly the least skilled, and increased returns to capital. This manifests itself as stagnant or falling real wages for the least skilled, particularly in the United States with its relatively unprotected labor market. At the same time, returns to capital, primarily in the form of business profits, have increased. This is apparent from trends in the share of GDP accounted for by corporate profits. In the United States, the share of profits has grown from 5.2 percent in 1992 to 7.5 percent in 2005, a 50 percent increase.

At the same time China's vast supply of labor and low wage costs have allowed it to produce and export products at much lower prices than competitors. This has had a deflationary effect on the world economy. Simultaneously, China's need for energy and raw materials has pushed up the prices of these commodities. The result has been a shift in the relative prices of (manufactured) goods and commodities. The resulting fall in inflation rates has allowed governments around the world to lower interest rates and expand credit. Furthermore, China could continue to exercise a pervasive influence on economic conditions for perhaps another two decades. It will likely take this amount of time to absorb the perhaps 200 million underemployed Chinese, currently in the rural sector, into the industrial economy. Until then, China will be able to maintain low wages and to export deflation.

Conclusions

This chapter has examined the economic significance of the large emerging economies of China and India. We have seen that the size and rapid growth achieved, by China in particular, has brought fundamental changes to the world economy. The principal impact has been dramatic changes in relative prices in labor, product, and commodity markets. Much of the interest and concern over the reemergence of China and India focuses on their potential rather than their actual impacts. Optimistic predictions highlight the growing market opportunities and the future strategic importance of these markets.

Our discussion has highlighted a number of important points. First, it is apparent that these countries have attracted a huge amount of interest and concern. The concerns are shared by developed and developing countries that fear the competitive threat that China and India bring. Developed countries are concerned about the loss of jobs through relocation and offshore sourcing. Developing nations, particularly in other parts of Asia, compete against China and India in overseas markets and for foreign investment. However, most of the available evidence suggests that China and India bring more benefits than costs, and that they offer huge opportunities for all business.

Second, the dynamism of these markets is readily apparent. They are evolving rapidly at rates not seen before. A unique characteristic seems to be the ability to simultaneously dominate low-skilled market segments while moving steadily up the value chain. However, much of the high-tech activity, particularly in the case of China, is under the control of foreign-funded firms.

Third, the extreme concerns expressed in some quarters are a little difficult to understand. As we have seen, China's economic position is in some ways less threatening than that of Japan in its heyday of the mid-1980s. The basis of the concerns may lie in the potential for these countries to go on growing and to combine their economic, political, and military influences. Unlike Japan or the other Asian Tiger economies, the resurgence of China and India will undoubtedly alter the balance of world power to the detriment of the current G8, leading industrialized nations.

Fourth, future relationships between China and India are very hard to predict. It has only been 40 years since these two countries were involved in a direct conflict. At the same time, they share many similarities and complementarities. Their sheer size means that they can continue to grow and develop independently. What we can say with confidence is that the most likely scenario is a mix of both competition and cooperation across a range of areas.

Fifth, the success of China and India could provide valuable lessons for other emerging economies. Neither country has followed the dictums of Western financial institutions and the so-called *Washington Consensus*, and neither enjoys the luxury of the relative insignificance that countries such as Hong Kong, Taiwan, and Singapore could exploit in international markets. The experience of China and India highlights the importance of engagement with the world economy; the need for inflows of capital, technology, and ideas; and the value of a huge and rapidly growing domestic market.

Implications for Management

1. By 2050, China and India are likely to exceed the United States as the two largest economies in the world.
2. The importance of China and India means that they are already primary drivers of the world economy. Business leaders cannot ignore developments in these economies.

3. For Western businesses, China and India provide complementary opportunities—China in manufacturing and India in services.
4. China and India have already changed relative prices and hence cost conditions in the world economy.
5. The rise of China and India will necessitate a rethink of business models in an environment where the largest markets are not necessarily the richest, where a cost advantage can be maintained for decades, and where competitive advantage can exist simultaneously in low- and high-tech products and services. These are essentially new operating conditions.

Discussion Questions

1. In what ways would a change in relative prices as described in this chapter affect business decision making?
2. What are the implications for international marketing of a future where the largest markets in the world are not also the wealthiest markets?

3

THE CHALLENGES OF DOING BUSINESS IN LEMs

Introduction

The substantial attractions of large emerging markets must be balanced against the considerable challenges of doing business in these economies. While any business venture faces challenges, the number and type of difficulties encountered in an emerging market are likely to be much higher and quite different from those experienced in developed markets. This is reflected in the expectation of higher returns (a *risk premium*) from investments in emerging markets. In this chapter we discuss the principal challenges that foreign businesses are likely to face in big emerging markets. We organize the discussion around five groups of difficulties that international businesses might experience. The first results from the considerable risks—political, economic, financial, and informational—that reflect the underdevelopment and rapid change characteristic of emerging markets.

The second group of difficulties is a reflection of the size and diversity of large emerging markets; it is rarely the case that all regions, industries, or groups will share equally in the benefits of development. The nature of this problem varies among markets. For China, the principal inequalities are locational, with the southern coastal regions enjoying much higher growth rates than the western or inland regions. India also suffers regional diversity but additionally has experienced significant differences in growth rates between older manufacturing industries like steel and energy and the newer sunrise industries such as software, business processes, and pharmaceuticals.

Third, investors should be aware of the competitive situation before they commit resources to a new business. In emerging economies, market structures and the competitive environment can change dramatically. Such changes can be triggered by government policy decisions with regard to import protection, the structure of industries, support for local firms, or as a result of trade and international commitments. Changes in consumer demand can also affect the nature of competition. Competition levels can increase significantly when industry opportunities are recognized by international businesses in many parts of the world at the same time, resulting in a clustering of investments and sharp rises in productive capacity. This was a problem in the Chinese beer market.

The fourth set of challenges is a manifestation of the underdevelopment of market institutions in many emerging economies. For China, a state-owned, planned, and directed economy rendered many of the institutions found in a capitalist economy superfluous. India, in operating a *mixed model economy* for almost 50 years, severely regulated and impeded the workings of market forces. Institutional deficiencies in both countries impede the efficient operation of product, labor, and capital markets, as well as the protection of intellectual property.

Finally, in this chapter we also consider a set of problems that arise simply because an international firm is a foreigner in an overseas market. These problems, which can range from hostile attitudes toward foreign business to a significant cost disadvantage on the part of foreign investors, encourage a variety of strategic responses to minimize the so-called *liability of foreignness*. While this problem arises in every foreign market entry, it is particularly significant in emerging markets characterized by unfamiliar business systems and practices, information deficiencies, and a predominance of personal relationships. To support the analysis, Table 3.1 provides a range of business environment indicators for China and India.

Risk in Large Emerging Markets

While all markets are risky, risk levels in emerging markets tend to be higher than average. In part, this is inevitable given that we define

Table 3.1   China and India: Business Environment

	CHINA	INDIA
Infrastructure		
Road density 2002 (km of paved road/1,000 sq km of land)	34	441[a]
Railroad density 2002 (km of track/1,000 sq km of land)	8	21
Electric power interruptions (average number per month)	5	17
Fixed lines and mobile phones per 1,000 people	247.7	43.8
Digital access index, 1= highest access	0.42	0.32
Spending on energy $ bn	54.2	8.7
% of GDP	3.8	1.4
Spending on transport, storage, and telecoms $ bn	73.5	9.7
% of GDP	5.2	1.6
Infrastructure Operating Cost		
Railways (U.S. cents per ton kilometer)	2.6	7.9
Electricity cost for industrial clients (US$ per kwh)	0.03	0.08
Financial Markets		
Percentage of the world's financial assets	4	<1
Financial depth (financial stock as a % of GDP)	323	137
Percentage of financial assets held in bank deposits	65	<50
None Performing Loans (NPL) as a % of all outstanding loans	25–65	15–20
Opacity factor score[b]	87	64
Base interest rate 2003 (%)	1.7	6.0
Labor Market Indicators[c]		
Flexibility of hiring index	17	33
Conditions of employment index	67	75
Flexibility of firing index	57	45
Employment law index	47	51
Number of (internal) migrant workers (millions)	100–150	11
Business Environment		
Corruption ranking 2004 (of 145 countries)	71st	90th
Percentage of management time spent on regulatory issues	8	14
Number of procedures to start a business	12	10
Time to start a business (days)	46	88
Cost to start a business (% of per capita income)	14.3	49.8
Number of procedures to enforce a contract	20	22
Time to enforce a contract (days)	180	365
Cost to enforce a contract (% of per capita income)	32	95

Table 3.1   China and India: Business Environment (continued)

Time to go through insolvency (years)	2.6	11.3
Cost to go through insolvency (% of estate)	18	8

[a] Of 65,000 km of national highways, 56% are two lanes, 35% are one lane, and only 9% are four lanes. Speed on two-lane highways is typically less than 50 km per hour.

[b] Opacity is a measure of the absence of clear, accurate, formal, and widely accepted practices in the world's capital markets. The higher the score the higher is opacity. The U.S. score was 36, and the Singapore score was 29.

[c] 100 = most rigid.

Sources: Data from Ahya and Xie 2004; PricewaterhouseCoopers 2001; UNCTAD (United Nations Conference on Trade and Development) 2005; World Bank 2004.

emerging markets as those experiencing rapid growth and transformation. Given these conditions, risks are likely to be greater than in a static or slow-growth environment. However, the nature of emerging markets also adds to the risks that businesses face. Their underdevelopment makes it very difficult to collate and validate market information. The importance of bureaucracy and vagaries of the judicial system create delays and uncertainties in contracting. Relatively unsophisticated and thin financial markets bring volatility to growth. Sudden policy reversals can also inject instability. Widespread corruption and opacity add to the costs and risks of business. Furthermore, both China and India have shown themselves to be vulnerable to some of the newer forms of uncertainty affecting the global economy, including viruses (SARS, avian bird flu), social unrest, and terrorism in the case of India. For all these reasons, risks in emerging markets create significant management challenges.

Volatility

There is certainly evidence of volatility in emerging markets, including India and China. While there has been a long-term decline in volatility, as measured by variations in output growth rates, it remains almost twice as high in emerging markets as in developed economies (IMF [International Monetary Fund] 2005). While it was once believed that volatility had only a limited impact on growth and welfare, more recent research (Martin and Rogers 2000; Ramey and Ramey 1995) suggests that volatility may impact growth in several significant ways. The experience of the 1997 Asian economic crisis also highlighted the very considerable costs that result from a sharp recession. The principal negative impact of volatility on growth is likely to be through a reduction in investment. Investment could be discouraged where volatility increases the difficulty of accurately predicting expected future returns. Similarly, credit restrictions triggered by excessive growth or inflation could substantially raise the cost of investment funds.

Output volatility could adversely affect consumer welfare through disruption of consumption patterns. The stability of consumption patterns is an important part of consumer welfare. Variability in consumption is two to three times greater in emerging economies than in the developed countries (Pallage and Robe 2003). Volatility is a particular problem for the poorest within emerging economies. The poorest have the greatest reliance on public services and are the least able to access alternative sources of income. Furthermore, the poorly skilled lack the mobility to take advantage of new employment opportunities that may arise in different sectors or regions. There is considerable evidence that poverty increases sharply during periods of recession (Laursen and Mahajan 2005).

Assessing the sources of volatility is important for policy purposes. Variations in output growth can result from global, regional, and country factors. Clearly, a government has the least control over the first two factors but significant influence on the third. Recent evidence suggests that emerging markets are most prone to regional, and particularly country-specific, influences on output growth (IMF 2005). This suggests two important implications. The first is that the long-term decline in volatility within emerging markets is primarily due to improvements in domestic economic management, fiscal and monetary policy, deepening of financial markets, and exchange-rate flexibility. Second, the effect of increased international integration on volatility may be limited. If global influences are the least important in determining volatility within emerging markets, then increased integration may carry few risks of this type.

Unfortunately the links among integration, growth, and volatility appear to be much more complex. On the one hand, openness can reduce volatility where it enables greater specialization and flows of intermediate products. Similarly, the transfer of best practices in domestic economic management can reduce output fluctuations. Access to a wider range of markets, particularly when business cycles are imperfectly correlated, can provide producers with a more diversified and stable set of buyers. More stable export earnings can facilitate the servicing of external debt. On the other hand, integration can increase volatility if it encourages excessive specialization and vulnerability to shifts in demand and prices. Economies that become highly specialized, such as Bangladesh, which depends on textiles and clothing for 85 percent of its total export earnings, are highly vulnerable to changes in the international policy regime. Similarly, growing integration is both a cause and a result of the increasing mobility of production. China's integration has triggered a massive shift of labor-intensive production, such as shoes and computer chips from Taiwan to the mainland. Failure to adjust to such shifts could result in significant downturns and output volatility. A further disadvantage of increased integration is the danger of a bunching of investment and the creation of excess capacity. The Chinese authorities have identified ten sectors, including aluminum, autos, cement, coke, steel, and textiles, with capacity problems. Where domestic policy initiatives include restrictions on output, the result is likely to be increased volatility.

There is little doubt that economic openness contributes to economic growth (Berg and Krueger 2003), but there are a number of structural characteristics that affect the nature of this relationship. One is the level of economic development. Recent research suggests that links between growth and volatility vary with the level of economic development (Kose et al. 2004). While the basic relationship between growth and volatility is a negative one, external integration appears to moderate this relationship, particularly for emerging economies. This research suggests that the more globalized an economy is, the greater its ability to withstand higher levels of volatility without this reducing growth (Kose et al. 2004). Furthermore, higher-quality institutions and a well-developed financial sector increase resilience to external shocks and are also correlated with better-quality domestic economic management. These findings raise an important implication for an emerging economy. They suggest that the growth benefits of openness are overwhelmingly positive, and that openness can be useful in containing the negative impact of volatility, particularly external sources of volatility. Where this openness can be combined with sound domestic economic management, the extent of volatility is further reduced. In combination, this can result in a virtuous circle as growth-enhancing investment is encouraged. Faster growth then induces further investment. For international managers it is important to understand the sources of economic volatility and in particular to carefully scrutinize the effectiveness of domestic economic management.

Country Risk

Country risk refers to the level of business risk experienced in a particular country. Country risk comprises a number of discrete elements of risk, which are likely to be interrelated. Chief among these in most emerging markets are political, economic, social, and informational risks.

Political risk results from political instability and conflict as well as the robustness of political, bureaucratic, and legal institutions. Like the risks arising from economic volatility, political risk is generally higher in emerging markets than in developed countries. Emergence, implying high rates of growth and significant transitions, is often associated with policy changes and creates the need to adjust to changing conditions. In both China and India, the greatest political risks relate to external claims and conflicts. China's aspirations with regard to Taiwan and disputed territories in the South China Sea constitute its greatest geopolitical risk. Ethnic conflict and the continuation of peace with Kashmir are India's key challenges.

A number of strategies to minimize political risk are available to international managers. Widespread are the use of a powerful local partner with strong political ties and the building of links with local politicians and officials. This raises the costs to a government of interference because it imposes costs on local organizations. It may also be useful for a firm to arrange funding or guarantees from major international organizations such as the World Bank or EXIM (export-import) banks. Few governments wish to offend such organizations. Where appropriate, political risk insurance can be purchased. Many investors insist on detailed legal documentation and often arrange, in the event of conflict, for legal jurisdiction in a major center such as London or New York. Strategic integration of a local subsidiary into global operations, and particularly a reliance on the overall business for market, supplier, and technological knowledge, can reduce the likelihood that operations will be targeted by political authorities. They stand to gain little from interference in such a situation.

Economic risks relate to the volatility of growth rates discussed above as well as problems that arise from exchange rate instability, poor infrastructure, insufficient savings, and labor shortages. Neither China nor India display particularly high risks in these areas, with the exception of India's infrastructure. China's currency is linked to the U.S. dollar and, despite a modest devaluation in 2005, remains strong backed by significant financial reserves. The Indian currency is considerably weaker than the yuan and long-term has declined against the dollar because it became quasi-market determined in March 1993. It was pegged to the U.S. dollar between 1955 and 1985 and now is best described as a controlled currency.

Both China and India enjoy relatively strong savings rates, and this translates into high investment rates. Fixed investment as a percentage of GDP is 42 percent in China and 24 percent in India (Table 2.1). China has the advantages of a higher domestic savings rate, a greater likelihood that savings will find their way into the financial system, and considerable external funds in the form of foreign direct investment. In this way, China has been able to make substantial infrastructure investments while India has lagged behind and suffers a lower quality of infrastructure. It is worth noting, however, that the fastest growing sectors of the Indian economy—software and business services—have been those least dependent on traditional infrastructure such as roads, rail, and energy supplies.

Neither country seems likely to face immediate labor shortages, although one needs to be careful in simply interpreting gross labor supply figures. In India in particular, the demand is for skilled labor. Rapid growth in a number of centers has increased demand and costs of suitable workers. China's labor market suffers two difficulties: its workforce is considerably older than India's and is aging faster, and the number of English-speaking graduates suitable for employment in international businesses is a fraction of the absolute number of graduates (Farrell, Laboissiere, and Rosenfeld 2005).

Social Risks

Social risks encompass ethnic and religious conflict as well as social unrest. Such risks are a concern in both China and India. Change in China has brought a considerable rise in social unrest and riots. Official figures show a clear upward trend in both the number and size of protests (*Economist* 2005c). India faces ongoing ethnic and religious conflict, a problem that has existed since independence more than 50 years ago. In recent years there have been Maoist uprisings in Chhattisgarh state and the northeast region more generally. Conflict between Muslims and Hindus erupted in the western state of Gujarat in 2002. Social unrest is a feature of both countries but is more firmly suppressed in China than in India.

Informational Risks

An enduring characteristic of emerging economies is the paucity of quality economic information readily available. The information problem in emerging markets has several components—there are problems with the amount of information, the quality of information, its timeliness, and the fact that it may not be available in English. The paucity of information available, often only half that normally expected in an advanced market, means that decisions must be made under severe constraints. This suggests the value of local knowledge, perhaps that held by a partner organization or a competitor. Economic information may also be of questionable quality and out of date. In such a situation, the use of multiple sources and multiple disciplines, where available, is a sound practice. In some cases it may be possible to cross-check data using seemingly unrelated measures. For example, growth figures might be validated using trends in energy consumption (Rawski 2001). Because there is likely to be a relatively fixed relationship between these two measures, they might provide an indication of the validity of official figures. Obtaining more contemporary data might require private collection or the commissioning of consultants. This can add significantly to costs. A similar cost problem arises if translation is necessary for information not available in English.

At the firm or industry level, other difficulties are likely to exist. Few emerging market firms create the types of management information commonplace in Western firms. Information on costs, suppliers, and customers is likely to be limited and not widely shared. The problem arises because these firms have relatively unsophisticated information management systems, and because business decisions depend more on experience or intuition than objective data. Where this is combined with a high level of centralized decision making, access to information is extremely limited. Further difficulties arise in a formal context, such as an acquisition or partnership. Divergence in local accounting and auditing practices from globally accepted standards means that great care must be taken in valuing assets and evaluating prospects. There is also a strong likelihood that contingent liabilities and favorable agreements may be undisclosed.

These conditions suggest a number of implications for international managers (Haley 2003). First, it is likely that any firm will have to ensure extra levels of due diligence to safeguard investor interests. This is likely to add to both costs and timelines. Second, it may be useful to extend risk analysis beyond the disciplines normally included in Western markets. It may be necessary in an emerging market to include senior executives, former government officials, banks, legal experts, consultants, and academics. A wide range of information sources not only gives more data, it may enable cross-checking of validity. Third, the informal nature of strategizing under conditions of uncertainty means that similar strategies might be observed largely as a result of imitative practices. This is a rational response under conditions of information deficiency, particularly if there are grounds for believing that industry leaders have access to inside information.

Corruption and Opacity

The nature of business systems in many emerging markets, with their emphasis on personal relationships, means that the danger of corruption is likely to be high. Corruption has been defined by the World Bank (1997b p8) as "the abuse of public office for private gain." This definition implies that corruption is primarily encountered when dealing with government officials and bureaucrats. While this is likely to be the case in most emerging markets, it is possible that demand for illicit payments might be made by private sector managers. In the absence of competing alternative suppliers, this is a cost that may have to be considered. Corruption takes a number of forms. It may involve payments to politicians and government officials to obtain access to public resources or services, to secure government contracts, to overcome regulatory hurdles or administrative delays, or to avoid regulations and liabilities. Corruption begins to blur into nepotism when officials demand appointment of themselves as "consultants," or relatives as employees.

It is commonplace to make a distinction between petty and grand corruption (Tanzi 1998). Petty corruption occurs when there is a widespread expectation among public sector employees of illicit payments. In many cases, such payments are seen as an additional source of income for low-paid employees. Petty corruption creates widespread uncertainty because individuals are unsure who, when, and what amounts to pay. This clearly distorts the workings of markets, even where bribes are used to facilitate transactions. Petty corruption is a redistributive tax, being particularly onerous for the poorest members of a society. Grand corruption involves the diversion of large sums of money by senior officials and political leaders. The level of theft can be so high as to seriously encroach on economic development. Well-known examples include the Suharto government in Indonesia and the Philippines under President Marcos. Transparency International estimates that Suharto stole between US$15 billion and US$35 billion in his 31 years of rule. Marcos is believed to have diverted US$5 billion to US$10 billion between 1972 and 1986. Grand corruption is also widespread among senior public officials. The Indonesian attorney general's office estimates that the country lost $2.35 billion in corrupt payments between 2002 and 2004. It is worth noting that this level of corruption continued well after the ousting of the Suharto government, and that this figure refers only to cases investigated. Although the nature of the problem makes it difficult to assess the cost of corruption, bribes paid by businesses in the year 2001–2002 are estimated at around \$1 trillion.

Corruption has a detrimental impact on both an economy and society. Clearly it involves a diversion of funds, often from the public sector to private hands. Grand corruption may exacerbate a country's debt levels if funds designated for debt servicing or repayments are lost. Corruption also distorts investment priorities. It encourages public officials to pursue large and complex projects where more opportunities for extortion exist. These may not be the most economically desirable projects and in extreme cases can be an ongoing drain on government funds. To generate opportunities for rent seeking, policy makers may be tempted to introduce protectionist policies creating situations of oligopoly or monopoly, adversely affecting economic welfare. Corruption also imposes considerable financial costs on the public sector. Bribes are not likely to form part of declared income, so tax evasion occurs. At the same time, illicit payments add to the cost of public works. For firms and consumers, corruption generally increases costs and uncertainty. Even where the firm is able to lower its production costs through payments to circumvent regulations, this is likely to create a social cost if, for example, health and safety or environmental regulations are flouted. Corruption also imposes a cost on society as illegal behavior becomes widespread and increasingly acceptable (Dearden 2003). It can also undermine democratic processes and institutions where these exist (Doh et al. 2003).

The persistence of corruption requires the availability of opportunities to extract illicit payments. Corruption depends on policies and institutions that create the opportunities. Where the state regulates prices, determines market structures and attractiveness through a process of licensing or approvals, and empowers bureaucrats to ensure conformity with regulations, there is considerable scope for corruption. This suggests the existence of market or institutional failure. If liberalization and deregulation are combined with market-determined prices, there would be few opportunities for rent-seeking behavior. Two institutional features of a country increase the likelihood of corruption being present. One is a political sector with a propensity to increase regulation and price controls. Here, political policy can be used to increase opportunities for extracting corrupt payments.

Second, the delegation of authority to bureaucrats creates a principal–agent problem whereby it is difficult to monitor and control the behavior of public officials. It is at this level that businesses are most likely to experience corrupt dealings.

It is readily apparent why corruption is a pervasive problem in many emerging markets. The development path pursued by the majority of emerging markets, following the experience of Japan and East Asia, emphasizes industrial policy and active government intervention in economic affairs. This gives public officials considerable discretion over a range of economic activities, and hence opportunities for extorting payments. With the exception of Singapore, emerging economy officials are not likely to be well paid. The Indian experience shows that corruption is highest in those departments enjoying financial dealings with the public (Palmier 1985).

Despite evidence of the considerable costs of corruption (Aidt 2003; Gupta et al. 2002; Mauro 1995; Mo 2001) it is a problematic crime. It is by nature highly secretive; it is extremely difficult to detect and quantify. Second, unlike most other crimes, there are no obvious victims. Rather, it involves a conspiracy against the state. Third, there is a low probability of detection when all parties believe that they gain and none has any incentive to denounce others. Fourth, it is a profitable business offering high returns for very little outlay and a low probability of detection. Few emerging countries have sufficient resources to effectively investigate and punish corruption (Palmier 2003). The dynamic nature of corrupt networks suggests that there are both incentives for expansion as well as limits on the efficacy of networks. To protect those involved, it is often necessary to extend networks. This in turn increases the need to find new opportunities for extracting payments. However, the expansion of networks increases the likelihood of both defection and detection. Larger networks are also more prone to opportunism, a condition that arises when some members seek to increase their returns from the network at the expense of others. Both China and India suffer from pervasive corruption. In 2004, China was ranked 71st and India 90th out of 145 countries ranked in terms of perceptions of corruption by Transparency International (Table 3.1).

Opacity refers to the extent to which an economic or financial system lacks transparency. The lack of transparency adds to business risks and the cost of capital. A recently developed opacity index combines the problem of corruption with indicators of the transparency of legal and financial institutions. Not surprisingly, as Table 3.1 illustrates, both China and India suffer problems of opacity, China in particular. This inflicts a considerable cost in attracting and servicing capital.

Corruption and Guanxi

China provides an excellent illustration of the practicalities of delineating corruption from the more general issue of relationships. Extensive market failures in China mean that considerable reliance is placed on the development of personal networks or *guanxi*. These networks are used to facilitate exchanges in the face of incomplete or malfunctioning markets. Individuals and businesses make considerable investments in developing and nurturing *guanxi* networks (Yan 1996). At the same time, corruption is a significant problem within Chinese society and has grown dramatically over the past two decades as the economy has been opened up. One estimate is that corrupt payments may be as large as 13 to 16 percent of GDP (Damon 2003). This problem was astutely recognized by former Chinese leader Deng Xiaoping's observation that if you open the window for fresh air, you have to expect some flies to blow in.

This famous statement recognizes that one cannot expect to enjoy the considerable economic benefits of liberalization without some of the accompanying evils, including corruption.

As China seeks to develop its legal and institutional structure, in part because of obligations incurred with WTO membership, *guanxi* networks and legal systems will coexist. One problem faced by international businesses is in understanding the cultural context of *guanxi* networks. Because legal systems remain underdeveloped and unproven, *guanxi* networks will continue to play an important economic and social role. Much of what would normally be defined as illegal activity from a Western perspective may constitute acceptable behavior in China. For example, *guanxi* is linked to gift giving, but unlike Western notions of giving a gift for a gift, the Chinese do not distinguish between gifts and favors. From a Western perspective, this blurs the fine line between relationships and corruption.

Despite the probable growth of institutionalized legal systems in China, it is likely that *guanxi* will continue to be an important part of the economic system. This is despite the fact that a legal system offers considerable efficiency benefits. Such a system encourages more transactions, offers lower transaction costs, and provides greater freedom in the selection of partners (North 1990). For example, operating only within a *guanxi* network imposes an opportunity cost on members because transactions with outsiders are not possible.

While institutionalized legal systems offer efficiency benefits, for a number of reasons it is by no means inevitable that such a system will displace *guanxi* relationships in China. First, the mere existence of a legal system may be a necessary, but not a sufficient, condition for its acceptance. In addition, the system must demonstrate its effectiveness. That is, to offer security, it must be able to show that it offers impartial application as well as the enforcement of sanctions. Failure in any of these areas threatens the credibility of the system. Second, and related to the first problem, is the fact that *guanxi* networks require members to undertake considerable investments, which become sunk costs. This creates significant inertia to resist change. Third, it is not possible to simultaneously operate a *guanxi* and a legal system with the intention of comparing their relative efficiencies. Such an experiment is simply not feasible. This means that any supplanting of the *guanxi* system requires either acceptance of its considerable inferiority or massive pressure from the state or international obligations to displace the system. Fourth, in the event of litigation, imposition of a legal system would shift advantage from former network incumbents to the well resourced. Sizable resources are required to pursue a commercial disagreement through the legal process. Fifth, it is by no means clear that powerful decision makers in China would support the shift to a supra-individual legal system. Such a move is unlikely to be in the best interests of those who have invested in, and who benefit the most from, existing networks. Finally, it is important to recognize that *guanxi* is much more than simply a mechanism for effecting economic transactions. Rather, it is deeply immersed in the fabric of society (Granovetter 1985). Cultural and social embedded-ness (DiMaggio 1994) is a further impediment to change (Schramm and Taube 2003).

The likelihood of the long-term coexistence of *guanxi* networks and an evolving legal system has important implications for inter-national investors in China. First, it suggests that barriers to entry into networks will continue to be a problem. These barriers encourage new businesses to seek new opportunities rather than try to break into existing relationships. This point is consistent with the rapid emergence of the services sector in India, which has not been subject to the same degree of government regulation as industry. Similarly, the most rapid growth of new business in China has occurred in the private sector, outside the large state-owned sector with its pervasive links between business, banks, and public officials. Second, inexperi-enced foreign investors will continue to seek local partners who offer the connections that are so valuable in facilitating business. While there are many drawbacks with joint ventures, they can facilitate entry into tight business networks. Third, the expansion of network connec-tions encourages cross-industry growth strategies and conglomerate family business forms. This has certainly been the case in India and a number of other emerging markets.

Economic Diversity

The experience of the large emerging markets has been a diverse one with respect to growth and the impact of internationalization. In most cases the benefits of openness have been overwhelmingly con-centrated in particular sectors, regions, or enterprises. One result of this has been growing income inequality as development has occurred. Unequal growth is manageable in some cases but is also linked to unemployment and social unrest.

From the perspective of international businesses entering an emerg-ing market, economic diversity can be a positive feature (Cavusgil et al. 2002). The size of large emerging markets such as China and India with populations in excess of one billion means that few investors are able to serve the entire market. In most cases it is necessary to focus on a specific location or market segment. For example, many consumer goods firms target the Yangste River Delta region, a prosperous area of China with a population of more than 360 million, a region bigger than most countries. Similarly, producers seeking to subcontract manufacturing or to source intermediate products might target the Pearl River Delta. A similar diversity is apparent in India with software and business process firms concentrated in cities such as Bangalore, Pune, and Hyderabad. A limited focus on particular cities or regions substantially reduces the setup time and costs associated with entering the country. From the host country's perspective, there is likely to be an expectation that the benefits created in one area will eventually trickle down to others, perhaps in the long run creating some equalization. Governments unable to wait for trickle-down to take place may assist the process through positive intervention. This was the case with China's Go West policy announced in 2000, which seeks to industrialize, repopulate, and transform the western region, one-sixth of China's entire land mass. During the first four years, more than US$50 billion was invested in a project that is likely to take 40 to 50 years to complete.

Inequality in China has certainly increased, quite dramatically since the early 1990s (Huang et al. 2003; World Bank 1997a). The Gini coefficient, a widely used measure of the dispersion of income, reached 0.458 in the year 2000, a high level in comparative terms and a significant increase over the 1992 level of 0.376. However, it is worth noting that China's reform was from the position of an overequalized society formed under socialism (Fan 2003). Growing dispersion between the richest and poorest is also evident. While the per capita income of the top 20 percent of income earners was 2.9 times that of the bottom 20 percent in 1990, it was 4.2 times higher by 1994. The Chinese authorities recognize the danger of increasing inequalities (*Economist* 2006g; Shaoguang and Angang 1999; Watts 2006). China is undergoing a number of transitions—from command to market, from rural to urban—and maintaining stability is fundamental to the success of these reforms.

The largest disparities are between urban and rural residents and among regions, particularly the eastern coastal regions and the inland areas (Deloitte 2004b). While incomes for all Chinese have risen in recent years, differential growth rates are increasing inequality. Growth rates in the coastal region have been 3 percent higher on average than those enjoyed in the central region. Farmers have seen a modest increase in their incomes, averaging 4.3 percent per annum over the period between 1985 and 2003, largely as a result of their ability to increasingly specialize in new agricultural activities such as orchard production and animal husbandry. At the same time, the rapid development of town and village enterprises (TVEs) has provided new earnings opportunities. However, incomes of urban residents grew much faster, averaging 8.7 percent between 1985 and 2003. In addition, urban residents have benefited from the continuing provision of low-cost housing and generous health and superannuation benefits.

Regional income inequalities have long existed in China (Lu and Wang 2002). In 1949, 71.5 percent of Chinese industry was found in the coastal areas and only 28.5 percent in inland regions (Park 1997; Shaoguang and Angang 1999). Today, the economy comprises three distinct regional areas (Kanbur and Zhang 1999; Lee 2000; Yao 1997). The coastal region is by far the wealthiest and enjoys a strong technological base, superior infrastructure, and a large supply of labor. The interior area encompasses a vast land area, rich in resources but underpopulated. The western region is the most remote, least developed, and poorest. The evidence suggests that income disparities between these regions have increased, particularly following economic reforms. By 2002 the average per capita income of Shanghai was more than 13 times that of Guizhou province. According to the 2005 China human development report (UNDP [United Nations Development Program] 2005) the ratio of per capita income in eastern to central regions rose from 1.42 in 1997 to 1.52 in 2003. A large part of the increase is attributable to the rapid growth of secondary industry in the most prosperous region (Zhang et al. 2001). In 2000, the eastern region attracted more than 85 percent of total foreign direct investment (UNDP 2005). Wage growth within new industries such as telecommunications, real estate, and finance has far outstripped that in agriculture and mining. Wealth inequality is also high. According to official figures, in 2005 China's richest 10 percent had 45 percent of the country's wealth while the poorest 10 percent had only 1.4 percent.

The Chinese authorities are particularly concerned with the negative effects of growing inequality. They recognize that reform has brought huge benefits, lifting more than 150 million people above the poverty line, but that it has also brought dramatic changes to attitudes and policy. Traditional communal values are being eclipsed by growing individualism and an emphasis on material well-being. At the same time, increased decentralization of fiscal policy has weakened the ability of the central authorities to undertake extensive redistribution. The rural–urban differential has triggered some predictable responses. One is emigration from the countryside. Between the early 1980s and mid-1990s, the share of China's population living in the countryside fell from 81 to 71 percent. Second, land is being converted from agricultural to commercial use at a rate of 0.5 percent per year. Third, a number of farmers are shifting into wage- or self-employment in non-agricultural activities, raising concerns about China's ability to remain self-sufficient in grain production. The suicide rate among China's farmers has increased and has been linked to low income levels and policy idiosyncrasies. In 1990, China accounted for 40 percent of global suicide deaths (Jamison 1999) and rural suicide rates are three times those in urban areas. More generally, there is apprehension that growing inequality will foster social unrest, particularly unrest among youth. In 2004, China had a reported 74,000 cases of social unrest involving more than 3.7 million people, up from 10,000 cases in 1994. The unrest appears to be widespread involving 337 cities and almost 2,000 counties in 2004 (*Economist* 2005c). The vast majority of these involve local grievances; there is little indication of orchestrated and coordinated dissatisfaction with government policies. Rather, corrupt profit-taking opportunities and rising unemployment seem to be the key triggers of discontent (see Box 3.1).

Box 3.1 Chinese Farmers Riot Over Crop Poisoning

Thousands of Chinese farmers overturned buses, smashed cars, and attacked policemen during a riot in a village in eastern China against chemical plants that they say are destroying their crops.

Villagers said that 3,000 police officers armed with electric batons and tear gas descended on the village of Huaxi before dawn on Sunday to clear roadblocks that villagers had set up to stop deliveries to and from chemical plants built on land where rice and vegetable farms once stood.

The scene was one of complete devastation and anarchy: 40 buses lay smashed in the grounds of a local school and 14 cars were piled upside down in an alley, some draped with police uniforms. There were unconfirmed reports that two of the elderly protesters died during efforts to disperse them, and more than 100 people were treated for minor injuries in hospital.

In a country where dissent normally brings swift retribution, the weekend riots were just the latest clashes between local authorities and farmworkers, who feel marginalized by the extraordinary growth of China's economy and the expansion of its industrial base deeper into rural areas.

The 13 chemical plants in Zhejiang, built during the current economic boom and operational since 2002, produce fertilizer, dyes, and pesticides. Farmers say that waste from the factories is poisoning the wells that provide their drinking water, and that the plants periodically release clouds of stinging gas. They also claim that the effluents are causing stillborn babies and birth defects. Chen Qixian, a Dongyang government spokesman, said that 1,000 officials had taken part in the operation to remove the roadblocks, which were set up on March 24 and had stopped production at the chemical plants. Hospitals treated 128 people, of whom 36 were still inpatients. Of these, three were villagers and the rest police or cadres. Five were seriously injured. The factories have suspended operations as many laborers are too frightened to report for work.

In China, farmers do not own the land; they receive 30-year leases from the state, which allows the government to reallocate the land for industrial use without the consent of the farmers if it is approved by the village committee. Farmers have been given compensation, but for many this is not enough.

Land grabbing and rural land rights are big political issues in China, and the government has made public commitments to bridge the gap between urban rich and rural poor. In a sign of how sensitive the Huaxi rioting became, the Zhejiang government took the rare step of punishing eight officials from Dongyang and Huaxi in December for failing to "preserve social harmony."

Source: Clifford Coonan, *Times*, April 12, 2005; *Independent*, March 8, 2006.

Tackling the problem of growing inequality will require a battery of policy initiatives. Public investment continues to be biased toward urban areas. This bias is reflected in early initiatives that first opened up coastal cities and established economic zones in this region. This gave the coastal region a considerable head start in terms of infrastructure and more liberal policies. This early advantage has been consolidated by an ability to attract the overwhelming share of inward investment. The lagging regions have not been helped by the fact that the Chinese authorities pay scant regard to the linkage effects of foreign investment. The result is negligible spillover of the benefits to other regions. At the same time, farmers face heavy taxes and higher costs as a result of health care and education policies that disadvantage them. While the official urban–rural wage gap in 2004 was 3.2 to 1 (Brown and McBean 2005), if the benefits that urban residents receive are added to the high taxes faced by farmers, the true gap is closer to 6 to 1. For individuals, upward mobility is difficult because of state underinvestment in education. China commits only 2 percent of GDP to education; the United Nations suggests that 6 percent is more appropriate. Restrictions on labor mobility further discourage investment in education and training and are an important factor behind rural–urban inequalities. Restrictions prompted by concerns about loss of agricultural labor and excessive strain on urban infrastructure and services means that considerable misallocation continues in labor markets.

In early 2006 the Chinese authorities announced a series of initiatives to address inequalities through the creation of a "new socialist countryside." This is to be achieved through the removal of the agricultural tax, increased agricultural subsidies, and additional funds for rural education and health care. This appears to represent a significant shift in policy focus, away from growth per se and toward more balanced growth. Balanced development will be an increasing concern as China seeks to maintain self-sufficiency in grain production while losing agricultural land to development and farmers to the cities. If United Nations forecasts are accurate that 7 of every 10 Chinese will live in the cities by 2050, self-sufficiency will be maintained only through huge increases in agricultural productivity.

Economic Inequality in India

Like China, India has also experienced growing inequality in the years since reform. This inequality is apparent in both geographical and sectoral terms. India is divided into 28 states and seven union territories, but very strong growth has been experienced in just four states—Gujarat, Karnataka, Maharashtra, and Tamil Nadu. While these four states account for only 25 percent of India's population and 35 percent of output, they attract 70 percent of FDI approvals. They are growing significantly faster than other states. High rates of growth have widened the gap between the very richest and poorest states. In the early 1980s Maharashtra, India's wealthiest state, had per capita income levels twice those of Bihar, the poorest state. By the end of the 1990s, the gap was fourfold (Kurian 2000). The four high-growth states have created a virtuous circle where their growth attracts considerable investment, both domestic and foreign, fueling further growth.

The superior performance of these four states can be explained by a combination of initial endowments and vigorous reform. Prior to the reforms, these states had economic structures biased toward services and industry rather than agriculture. Because the reforms favored services and industry and not agriculture, these same states experienced higher growth rates. Their coastal locations also enabled them to benefit from the more liberal trade regime after 1991, and they contain more export businesses than other states. Because deficient infrastructure is such a constraint on growth in India, it is not surprising to find that the high-growth states all have better-than-average levels of infrastructure provision (Kurian 2000). This advantage is reinforced by the greater fiscal responsibility shown by these states; their government debt levels are lower than the all-India average. These states also benefit from having some of the largest cities, such as Mumbai and Chennai, which have benefited considerably from the more liberal environment.

At the same time, the regional governments of these high-growth states have been at the forefront of policy initiatives to boost growth. Prior to the reforms, the Indian economy was highly centralized and much of state policy consisted of lobbying for public investment or to secure the licenses necessary for private investment. Now greater decentralization means that state governments compete to attract investment. Many states do this simply on the basis of generous incentives. However, the more successful state governments are now tackling some of the underlying difficulties in their business environments. Moves to establish "one-stop shops" to facilitate business registration and computerization to lower compliance costs and improve transparency are beginning to show benefits. Some states have invested in improvements in infrastructure, particularly power provision. Karnataka, which includes the high-technology center of Bangalore, has boosted investment in education and training capacity and created a number of new technology parks (Commonwealth of Australia 2001).

Diversity is also apparent among industrial sectors in India. Effectively, the country comprises both an old and a new economy (Commonwealth of Australia 2001). The old economy includes agriculture, manufacturing, mining, and infrastructure. The new economy, in contrast, is dominated by services, such as information technology and communication, hotels and restaurants, and finance. The new economy has grown much faster than the larger old economy. During the postreform period, growth rates in the new economy have been, on average, 60 percent higher than in the old economy. As a result, the share of the new economy rose from 12.9 percent of GDP in the 1980s to 18.8 percent by the end of the 1990s. Growth rates in the old economy actually declined in the 1990s, with the exception of manufacturing, which enjoyed some of the benefits of reform and liberalization.

The growth of the new economy again reflects the peculiarities of development in India. While sectors such as IT clearly benefited from high rates of technological change, much of the differential growth rate is a result of the ability of the service sector to avoid some of the considerable impediments that constrain growth in India. Services are less reliant on India's weak infrastructure, particularly transport, power, and ports. Their capital requirements are lower, making it easier to expand the business in an environment of costly finance. They are able to avoid many of the restrictive labor market regulations that burden goods producers. Finally, the new service industries are less encumbered by India's bureaucracy with its onerous regulations, recurrent inspections, and excessive compliance costs.

This diversity of performance by region and sector is likely to be reflected in a similar diversity of opportunity for international businesses. Many consumer goods manufacturers will be attracted to the wealthier and faster-growing states. The fact that these same states have been foremost in reforming policies and tackling deficiencies in the business environment makes them doubly attractive. Like China, the geographic and demographic scale of India encourages niche or geographically constrained business strategies. Similarly, the prospect of continued high growth in the new service sector makes these industries attractive to international investors. However, these are the very industries populated by some of India's largest and most competitive firms, particularly in information technology. There may also be openings in manufacturing, which is still relatively underdeveloped in India, accounting for just 16 percent of GDP, a far lower percentage than in many other Asian economies. Opportunities to improve agricultural productivity and to access India's considerable mineral wealth mean that the old economy will continue to be important.

Like China, India has recently announced a new initiative to assist the poorest segments of the rural population (Patel 2005). The rural employment guarantee scheme promises to give 100 days work each year to 60 million of the poorest families at a rate of 60 rupees ($2) a day. India's rural poor, more than 250 million, have incomes of less than $1.50 a day. The cost of the initiative is likely to be high, as much as $39 billion. Critics have raised concerns about the effectiveness of providing public work to the least skilled. They also draw attention to the danger that much of the money could be siphoned off by officials and middlemen before it reaches the poor. Like China, India is concerned with spreading the benefits of higher growth to those least likely to benefit directly.

Competition in Large Emerging Markets

Successful entry into an emerging market requires that the investor undertake a comprehensive competitor analysis. While at first glance it might seem that competition in such markets is likely to be under-developed, this is rarely the case. Competition is offered by a number of different groups of firms, primarily indigenous businesses and early mover investors. It is also likely that many competitors will be of types less likely to be encountered in developed markets. The long history of socialism and government intervention in China and India means that industrialization was managed through state-owned enterprises and favored private entrepreneurs. The result is a number of indus-tries—steel, banking, and consumer electronics—dominated by state-owned businesses. State-owned enterprises (SOEs) pursue goals that are likely to differ from those of international businesses. SOEs are more concerned with maintaining employment than securing a strong financial return. They may incur losses that do not have to be repaid and can readily secure low-cost funds to add to capacity. In India, a system of licensing and import protection has created a number of very large, diversified family conglomerates, such as the Tata Group, which operate across both traditional and new emerging industries.

It is also important to understand that these competitors are mov-ing aggressively to take advantage of the opportunities offered by high rates of growth. In particular, many are involved in technological and competitive upgrading. There is little doubt that Chinese automobile manufacturers, both domestic and foreign-funded ventures, present a threat to many of their competitors as China becomes a significant vehicle export base. India's growing competitiveness in information technology, pharmaceuticals, and biotechnology is readily apparent.

However, the strength of entrenched domestic firms is by no means assured. Continuing deregulation and liberalization, often an obliga-tion of multilateral trade agreements, is changing market structures, creating huge opportunities for new entrants. In China's banking industry, the four largest and hugely advantaged state-owned banks have lost 20 percent of their market share over the past 15 years (Fan 2003; Holz 2003). The banking industry is one of the weakest in China, saddled with bad debts and underperforming assets. Heavy-handed government intervention results in a massively inefficient allocation of funds. Even where the dominant firms are foreign funded, as in the Chinese car industry, late entrants providing smaller vehicles customized to emerging needs have captured considerable market share. Equally important are the opportunities that arise as markets develop. The requirement for new personal and business services, such as real estate and management consulting as markets evolve, creates vast new opportunities that are particularly appealing to foreign investors.

In some cases, strong competition is provided by domestic firms. This is certainly the case with the Chinese personal computer industry (*Business Week* 2004d). The PC market is a very attractive one, with sales increasing by 29 percent between 2004 and 2005. It is expected to continue to grow at such rates until the end of the decade. In 2004 the top three companies by market share were all Chinese: Lenovo, with a share of 25.1 percent; Beijing Founder Electronics (9.9 percent); and Tsinghua Tongfang (7.4 percent). Multinational producers, such as Dell and HP, held 7.4 percent and 4.8 percent, respectively. Over the past three years, Dell's share has slipped because it is seen to be too focused on China's biggest cities and corporate customers. There are also doubts about the suitability of its direct sales model if it moves into smaller cities. On the other hand, Lenovo has enjoyed strong growth and gains in market share since it introduced its Yuanmeng line of low-cost PCs. These products have been targeted at the lower-income rural market with the marketing message that they are an educational tool and an investment in a child's future education. Despite a cost that is approximately equal to the annual average rural household income, Yuanmeng PCs now account for 70 percent of all desktop computers sold by Lenovo. This success provides a valuable business model for eventual exports to other emerging markets such as India, Brazil, and Russia.

In other cases, such as TV manufacturing, domestic firms have moved quickly to emulate the products of multinational pioneers. In the Chinese TV market, Toshiba enjoyed strong market leadership in the 1990s until its success triggered a wave of investment by other multinationals such as Sony, Panasonic, and the South Korean producers Samsung Electronics and LG Electronics. Foreign manufacturers moved out of lower-value units in 2001 and 2002 and now enjoy a 70 percent market share of high-end TVs. However, this has not discouraged domestic producers. The industry has gone through considerable consolidation. In 1995 there were more than 200 brands in the Chinese home-electronics industry. By 2002 this was down to about 20. The more traditional Chinese TV manufacturers—Changhong, Skyworth, Konka, and TCL—have also lost ground to new upstarts such as Amori, Hisense, Haier, and Shinco.

The Chinese beer industry illustrates a competitive situation of investment clustering and considerable excess capacity. The market is both large and, compared with the more advanced economies, growing rapidly. Between 1997 and 2003 the Chinese beer market grew by 17 percent and is now the world's second biggest market by volume. Future growth is also considerable. Currently, Chinese per capita consumption is just 40 percent that of South Korea or Japan. The industry is very fragmented, with most brands being regional or subregional. Foreign investment has triggered industry consolidation. The number of breweries has halved from about 800 in 1988 to the current 400 or so. The top 10 brewers now hold more than 50 percent of the market compared with just 22 percent in 1996.

International breweries first entered the Chinese market in the 1980s. This first wave, based on adding new capacity and selling foreign brands, was not that successful. Indeed, a number of major players withdrew from the Chinese market. A second wave of foreign investment began in 2002 and is distinguished by its focus on acquisitions and the retention of local brands (Rowley 2006). Total investment over the period between 2002 and 2004 was more than $700 million and involved SAB Miller, Interbrew, Heineken, Carlsberg, and Anheuser-Busch. There are now more than 50 foreign brewing ventures accounting for almost 20 percent of all breweries.

However, locally produced brands dominate the market, accounting for an estimated 90 percent of all consumption (*Business Week* 2004e). Leading breweries include Tsingtao with a 13 percent market share, Yanjing (10 percent), and Zhuijiang. While premium brands are growing strongly, they represent a small percentage of the market. Foreign brewers are finding it difficult to make profits in a situation of overcapacity; beer production exceeds consumption by some 40 percent. The result has been intense price wars. Furthermore, exceptionally high transport costs make building regional or national brands very difficult. Even large domestic producers are consolidating. Yanjing Beer recently bought a substantial stake in Huiquan Beer, enabling Yanjing to remain the only leading Chinese brewery without a foreign stake. Low-scale producers such as the Japanese are finding it difficult to increase their presence because the most attractive acquisition targets have already been taken.

The Indian motorcycle industry, which produces around five million bikes each year, has attracted a number of international competitors including Honda, Yamaha, and Suzuki from Japan and Piaggio from Italy. While Hero Honda is the market leader, a domestic firm, Bajaj Auto, has gained market share in recent years and is a strong second contender. While the company benefits from continuing protectionism, the Indian motorcycle industry was opened up in the 1980s.

All of these situations suggest that foreign investors entering emerging markets may find them attractive in terms of size and growth, but this must be understood in the context of a likely high level of competition. Competition is provided by domestic and other foreign investors who tend to be attracted by the same opportunities. Domestic firms in markets such as China and India often have a long, if sometimes undistinguished, history and may enjoy considerable state support. The evidence from the examples we have briefly considered suggests that in a number of cases they enjoy a strong understanding of consumers and are capable of rapid upgrading. Their competitive strength should not be underestimated.

Market Failures

A characteristic of almost every emerging market is the absence, or at least underdevelopment, of markets and supporting institutions. These are commonly termed *market failures*. Market failures influence business strategy and structure. As indicated above, ineffective markets in information in China encourage considerable investments in personal networks (*guanxi*) and mean firms prefer to trade with businesses with which they are already familiar. Dependence on relationships encourages outside investors to seek out well-connected local partners. In India the widespread use of licensing, price controls, and protectionism encourages conglomerate business organizations. India's largest business group (Tata) comprises 93 companies in seven business sectors as varied as engineering, energy, financial services, and tea production.

Market failures in emerging markets are widespread in labor, product, financial, infrastructure, and intellectual property markets. Market failures typically add to transaction costs, increase uncertainty, and require innovative responses. In most cases they are not insurmountable, but they are likely to present considerable challenges to outsiders unfamiliar with local business systems and practices.

Labor Market Failures

Labor market failures result from problems with mobility, adjustment, and quality of workers. China has long had policies restricting labor mobility, particularly in the movement of workers between provinces (Zhao 2005). In India, pervasive regulations, impacting particularly on larger organizations, have created a dual labor market. The official sector, comprising primarily the public and private corporate sectors, represents only about 10 percent of the Indian workforce. The vast majority of workers, some 90 percent, are found in the unofficial sector. Regulatory interventions have created a situation where wages and conditions in the official sector are too generous, while those in the unofficial sector are insufficient. Under the Industrial Disputes Act of 1947, any company with 100 or more employees must obtain local state government approval before making any layoffs. The result has been both growth in the unofficial sector and stagnation of larger manufacturing firms. Indian manufacturers with 100 or more employees added only 25,000 full-time jobs in the decade between 1993 and 2003, a tiny fraction in an economy with 10 million new labor force entrants each year (Kripalani 2003).

While both China and India have attempted to improve adjustment processes in their labor markets, there are still obstacles. China would be unable to cope with a massive wave of rural-to-urban migration. Similarly, rapid restructuring of its overstaffed state-owned sector would, at least in the short to medium term, create an unacceptable level of unemployment. It is hard to conceive of India's labor aristocracy giving up its favorable terms and conditions by allowing new entrants.

Problems also exist in terms of the number and quality of workers available to the development process, particularly the highly skilled. The skills possessed by many traditional Chinese managers are not necessarily those demanded in an increasingly open and competitive economy (Xue and Enderwick 2005). Furthermore, the pool of potential talent may be far smaller than that suggested by demographic data. Research by the McKinsey Global Institute suggests that fewer than 10 percent of Chinese job candidates may be suitable for employment in a foreign company. The reasons for this include poor English, an educational bias that favors theory over practice, a lack of world-class graduates in business disciplines, and widespread geographical dispersion of educated workers (Farrell and Grant 2005). More generally, while relative wages are low in an economy such as China, so is labor productivity (Wu 2001).

Product Market Failures

Product market restrictions exist in many emerging markets as a result of government protection and ownership. China's vast state-owned sector, while declining in relative terms, has long enjoyed a virtual monopoly in the commanding heights of the economy controlling the steel, energy, machinery, armaments, textiles, telecommunications, and banking industries. This is beginning to change as WTO membership requires many of these industries to be opened up, allowing import competition and foreign direct investment. Such changes are expected, through competition, to lower prices and improve quality. India has long cosseted its economy with pervasive trade protectionism and restrictions on foreign direct investment. The allocation of production rights in more than 800 product classes to only small firms has artificially pushed up costs and prices as undersized establishments have been unable to achieve economies of scale. Competition is increasing significantly in a number of Indian sectors. Between 1991 and 2003 the number of competitors in telecommunications increased from 2 to more than 15. The domestic airline industry has increased from one to eight competitors over the same period (Sinha 2005a). Again, a more open trading and investment environment offers the best hope for reducing product market distortions. In the future, India will need to deregulate politically sensitive industries such as retailing, banking, and the media.

Financial Market Failures

China's financial sector in particular suffers considerable elements of market failure. State ownership of the major banks, directed lending to inefficient state-owned enterprises, and a lack of alternatives for individual savers has brought massive wastefulness in financial markets. While private savings in China exceed $1.4 trillion, these languish in banks, inaccessible to the many new private businesses seeking to fund growth. While private businesses and collectives now account for almost half of China's industrial output, they account for only 20 percent of loans by value. With nonperforming loans perhaps as high as 40 percent of all loans, and just 2 percent of China's population accounting for more than half of all deposits (Pitsilis et al. 2004), Chinese banks remain fragile. Because banks still account for 80 percent of all credit, this is a considerable obstacle to an efficient financial sector. Nonperforming loans form, on average, 15 to 20 percent of all loans in India, and less than half of all Indian savings are held in banks (Farrell and Key 2005).

India may have lower domestic savings and attract a smaller share of foreign direct investment than China, but it does appear to use its capital more efficiently. With an investment rate half that of China, India has had an average growth rate two-thirds that of China. India's more efficient use of capital may be due, at least in part, to its lower level of development. In the early stages of liberalization, there are likely to be many productive applications for capital. India's banking system is also more efficient; foreign and privately owned banks now have a market share of around 25 percent (Farrell and Lund 2005).

Infrastructure Failures

Infrastructure investment is a critical component of development, particularly in the case of large countries such as China and India. Infrastructure bottlenecks can dramatically constrain growth and in the case of India are thought to have favored the development of the service sector, particularly software and business process services, which are less dependent on infrastructure, such as power, ports, and roads, where India is seen as weak. Evidence on infrastructure spending highlights India's difficulties. In 2003, China's spending was US$150 billion, some seven times higher than India in absolute terms and three times higher as a proportion of GDP (Morgan Stanley 2005). Underinvestment and poor management mean that with the exception of telecommunications, infrastructure costs in India are considerably higher than in China. Average electricity costs are twice as high, and railway transport costs are three times those in China. Investors face additional costs in that many provide their own alternative power sources in the form of generators and face considerable delays in the transfer of supplies and products. Infrastructural weaknesses also impose a cost on the country, constraining growth and export performance. India's share of world merchandise exports in 2003 was just 0.7 percent, well below China's 5.9 percent (Table 2.1).

Intellectual Property Rights Failures

The effective protection of intellectual property is an instrumental concern for many foreign investors, particularly those operating in higher technology or consumer-branded industries. Failure to protect intellectual property can result in considerable revenue loss and damage in the marketplace where counterfeit products appear. This is a problem in many emerging markets and imposes huge costs on producers of software, media, and fashion products. The most serious offenders are often found in Asia. Measures of the security of property rights highlight weaknesses in both China and India. Where a score of 10 implies the most security, China was rated at 4.1 and India at 6.0, compared with the United States at 9.2 (Gwartney et al. 2002). In recent years India has moved to strengthen intellectual property protection in a range of areas including patents, trademarks, and copyright. China, as a result of obligations arising from WTO membership, is also committed to strengthening intellectual property protection.

However, estimates of the extent and costs of piracy suggest that both countries are major violators with little evidence to suggest that the problem is being addressed. Estimates from the U.S.-based International Intellectual Property Alliance (2004) suggest that piracy rates in China are over 90 percent for commonly counterfeited products such as motion pictures, music, and software. Rates in India are lower, averaging 60 percent. However, the size of these markets means that losses are substantial. In 2004, China accounted for more than 20 percent of total estimated losses; India accounted for almost 4 percent. Of more concern is the trend in these figures. Between 2000 and 2004, the share of total losses accounted for by both countries increased, in the case of China from 13 to 20 percent. In part this reflects their rapid growth as consumer markets but is disturbing in light of stated aims to curb the problem. Clearly, any producer of copyrighted products or material needs to be very wary of piracy in these markets (see Box 3.2 below). Reliance on litigation is unlikely to be sufficient where enforcement is weak, and Western companies are urged to move to more offensive strategies in tackling the problem (Dietz et al. 2005). The experience of Pfizer in attempting to enforce its intellectual property in Viagra is that such processes are expensive, slow, and unpredictable. Interestingly, in this case the Chinese imitators actually worked together to bring a collective case (Balfour 2006).

Box 3.2 European Luxury Brands Challenge Chinese Pirates

Burberry, Chanel, Gucci, Prada, and Louis Vuitton have fired a legal broadside against Beijing's Silk Market, the reputed flagship of trademark piracy in China. Normally commercial rivals, the five luxury European brands have taken the unusual step of joining forces to file a lawsuit against the sprawling shopping emporium, which is immensely popular among foreign tourists because of its reputation for offering high-quality counterfeit goods at a fraction of the price of the genuine article.

According to the *Beijing Times*, the companies are demanding 25 million yuan, a little over $3 million, from the operator of Xiushui Haosen Clothing Market and five of its stallholders. Although the sum involved is relatively small, the high-profile case is likely to be a test of China's global commitment to protect intellectual property rights.

The Silk Market is usually cited as the prime example of lack of enforcement. When the first few stalls appeared in an alley next to the U.S. Embassy in 1985, they were initially welcomed as a sign of China's nascent embrace of capitalism. But the traders quickly realized there was more money to be made from fake brand name goods than the traditional silk products that gave the market its name.

The Beijing government denies that there is a problem. During 2005 the market was moved indoors from the cramped alley to a new purpose-built five-story mall with space for 1,600 stalls. The authorities said they would severely punish any outlet that offered pirated products, but the plaintiffs in the latest lawsuit claim to have six large boxes filled with evidence in the form of fake bags and clothes. "Though the market operator had promised to weed out counterfeit goods in the market, it failed to keep these knock-offs out," the plaintiff's lawyer, Gao Hualin, was quoted as saying in the *China Daily*. "The company takes no measures to fight against counterfeiting, and facilitates stalls in selling fake brands."

Source: Jonathon Watts, *Guardian*, November 4, 2005.

Disadvantages of Foreignness

Any foreign business entering an emerging market faces additional costs resulting from its lack of familiarity with the local business environment (Zaheer 1995). These costs arise from geographical disadvantage (transport and communication costs), cultural differences, and institutional distance (lack of familiarity with local institutions). Because domestic firms do not incur them, the international investor is disadvantaged. While it has long been recognized that international businesses possess strong firm-specific advantages that can be used to offset these costs (Buckley and Casson 1975; Dunning 1992), the rational firm will still seek to minimize the costs of foreignness where possible.

Understanding of institutional distance has made only limited progress. It is broadly accepted that the more remote a host country is from the organizational core of an international business, generally its home country, the greater will be the differences in culture, regulations, and business practices the firm will have to reconcile. Similarly, the greater are cultural differences between the two countries, the more difficult adaptation is likely to be. However, physical distance is not a reliable indicator of institutional distance. While the physical distance between Britain and Australia is considerable, institutional differences between the two countries are much less than between Britain and Russia, which are physically much closer. Similarly, the concept of *psychic distance* widely used in international business (Johansen and Vahlne 1977) emphasizes cultural differences and pays scant regard to other institutional differences.

Scott (1995) provides a helpful characterization by separating the regulatory, normative, and cognitive elements of institutional distance. Regulatory aspects are concerned with the basic rules that guide business activity, the legal and regulatory framework, and how effectively these are monitored and enforced. Cognitive elements relate to cognitive patterns prevalent within a society and broadly shared social practices. These first two elements are often conveyed through the concept of a business system. The third element, normative aspects of a society, equates to commonly defined cultural characteristics and comprises values, beliefs, and norms.

The challenge for an international business entering an emerging market is to understand how institutional distance is likely to affect its operations and how to achieve the most effective adaptation possible. The firm faces a twofold challenge. On the one hand, institutional distance between the home and host country will affect the ability of the business to transfer and exploit its firm-specific competitive advantages. Because these are typically embedded in corporate processes and practices, institutional distance will inhibit the transfer and adoption of such practices (Kostova and Roth 2002; Kostova and Zaheer 1999). On the other hand, issues of institutional distance are likely to exist between the foreign affiliate and its local environment because the affiliate is subject to pressures from the parent organization. This sets it apart from indigenous businesses and complicates the processes of achieving local acceptance.

Institutional distance affects strategic choices made by an international business. For example, if competitive conditions dictate the need for effective transfer of competitive advantages, but institutional distance is high, the firm may opt for a greenfield wholly owned subsidiary because this facilities internal coordination and control. On the other hand, if attaining local acceptance is paramount and significant cognitive and normative differences exist, the investor is more likely to form a collaborative relationship with a local partner who can provide a cognitive and cultural bridge.

Luo (2002) suggests two broad responses to the problem of foreignness—a defensive and an offensive approach. The defensive approach centers on reducing the international firm's dependence on the local environment and exposure to the uncertainties it produces. This can be achieved in a variety of ways. One is to rely on fully specified contracts. These are designed to safeguard the rights of the investor. In the absence of a fully developed commercial legal system, contracts offer some safeguards against the vagaries that can arise when stakeholders act in an arbitrary manner. A second mechanism is to integrate operations within the parent organization, again reducing dependence on the local business environment. The subsidiary may obtain inputs from, and provide outputs to, other parts of the same organization. As well as vertical integration, parental control can be achieved through the use of high-control entry modes, such as a wholly owned subsidiary, and by limiting the autonomy of subsidiary management. Local interaction can also be reduced by standardizing output, minimizing the need to understand the local market, and customizing products and services.

While defensive approaches can assist in reducing the liability of foreignness, they are unlikely to be the preferred approaches in a large emerging market. The size and attractiveness of China and India mean that an international investor is likely to enter such a market with the intention of servicing and developing that market over the long term. That would suggest the benefits of an offensive rather than a defensive approach. Offensive approaches attempt to reduce the costs of foreignness by encouraging the firm's integration into the local market. This can be achieved through networking whereby the firm's management builds relationships with local stakeholders, including public officials. Local contacts provide information that can help the firm understand and adapt to the local business environment. A second mechanism to increase local acceptance is through increased resource commitment. The commitment of resources can offset the weakness of international businesses when compared with local firms in terms of market power, company image, and institutional support. Resource commitment also increases the firm's local legitimacy as it is increasingly seen in local terms. Finally, increased local sourcing of inputs aids local acceptance while simultaneously reducing vulnerability to exchange rate shifts. Increased indigenization of management at the expense of expatriates offers both lower costs and increased acceptability.

While most international investors are likely to use a combination of defensive and offensive approaches to reducing the liability of foreignness, our discussion suggests that for a large emerging market, offensive approaches offer the best match with strategies that place countries such as India and China at the center of competitive positioning.

Market-Making Investments

The discussions on market failure and the disadvantages of foreignness have highlighted two situations where an international business entering an emerging market is likely to incur additional costs when attempting to both overcome market failure and achieve local acceptance. We can integrate these types of investment through the concept of market-making expenditures. Because emerging economies are distinguished by both market failures and institutional distance, early entrants to these markets need to overcome these obstacles to success. We suggest that they do this through investment in overcoming market failure, investments that also contribute to their legitimacy in local markets. We define *market-making expenditures* as expenditures that entrants must make to create, educate, and develop the markets that they enter. This concept differs from the more traditional idea of *pioneering costs* (Carpenter and Nakamoto 1989) in three key ways. First, pioneering costs refer to costs that are primarily attributable to the higher levels of uncertainty that are faced by early entrants. The price that early entrants pay is an environment that is less predictable than that enjoyed by later entrants. This difference arises from institutional and policy development over time and the opportunities for learning that result from incumbency in the market, for example, the ability to learn from the experience and mistakes of early entrants. Second, the concept of market-making expenditures allows for investment in the creation of competitive advantage and not simply the incurrence of higher transaction costs. In this way, the concept encompasses one of the key advantages associated with early entry—the opportunity to undertake preemptive investments (Lieberman and Montgomery 1988). Thus market-making expenditures may be seen as either a cost or an investment. Third, market-making expenditures are discretionary and are under the control of the investing firm. As such, they form part of the strategy process, as compared with pioneering costs, the extent of which are primarily determined by market and competitive conditions.

As mentioned above, market-making expenditures can take the form of a cost or an investment. Cost elements of market-making expenditures are similar to pioneering costs. Of greater significance are the investment aspects of market making. Here we may distinguish between proprietary and nonproprietary investments. Proprietary market making investments are those that are specific to the firm and cannot be enjoyed by others. An example is provided by local adaptation of a potential product that subsequently enjoys enhanced appeal in the host market. Provided intellectual property rights are enforceable, such investments should yield a return only to the firm owning the rights. In contrast, some market-making investments generate returns to a number of firms in the industry. This is likely, for example, in the case of the creation of a supply base.

When considering emerging markets we can distinguish seven principal categories of market-making expenditures. These relate to host-country government relations, local product adaptation, creation of a supply base, investments in distribution, the establishment of after-sales service facilities, employee training, and buyer education. Clearly, all of these refer to stages of value adding in market processes. In many emerging markets, these elements may be incomplete or underdeveloped. For example, an international automobile manufacturer entering the Indian market cannot be assured that there will be a potential supply base comparable in terms of numbers, experience, quality, or performance with what might exist in the home country. As a result, the investing firm may incur expenditures to help build this base, perhaps by bringing suppliers from the home country or by assisting in the upgrading of local firms. The concept of market-making expenditures may be a useful approach to understanding how international businesses can overcome the problems of market failure and the liability of foreignness which they are likely to face in emerging markets.

Conclusions

This chapter has examined some of the major challenges that international businesses are likely to experience when operating in emerging markets such as China and India. In large part, these challenges result from the underdevelopment of markets and institutions in these economies, as well as their high rates of growth. Many of these challenges are faced by all firms—high levels of risk, growing economic inequality, and market failures, for example. Others, such as the disadvantages of foreignness, are unique to international investors. Some challenges vary in degree from those likely to be experienced in developed home markets. This is the case with informational deficiencies, which mean that decisions in emerging markets are often made with insufficient, outdated, or unreliable data. The potential investor must weigh these challenges against the considerable opportunities that emerging economies offer. The very high levels of direct investment in China, and growing levels in India, suggest that in many cases the trade-off appears favorable. In such cases, strategies should seek, wherever possible, to overcome the challenges.

Implications for Management

1. The considerable attractions of LEMs should be evaluated in the light of the significant challenges that such markets bring.
2. The most common set of difficulties result from elements of market failure, with which Western businesses may have little experience.
3. The growth and development processes of LEMs are accentuating differences—by region, by industry, and by skill level. In the absence of comprehensive social safety nets, these may mean future problems.
4. Emerging markets are likely to be competitive markets. Many international businesses have entered these markets, and the competitiveness of local firms is increasing rapidly.
5. To successfully serve emerging markets, firms may have to undertake market-making investments. Capturing the returns on such investments is not always easy.

Discussion Questions

1. You are advising a large Australian beer manufacturer about entry into the Chinese market. The company is concerned about the paucity of market information available. Suggest ways in which such risks can be reduced.
2. In a world of brand loyalty and the importance of image, is foreignness really a disadvantage in markets like China and India?

4

THE EVOLUTION OF LARGE EMERGING MARKETS

Introduction

The defining characteristic of an emerging economy is change. In simple terms, such an economy is evolving, increasing living standards, and developing its economic and institutional structures. This means that an emerging market today is likely to be quite different from how it was 10 years ago and how it will be a decade into the future. While this statement is true of all economies, it is the pace and direction of evolution within LEMs that sets them apart.

Over time the pace of economic development has accelerated. A widely used measure of economic development is the doubling of per capita income. The time it took to achieve this in the United States from 1839 was 47 years, less than the 58 years it took Britain starting around 1780. Japan took 34 years commencing in 1885. More recently, South Korea achieved a doubling in the 11 years beginning in 1966. China's income growth has been little short of miraculous. Per capita income doubled in the nine years between 1978 and 1987, doubled again in the subsequent nine years, and has doubled again since then. India's performance has been a little weaker, with per capita income doubling once over a 25-year period; at current growth rates it should double again in about 15 years.

There are two principal explanations for the acceleration in economic development. The first is simply that later developing countries have been able to learn valuable lessons from those that went before them. Over the past two centuries the development of what are now the advanced, wealthy OECD (Organization for Economic Cooperation and Development) nations, and more recently the Asian

Tigers, have provided some development guidelines. For example, history suggests that a market economy is likely to outperform a planned economy, and this is increasingly the case as production activities become more information intensive and sophisticated. History also shows no recorded examples of economies that have achieved significant development under conditions of autarky; openness to trade, technology, and ideas appears to be a prerequisite for rapid growth. Furthermore, recent development research has highlighted the multiplicity of factors that can contribute to or inhibit growth, particularly the idiosyncrasies of institutions (Acemoglu et al. 2001; Rodrik et al. 2004). This suggests that there is no single development model or any simple policy prescription for development. Both China and India have followed different development paths and neither conforms precisely to neoclassical economic dogma.

The second factor linked to the acceleration of economic growth is the importance of foreign resources in facilitating the development process. Additional resources are essential to the growth take-off, whether these are the result of domestic savings or the inflow of foreign resources. Both China and India have relied heavily on foreign resources to drive their new industries. China's preference has been to attract resources bundled in the form of foreign direct investment. Such investment, under the control of international businesses, brings capital, management skills, technology, and overseas market access in one relatively low-cost transaction. Investment by overseas Chinese has powered the growth of labor-intensive, small-scale industries such as clothing, shoes, toys, luggage, and sports goods. Multinational enterprises have been at the forefront of higher technology and large-scale activities such as automobiles and electronics. India has followed a different path and has been successful in attracting service jobs and processes that have been performed by its larger domestic enterprises. This transfer of work through offshore sourcing has brought valued resources in the form of technology, quality improvement, and access to buyers.

Economic Evolution

The future direction of development in emerging markets raises a number of significant issues. The first is reliance on the same sorts of models that have described development in the most advanced countries. It would be extremely difficult to predict the future shape and direction of economies such as the United States, Japan, or Germany. We have no historical precedents to guide us in understanding how these economies will evolve. However, in the case of today's emerging markets we may be able to draw useful lessons from the past experience of the now wealthy countries. This is not to suggest that their economic development will be identical; rather, the suggestion is that there are sufficient generalities to draw some tentative conclusions. The generalities are to be found in four principal areas: macroeconomic stabilization, liberalization of the external economy, privatization of former state-owned businesses, and the creation of market-supporting rules and institutions.

For any nation seeking higher growth and development, macroeconomic stability is a precondition. Without such stability, domestic economic agents will be reluctant to commit capital and effort to the development process, and it will be difficult to attract external resources. It is not surprising that some of the poorest economic performers are also those countries identified as being most in danger of failing in a broader political sense. In many cases the sources of failure—whether political, social, or economic—can be traced back to economic instability (Norton and Miskel 1997). Before economic reform can be pursued, economic stability must be achieved. Such stability requires control over inflation, excessive government expenditure, an unsustainable trade deficit, or currency fluctuations.

Second, most nations will move to liberalize their economies, that is, to open themselves to external trade and exchange. There are no contemporary examples of economies that have enjoyed rapid growth and development while shunning the rest of the world. Economic development and autarky simply do not coexist. Liberalization enables an economy to receive additional resources (capital, technology, ideas, and management skills) and to trade products and services in which it has a comparative advantage. As well as encouraging further specialization and the associated benefits of higher productivity, trade also imposes a discipline on domestic producers. Because they are forced to meet the demands of global consumers and face competition from many quarters, such firms, if they are not subject to government support and protection, must achieve high levels of efficiency.

Third, the considerable costs of public ownership mean that privatization of the means of production is a widely adopted element of most economic reform packages (Megginson and Netter 2001). The economic case for privatization is compelling. It is expected to increase allocative efficiency through improved output and lower prices, as well as improve productive efficiency (the way that resources are used within the organization). It achieves this through the provision of market-based incentives (the threat of failure or takeover), the establishment of profit as the primary organizational objective, and the elimination of political interference (Boycko et al. 1996; Vickers and Yarrow 1991). The case for privatization has been spurred by the negative experiences of many countries with state ownership, particularly in the third quarter of the past century. Furthermore, the burden that SOEs (state-owned enterprises) have imposed on China through low productivity, excess employment, and bad debts offers a salutary lesson for other countries. Perhaps not surprisingly, in the past 2.5 decades the share of global GDP produced by state-owned enterprises has declined from more than 10 percent in 1979 to less than 6 percent by 2001 (Megginson and Netter 2001).

Fourth, as almost all emerging economies place growing reliance on a market system, market-supporting institutions and rules are necessary. Such rules and institutions are designed to help transmit information, enforce property and contractual rights, and manage competition, thereby lowering the costs and uncertainty of transactions and facilitating investment and growth (World Bank 2002). There are fundamental difficulties in making predictions about desirable institution building. This is true for a number of reasons. One is the problem of defining what we mean by *institutions*. For North (1990), institutions establish the "rules of the game" providing constraints on political, economic, and social interactions. In this way, "good" institutions are those that provide incentives for efficient transacting.

A second problem is confusion among the forms and functions of institutions. Institutional forms describe the structure of institutions. For example, while India has a political democracy, China is characterized by political authoritarianism. The functions of institutions appear to be of more importance than their form (Aron 2000). Mainstream economics highlights property rights as the key institutional function in a market economy.

A third problem with understanding institutional evolution stems from wide agreement that simple transplantation of institutions is unlikely to be successful. The appropriateness of institutions is influenced by a range of factors, including culture, history, tradition, and geography. Like imported technology, some adaptation to local conditions is generally necessary. Institutional structures contain significant tacit elements, which are difficult to replicate. These tacit elements may even be embodied in the workings of other, complementary institutions. However, this does not mean that institutional arrangements in other countries are irrelevant. There is evidence that emerging economies have learned from the more advanced economies. Chang (2002) suggests that the level of institutional development of a number of emerging countries today exceeds that displayed by the leading countries when they were at similar levels of economic development.

There has been a tendency to generalize Western institutions—an independent judiciary, a sophisticated stock market with takeover opportunities, an independent central bank, flexible labor markets, and shareholder-driven corporate governance—in the belief that these best meet universal needs (Chang 2005). In some cases, these have been promoted as a condition for assistance by international financial institutions (Kapur and Webber 2000). However, there is also evidence of the widespread voluntary adoption of Western-type institutions, particularly the rule of law, in many parts of the world (IMF [International Monetary Fund] 2003).

More generally, there are likely to be complex interactions among institutions and policies within an emerging economy. On the one hand, the effectiveness of policy outcomes depends, at least in part, on the quality and consistency of the institutions that are used to deliver these policies. In the extreme case, good policy can be rendered ineffective through weak institutions. On the other hand, and of particular relevance to this discussion, is the likelihood that policies impact on institutional development. Policies that emphasize openness to trade and foreign investment, competition, and transparency are associated with stronger institutions (IMF 2003). Powerful demonstration effects on institutional development are transmitted though regional trade groupings and multilateral organizations such as the WTO (World Trade Organization). The latter has certainly influenced the form and pace of institutional capacity building in China.

While we can conclude with some confidence that most emerging markets are likely to evolve along the lines outlined above (achieving macroeconomic stabilization, opening up their economies, elevating the role of markets and the private sector, and investing in market-supporting rules and institutions), development is unlikely to be homogeneous. There are many specific factors that inhibit development convergence.

One is the considerable influence of historical and geographical factors. New institutions and institutional reform do not occur within a vacuum; in most cases institutional innovations are layered upon, and facilitate adaptation of, long-standing arrangements. A number of recent studies have provided fascinating insights into the importance of history and geography in determining the form and effectiveness of institutions (Acemoglu et al. 2001; Beck et al. 2003; Easterly and Levine 2003; Engerman and Sokoloff 1997; La Porta et al. 1999).

Second, as our discussion suggests, there is no universal development model that can easily be applied by an emerging economy. The fact that development success continues to be highly concentrated and that development convergence is not occurring suggests that liberalization per se does not yield the growth it promotes. There is not even agreement on the appropriate policies to be followed (Moisés 2000). In fact, the paths followed by successful, high-growth economies such as China, Mauritius, and Botswana have been substantially different. Furthermore, there seem to be advantages in applying unorthodox policies that run contrary to the neoliberal ideal. Policies of selective protectionism, industry targeting, and industrial upgrading, as pioneered by the Asian Tiger economies and now epitomized by China (Rodrik 2004), seem to work. China has been extremely successful in attracting foreign investment while at the same time imposing ownership and local content requirements. It still controls its exchange rate and restricts international financial transactions. India restricts production of a large number of commodities to small domestically owned firms and operates a highly restrictive labor market. All these policies go against the generic advice usually offered to emerging economies—privatize, liberalize, and deregulate. Yet in terms of changes in both share of manufacturing value added and manufacturing exports over the period between 1980 and 2000, the East Asian region, including China, enjoyed by far the strongest growth (Lall 2004). The contrasting experiences of East Asia and Latin America are illuminating. While the Latin American region was the first and fastest to liberalize, and East Asian growth was linked to a far more interventionist policy, the latter enjoyed much higher growth rates (Lall 2004).

Third, technology means that the evolutionary paths of late developing economies may be characterized by a skipping of stages. The availability of new communication technologies such as mobile phones means that emerging countries may not need to make the same investments in copper cabling that were necessary 20 years ago. Such leapfrogging is simply one manifestation of technological progress and the process of learning from the experiences of predecessors.

Finally, as suggested above, differences in policy emphases will result in differences in the development process. While both China and India have adopted gradualist approaches to reform, China's innovative experiments with hybrid institutions and policies such as town and village enterprises and land reform, as well as China's ability to attract resources and expertise from the overseas Chinese community, have created a very different development trajectory from that of India. Similarly, each emerging economy faces a different set of threats or constraints, which may frustrate or otherwise vary the development process. India's inadequate physical infrastructure has discouraged manufacturing development, but encouraged IT-based services. China's continual weaknesses manifest in the state-owned sector have handicapped its banks, frustrated the funding of private business, and ensured a high level of intervention in financial markets.

Conceptualizing LEM Evolution

Despite the many idiosyncrasies discussed in the previous section, we suggest that it is still possible to draw some general conclusions about the future development of emerging economies. The conceptual framework of this reasoning is set out in Figure 4.1.

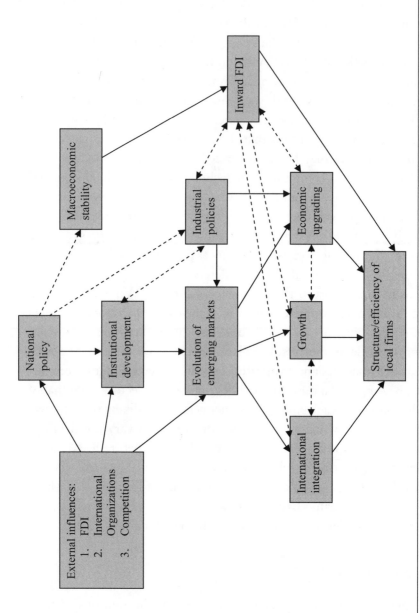

Figure 4.1   Dynamics of Emerging Market Evolution

As Figure 4.1 shows, the evolution of an emerging economy is subject to both external and internal (policy) influences. The principal external sources emanate from international organizations, competition, and foreign direct investment. International organizations—particularly those responsible for trade, aid, and finance—are likely to express strongly held views on appropriate policy. In recent years, the dominant position has been summarized in the idea of the *Washington consensus*—a set of beliefs that set out what are seen as the essential and fundamental elements of development policy (Williamson 2000). While this term has been interpreted in a variety of ways, and beyond its original coverage of Latin America, it provides a succinct summary of the neoliberal perspective. Countries are advised to liberalize their external economies, deregulate and privatize industry, and pursue prudent monetary and fiscal policy. Other international institutions, including regional trade and investment agreements, also influence the development process through the creation of opportunities and the imposition of constraints.

The combination of globalization and liberalization has undoubtedly increased levels of competition in the world economy. Competition comes from both national and international businesses. Freer access to emerging markets, whether in the form of imports or inward investment, has put considerable pressure on domestic enterprises and the ways in which they develop. Competition to attract FDI, technology, and infrastructure adds to the difficulties of driving development and in many cases the inducements that host-country governments must provide.

The importance of foreign direct investment as a driver of growth and development means that it is likely to exercise a major influence on any emerging economy that chooses to develop in this way. Historically, FDI has been instrumental in the rapid growth of Singapore, the Republic of Ireland, and Costa Rica, for example. Currently, it is at the very heart of China's industrial development and upgrading. Its centrality means that we will return to this influence later in this section.

External influences are interpreted within the context of domestic policy. While it is accepted that external factors can constrain domestic policy discretion, there remains considerable freedom for domestic management (Lall 2004). As Figure 4.1 suggests, the initial task of effective national policy is to attain macroeconomic stability. This means adequate growth, a manageable level of inflation, an acceptable external and fiscal balance, and an attractive business environment. Countries unable to achieve such status tend to be categorized as failed or failing states, displaying very low levels of income and rates of growth (Foreign Policy and the Fund for Peace 2005).

Once economic stability has been achieved, two further developments may be expected. The first is the likelihood of increased inflows of FDI. Economic stability contributes to a business environment that is clearly more attractive to international business. However, while economic stability may be a necessary condition for attracting FDI, it is unlikely to be sufficient. The extent of inward investment depends on the existence of locational advantages—features of the host location that attract foreign investors. Such features include a large and growing market, the existence of unique resources or capabilities, or the opportunity to access lower-cost resources. Clearly, China and India share some of these features—both are large and rapidly growing markets, both offer the opportunity to lower costs in manufacturing (China) and services (India), and both have unique human resources.

The second likely development is investment in institutional capacity building. As an economy is liberalized and greater reliance is placed on the workings of markets, relevant institutional supports are necessary. The key institutions relate to protecting property rights, encouraging competition, and ensuring that private-sector agents face appropriate incentives and constraints. India has long had a reasonably robust set of institutions underpinning business behavior. The contractual and justice systems are well established and regarded. It has an independent media, which provides a valuable counterbalance to the actions of business and public officials. India's institutional weaknesses are the excessive regulation of business activities and the operation of the labor market. Recent moves have seen a strengthening of intellectual property rights.

China faces a much greater challenge in developing market institutions. Constraints on the mobility of labor, financial markets, and private enterprise continue to impede efficiency. Recent moves to open up financial markets; to facilitate merger activity; and to relieve banks of crippling, nonperforming loans to state-owned enterprises suggests that there is now a recognition of the need to facilitate market operations. The establishment in 2001 of the same rights to private business as those accorded to state-owned firms was a major step forward. However, financial constraints on managerial behavior including the takeover threat or bankruptcy remain rare.

As Figure 4.1 illustrates, there is a link between industrial policy and institutional development. The direction and emphasis of industrial policy strongly influence the development of institutions. For example, China's reliance on inward investment and, in particular, its desire to maximize spillovers of technology and management skills to local businesses meant that the preferred form of foreign involvement was through joint ventures. In turn, this meant the selection of preferred local partners and support for their development. The policy focus on local content also meant that domestic suppliers and clusters were fostered. China's emphasis on export markets meant that early industrialization took place in the coastal cities, and the creation of free trade zones were essential to the success of such a policy.

The importance of industrial policy in the evolution of emerging markets is evident in Figure 4.1. Recognition of the role of such policy suggests that our conception contains both structuralist and neoliberal elements. The conception suggests that merely opening up markets is not likely to be sufficient to ensure growth and industrial upgrading. Discretionary industrial policy (the structuralist element) is also necessary. While economic liberalization has made it more difficult to implement some elements of industrial policy—local content, protection of infant industries, performance requirements on foreign investors, for example—it is still possible to utilize other policy aspects. Of particular importance in the global era are policies that facilitate technological capability. This includes both building initial capability and subsequent deepening or upgrading (Lall 2004). Furthermore, such policy should be discretionary. Because learning externalities vary with the type of technology and absorptive capacity of the host country, a blanket policy is not likely to be successful. Industrial policy is likely to target both factor and product markets. Correction of failures in factor markets as well as maximizing coordination between factor and product markets are areas government efforts should target (Lall 2004).

Industrial policies are related directly to industrial upgrading and indirectly to the role that is played by foreign direct investment. The effectiveness of industrial policy is instrumental in influencing international integration and the growth rate. Policy instruments, including trade and foreign investment policy, protectionism, and involvement in bilateral and multilateral trade agreements, will determine the extent to which an economy is internationally integrated. As discussed in Chapter 3, international integration is likely to be beneficial to an emerging economy, although it is important to ensure that the terms of involvement are favorable (Chase-Dunn 1975). The experience of the Asian Tiger economies of Hong Kong, Taiwan, Singapore, and South Korea shows the importance of discretionary industrial policy in their economic upgrading. International linkages were of particular importance to the Asian Tiger economies. Policies on foreign direct investment were used either to maximize spillovers to domestic firms (Taiwan, South Korea) or to create a largely autonomous, internationally competitive foreign-controlled industries (Singapore). International market involvement through exporting (Taiwan, Singapore) or a combination of trade and outward investment (South Korea) were used to bring discipline to policy and to ensure efficient resource use.

A combination of the spillovers from inward investment, international competition, growth opportunities, and economic upgrading comprises the key determinants of the structure and efficiency of local firms. The contrasting experiences of China and India are illustrative here. China has followed a far more internationally oriented development path than India. Early opening of the economy, the targeting of export activities, and immense success in attracting foreign direct investment means that by almost any measure China is far more internationally integrated than India (see Table 2.1). There are also industries such as light manufacturing where China has a clear comparative advantage. The downside of the strategy is that China has few globally competitive domestic enterprises. It also carries an expensive legacy of regionally based, state-owned enterprises that lack sufficient scale or competitive pressure to attain international competitiveness (Nolan 2001). Those that have ventured overseas have enjoyed government support—both political and financial. Economic upgrading, for example in the case of technologically sophisticated exports, is largely in the hands of foreign-controlled firms.

India, in contrast, has followed a far more protectionist path. Restrictions on foreign investment and import competition have enabled the development of a number of large, and now increasingly competitive, domestic firms. Where capital and market entry barriers are high, in vehicle manufacturing for example, selective foreign collaboration has been allowed. However, lower levels of competitive pressure have resulted in many inefficient firms; restrictive regulatory policies have also created many suboptimally sized firms (MGI [McKinsey Global Institute] 2003a).

Differences in these development paths have prompted a lively debate as to which one is likely to prove superior in the long run (Ahya and Xie 2004; Huang and Khanna 2003; Khanna 2004; Woetzel 2004b). Huang and Khanna (2003) argue that India's encouragement of domestic entrepreneurship is likely to provide it with a stronger foundation for future growth than China's development based on the attraction of foreign direct investment. They wonder why China, which attracts twenty times more FDI and has a domestic savings rate twice that of India, enjoys an average growth rate that is only 50 percent higher. The answer, they argue, is that FDI in China focuses on the lower end of technological sophistication and enables the continuation of a severely flawed capital market. Policies that attempt to maintain the continuing operation of a grossly inefficient SOE sector contribute to widespread waste of resources.

The argument that entrepreneurship is superior to a development model based on the attraction of inward investment is based on an extremely narrow view of the development process. It assumes that new activities are easily identified by domestic entrepreneurs because they are consistent with existing comparative advantage. Similarly, entrepreneurs are assumed to have access to the necessary funds, scale, and overseas market opportunities to succeed. The reality of development is quite different. Recent research has highlighted the importance of self-discovery in the development process (Hausmann and Rodrik 2003). *Self-discovery* refers the process of determining what goods and services a country should produce. Understanding the activities in which a country should engage determines future specialization. Such determination is no longer simple; in today's global economy it depends on more than just natural comparative advantage. Because of the mobility of capital, skills, technology, and discrete production processes, countries have a wide range of economic choices, the appropriateness of which they can influence through decisions on investment in infrastructure and capabilities (Gomory and Baumol 2000).

This view of development is supported by recent empirical evidence that reports a tendency, in the early stages of development, for economic activities to initially become more diversified before converging around comparative advantage (Imbs and Wacziarg 2003). This evidence is consistent with the self-discovery concept and an assumption that technology is neither fully known nor codified. Even technologies that are well established in the advanced countries are likely to require adaptation to the different cost and resource conditions that exist in an emerging economy.

The challenge for an emerging economy is that self-discovery is a process that is undersupplied. This is because it requires considerable investment and offers no guarantee of full appropriation of the returns. Discovering an appropriate economic activity or modifying technology to local conditions requires significant investment. Appropriating the return on such an investment is difficult when it may not be possible to protect the technology (because it is primarily a new application); entry of competitors is easy; and commercial success may require knowledge of, and access to, overseas markets. Under these conditions economic development may be slow and government intervention warranted. In particular, government policy should focus on encouraging entrepreneurial investment initially and production rationalization (to achieve economies of scale) subsequently (Hausmann and Rodrik 2003).

The argument of Huang and Khanna (2003) ignores these complexities of entrepreneurship in an emerging market. They conclude that individual entrepreneurs (as in the case of India) offer stronger growth prospects than state-owned enterprises or foreign direct investment (the path followed by China). However, when we factor in the market failures associated with the self-discovery process, this conclusion becomes tenuous.

The reality of entrepreneurship in India seems to be a good deal less optimistic than the position held by Huang and Khanna (2003). Many of the large private-sector family businesses, which have driven India's recent growth, were established under a licensing regime, which, like South Korea, favored existing entrepreneurs. Many of the new sectors opened to private investors were effectively "winners" picked by the government through a combination of industry targeting and ongoing protection. Barriers to entry meant that there were few incentives to ensure efficient production. The result has been a growth of large, diversified, but necessarily efficient businesses. Where these same firms, such as Tata, have entered new industries including call centers and business process outsourcing, the discovery processes have been undertaken by firms in the advanced economies that have sought to lower costs by outsourcing. The manufacturing outsourcing model was well established in Mexico and parts of Southeast Asia long before the Indian service sector was created. In the same way, where industry rationalization and technological updating were required, the Indian government has sought input from foreign investors. The Maruti-Suzuki joint venture has been instrumental in driving improvement in the Indian motor vehicle industry (MGI 2003a). More generally, the development of competitive Indian businesses in engineering, pharmaceuticals, and business services appears to be based more on imitation than on genuine discovery.

According to Huang and Khanna (2003), the development path pursued by China offers both a less sustainable model and a significant loss of economic sovereignty. The effective absence of a local entrepreneurial class, destroyed by almost 50 years of communism, means that reliance has been placed on foreign investors in both the development of new industries and rationalization of state-owned enterprises. However, it is important to recognize that the first wave of inward investment into China, particularly between 1978 and 1991, was largely undertaken by overseas Chinese based primarily in Hong Kong, Taiwan, and Singapore. These overseas-based entrepreneurs were eager to exploit new low-cost opportunities as they faced rising costs in their home markets. In a way that India has never been able to emulate, China attracted back many of the successful entrepreneurs who had fled the mainland after 1949. These entrepreneurs brought capital, proven production techniques, and strong sales in overseas markets. Their ties with the mainland meant that they were particularly effective in "discovering" new production possibilities.

The growth of FDI after 1991, and a broadening of source countries including Europe, Japan, and the United States, brought an alternative to domestic entrepreneurship. In many ways international businesses are very well placed to drive the discovery process in an emerging economy. They possess the technical knowledge necessary to determine new profitable opportunities in an emerging market. They are also equally knowledgeable regarding likely demand for such products in a range of overseas markets. International businesses have the resources (capital, technology, and management) to overcome local market failures and to achieve minimum efficient scale. The latter is an important consideration in China, where the emergence of national firms capable of competing successfully in global markets has been frustrated by four decades of policy that geographically dispersed productive capacity in response to perceived security threats.

International businesses also bring an important set of incentive mechanisms that ensure efficient operations. Many of these are integral elements of their day-to-day operations. Internal trade—the supply of components from one affiliate or the parent to another—is generally undertaken when this is the most cost-effective option. The widespread use of management practices, such as best practice, benchmarking, and the transfer of employees, contributes to the high levels of efficiency associated with international businesses (Dunning 1992). Because they are private businesses, multinational enterprises are also subject to the ultimate market discipline of takeover, bankruptcy, or withdrawal. This is well illustrated in the case of the Chinese brewing industry, where a number of international businesses, including Fosters, Lion Nathan, and San Miguel, all exited the industry as a result of intense competition. This discipline is generally not one that impacts state-owned firms or the large family businesses of India, which may choose to cross-subsidize an ailing division.

The contribution of international businesses to the development of the Chinese economy was strengthened by the use of discretionary industrial policy. The insistence, in the early years of opening, on joint venture operations, and more recently on the fostering of consolidation, has encouraged positive spillovers from the foreign-owned to the domestic sector. Similarly, requirements on local sourcing have also facilitated the development of local capability as well as technological and quality upgrading. Industrial policy has also recognized the importance of appropriate sequencing. While Chinese capital markets have been criticized as being inefficient (Farrell and Key 2005), the reality of development is that generally new activities need to be discovered before they require full financing. This has allowed the Chinese authorities to postpone financial reform. Membership in the WTO has accelerated inward investment flows while providing a breathing space until financial reform becomes compulsory.

Our discussion suggests that India and China have pursued different paths of economic development. While India has encouraged domestic entrepreneurship, China has placed far greater reliance on FDI. When we look at the reality of development, it is not apparent that one path is necessarily superior to the other. The argument that encouraging domestic entrepreneurship will provide a stronger foundation for long-term development is not persuasive. Available evidence certainly does not support this view. In quantitative terms, China's exports are 7.5 times larger than those of India. Analysis of the composition of exports reveals that China's trade structure is far more technologically sophisticated than might be expected for a country at its stage of development (Rodrik 2006). Discretionary industrial policy, when used and structured appropriately, can ensure huge benefits from a policy based on the attraction of foreign investors. India's attempts to attract more FDI have not been that successful, and it faces a huge challenge in competing with China for a greater share of such investment.

Obstacles to Emerging Market Evolution

While we can draw some general conclusions about the evolution of emerging markets, it should be apparent that numerous factors impact on the pace, direction, and form of development. Indeed, forecasts of the growing role of big emerging markets in the world economy are based on an explicit assumption that these countries will maintain growth-friendly policies and develop appropriate supportive institutions (Wilson and Purushothaman 2003). However, the reality is that a number of factors could frustrate the evolution process (*BusinessWeek* 2005e; Deloitte Research 2004b; Wolf et al. 2003). We can classify such factors as being either external or internal to an economy. They may also be common to a number of countries or unique to a particular country.

External Factors

External influences that are likely to affect the evolution of an emerging market stem from decisions or actions taken in other countries or overseas organizations. At the present time, the most significant threats are those linked to the new protectionism that has become apparent in a number of developed countries, as well as simmering political and strategic threats.

The New Protectionism The very success of China and India in the world economy creates the danger of a negative backlash. As these countries increase their share of exports to the advanced countries, and as work is transferred to lower-cost locations and massive trade imbalances continue, politicians have agitated to control what are increasingly seen as unacceptable costs. This has created a *new protectionism* apparent in the past couple of years. This protectionist sentiment is now found in a number of advanced economies and appears to be the result of a growing disquiet with globalization, of which the rise of China and India is simply one manifestation (Bachman 2006; Stewart 2006). There are several considerations that are fueling growing protectionism. One is the extremely high rates of export penetration that China in particular has achieved (Chat et al. 1999). China is now recognized as the world's factory, producing more than half the world's cameras, 30 percent of all air conditioners and televisions, and 25 percent of the world's washing machines (Deloitte Research 2003). When quotas on clothing and footwear were eliminated at the beginning of 2005, Chinese firms moved quickly to substantially increase their market shares in both the United States and Europe.

Europe attempted to restrict lingerie imports (Elliott 2005) and has faced calls to protect the footwear industry, which saw imports from China increase by 700 percent in the first half of 2005 (Buck et al. 2005). As a result of the pressure from domestic producers, China and the EU (European Union) agreed voluntary quotas on selected textile products, which will offer some protection until 2008. While these concerns seem very similar to the competitive threat posed by a rising Japan in the 1970s and 1980s, there are reasons to believe that the China onslaught may be more difficult to contain. For one thing, China's ability to undercut costs is much greater than Japan's ever was; undercutting of U.S. costs by 60 to 70 percent is possible by Chinese firms. China has a much larger labor force enjoying fewer protections than Japanese workers, meaning that the cost advantage is likely to persist for much longer. China is also waging a much broader attack on world markets within a wide range of product categories. Its businesses appear highly adept at moving quickly into new product lines and rapidly acquiring market share.

Similar threats have been faced by Indian service providers, which have seen a backlash over the growth in outsourcing, including restrictions on the transfer of U.S. government service work to India. However, recent evidence suggests that the concerns may have been exaggerated. Technical employment in the United States, particularly within higher-value activities, appears to be growing while outsourcing of lower-value tasks continues (Naughton 2006).

A second area of concern is the recent expansion of Chinese and Indian companies overseas. Chinese businesses are sometimes seen as enjoying an unfair competitive advantage resulting from state ownership, subsidized financing, and close political ties. These concerns led to the thwarting of a proposed $18.5 billion acquisition of California oil company Unocal by China's CNOOC. Haier was also unsuccessful in its attempt to acquire its U.S. rival, Maytag. In contrast, TCL Corporation acquired the venerable U.S. brand RCA, and Lenovo (formerly Legend) was successful in its acquisition of IBM's personal computer business. Having a Hong Kong listing may have affected Lenovo's perception in overseas markets. However, this deal did trigger a security probe, and more recently there has been a security concern with the possibility of the U.S. State Department purchasing

16,000 computers from Lenovo (Fioravante 2006). Where ownership or links are unclear, as in the case of telecommunications manufacturer Huawei, which is suspected of having close military ties, problems can result. The authorities restricted its expansion plans in India (*Economist* 2005d). In 2004, the U.S. authorities imposed a 25 percent antidumping duty on appliance manufacturer Sichuan Changhong Electric, not because it was selling below cost but simply because its state ownership was thought to provide an unfair advantage (*Business-Week* 2005f).

Third, there is a widespread view that the Chinese currency, the yuan, is undervalued. This is reflected in a rising trade surplus and a continuing ability to attract investment inflows. China is under pressure to revalue. This pressure comes from both Japan and the United States, which run considerable trade deficits with China, and from neighboring Asian economies that are struggling to maintain competitiveness against China. China is resisting calls for a currency adjustment because it is so dependent on exports to fuel continuing growth. Furthermore, any revaluation would disadvantage local businesses servicing domestic demand as imports become cheaper in local currency terms.

China faces considerable pressure as a result of the huge U.S. trade deficit. This, it is argued, results from China's ability to supply products at prices that other countries cannot match, as well as its adherence to an (undervalued) fixed exchange rate policy. While it is easy to place the blame overseas, the reality is that the U.S. trade imbalance reflects excessive consumption and insufficient saving by Americans. It is also difficult to reconcile the facts that the U.S. economy is far larger than that of China, and that U.S. foreign investment into China is thirteen times higher than investment going the other way, with the reality of the continuing trade deficit. It is not at all clear that the maintenance of an undervalued currency is in the best interests of China (Deloitte Research 2004b). Low interest rates and high levels of bank lending have fueled both inflation and excess productive capacity. A sizable revaluation would not only address these problems but would help correct the U.S. trade imbalance as well as offer Chinese consumers lower prices on imported goods.

In part, protectionist calls reflect anxiety about the continuing validity of conventional trade theory. Trade theory suggests that as a high-wage economy such as the United States imports simple products or outsources low-skill work, this releases resources that can be reemployed in higher-value-adding activities. In addition, consumers in the high-wage economy benefit from the lower prices of imported goods. While in theory this appears attractive, recent experience suggests that the nature of international economic exchanges may be changing (Roach 2006). Workers who have been displaced in the United States, for example, have struggled to gain more skill and higher-paying jobs. Indeed, the evidence suggests that such workers can expect a wage cut and may face pressure for work intensification to match lower-cost competitors. Furthermore, increasingly it is white collar, moderately skilled jobs that are shifting overseas as Indian and Chinese engineers and programmers offer comparable skill levels at much lower pay rates. Income is being redistributed from labor to capital, and the real wages of the least skilled have fallen both absolutely and relatively (*Business-Week* 2004b; Dapice 2006). However, it would be naïve to believe that globalization is solely responsible for this. At the same time there has been considerable substitution of capital for labor. In the advanced countries, manufacturing employment is declining at the same time that manufacturing output is increasing. This is not consistent with a belief that all such work is being transferred overseas; rather, it suggests an upgrading of manufacturing output and displacement of labor by capital. Interestingly, countries such as France, less directly impacted by the rise of China and India, are also struggling to adjust to the pressures of globalization (Sabatier 2006).

Military and Strategic Threats   The rise of China and India has created strains for international relations, particularly in the Asian region. India and Pakistan have fought three times since their separation in 1947, and relations over Kashmir continue to simmer. While relations appear to have improved in recent years, growing Muslim militancy and lingering Hindu nationalist attitudes mean that a flare-up remains a worrisome possibility. For China, Taiwan remains the main external threat. While economic links between the two economies have increased significantly, political questions continue to be a major source of tension. While China is committed to military intervention if Taiwan declares independence, its policy focus in recent years has been far more subtle. The emphasis has been on ensnaring Taiwan through growing economic and social interactions. For example, China is pushing for normalization of trade aviation and postal services. At the same time, its proposal for an ASEAN-China free trade zone would bring the two countries much closer. A peaceful solution is preferable to other parties because military action would invariably trigger U.S. and possibly Japanese involvement with massive implications for trade and financial stability. One effect of growing economic integration is to substantially raise the costs to both parties of conflict. Taiwan is an extremely open economy with a trade level close to 75 percent of GDP. It also imports 95 percent of its energy needs. This makes Taiwan extremely vulnerable to any trade blockade. Two-way trade between Taiwan and the Chinese mainland is now worth some US$30 billion. Estimates of Taiwanese investment in China suggest a base value of at least US$100 billion. Discounting political and military considerations, the purely economic costs of any protected conflict would be considerable for both sides.

China also faces several other areas of potential tension in the region. One results from its desired access to energy resources and maritime claims in the South China Seas. These claims are contested by a number of other countries including Malaysia, the Philippines, Indonesia, and Vietnam. A second potential source of conflict could be with India if there is a perception that China is fueling the Kashmiri problem through its military and technical support of Pakistan. The Sino–Indian dispute of 1962 has left a legacy of considerable distrust between the two sides.

While there is a 1,000-year history of conflict between China and Japan, relations have been particularly troublesome in recent years. Japanese interpretations of wartime history triggered widespread anti-Japanese protest across China in April 2005. However, the underlying problem appears to be one of leadership in the Asian region. Japan has both the military capability and economic strength to challenge China's growing influence in the region and appears to be moving away from its traditional postwar pacifism. China has sought to frustrate

Japan's attempts to gain permanent membership in an expanded UN Security Council. Japan has also made clear its willingness to defend Taiwan in the face of any Chinese aggression toward the disputed island. It has also impeded China's attempt to become a member of the Inter-American Development Bank. Both countries are competing to secure energy resources, particularly large gas deposits within the East China Sea as well as the disputed Senkaku/Diaoyu Islands.

Many of the smaller Asian economies are fearful of China's power and have attempted to enmesh China in the regional apparatus of Asia. China sees this as an opportunity to extend its economic power in particular. Both Japan and India have strengthened relations with the United States and are actively contributing to current international problem areas including Iraq and the war on terrorism. Perhaps the biggest obstacle to China's regional ambitions is its lack of political democracy. While its neighboring economies are based on the rule of law and adhere to regional and international rules and norms, this is not the case in China. As has been noted, China may be driving economic unity within Asia; politically it is divisive (Twining 2005) and appears to have prompted growing nationalism within a number of Asian countries.

Internal Factors

Economic development may also be threatened by a range of internal factors that are, potentially at least, capable of being influenced by national policy decisions. A number of these are shared by emerging markets; others are unique and reflect specific conditions in a particular country. The most common shared issues are the threat from rising inequality, maintaining reforms, achieving sustainable growth, and the likely impact of AIDS/HIV.

Inequality   The inequality of development in both China and India is causing concern. The widening income gap between the wealthy and the poorest has triggered discontent and protest. In China the level of civil protest has risen steadily in recent years (*Economist* 2005c). There seem to be two distinct causes of discontent. One is a result of industrial restructuring and involves workers in heavy industries such as steel, predominantly located in the industrialized northeast. Between 1998 and 2002, 26 million Chinese workers were laid off from state-owned enterprises (Smyth et al. 2005). In response to such protests, which emerged around 2002, the authorities have slowed down the pace of restructuring. In addition, they have sought to attract further foreign investment into industries such as telecommunications, tourism, and light manufacturing in an attempt to accelerate the rate of new job creation. The problem with this is that the sorts of jobs created, and the locations they favor, do not match the needs of the newly unemployed. The encouraging feature for the authorities is that there is no evidence of the emergence of a regional or national labor movement (*BusinessWeek* 2002a). Nor do the employment-related protests appear to be directed at the state; rather, the focus is senior management and local officials (Whyte 2000). While India has not experienced the same level of sustained labor protest, there have been isolated incidents that could negatively impact international investment. In July 2005 a violent protest at a Honda Motorcycles and Scooters India, Ltd. plant in Guragon, Haryana state, received international press coverage. Because of differences in political systems between China and India, social unrest has contrasting implications. In China, unrest is seen as a direct threat to the political authorities. As such, it is likely to trigger either a sympathetic policy response or increased repression. In India, in contrast, democracy means that such discontent can be managed but may hinder the reform process (*Economist* 2005e).

The second source of social discontent in China is found in the rural population with peasant farmers who have little to show from years of rapid growth. The Chinese model of development, with its focus on high growth, the encouragement of private enterprise, and strengthening property rights, favors an urbanized middle class. Peasant farmers have seen their incomes slip relative to others as urban income growth over the period between 2000 and 2004 was twice that of the rural sector. The result was that by 2004 rural net per capita income was less than one-third of the urban level (Yu 2005). Belatedly, the authorities have recognized the danger and in February 2006 announced a new policy initiative of increased rural investment, agricultural subsidies, and improved social services designed to address the growing income gap (Watts 2006). India has also moved to address the needs of its rural population, many of whom have seen little benefit from the country's increased global integration (Einhorn 2005), with the introduction of an ambitious work-guarantee scheme.

Continuing Reform If they are to achieve the growth rates required to drive job creation and fund social and infrastructure expenditures, both China and India need to ensure that economic reform continues. Failure to undertake the necessary reforms means that it will be difficult for either country, India particularly, to achieve the growth rates that underpin the optimistic forecasts suggesting that these countries will become economic superpowers. For example, a Goldman Sachs study assumes India can grow at an annual average rate of 8.5 percent, which is far higher than the 6 percent it has averaged over the past two decades. For China the key reform challenges continue to be state-owned enterprises and the banking system. These are certainly areas that concern executives doing business in China (Orr 2004). The significance of state-owned enterprises in China is a result of five decades of state intervention and central planning. Public ownership means that they face incentive structures quite different from those of commercial enterprises. They are obliged to maintain employment; losses are covered by government handouts; and cheap financing means that they can easily expand capacity, in many cases creating excess capacity and depressing product prices. The most troubled industries include armaments, metals, machinery, coal, and textiles. Their performance reflects this set of incentives. In 1998 SOEs received subsidies in excess of 150 billion yuan to generate profits of 49 billion yuan (Lingle 2000). In 2001 there were 174,000 SOEs, more than half of which had losses. The state strategy has been to encourage the growth of non-state businesses with the aim of reducing the importance of the state-owned sector. By 2002, non-state businesses accounted for 83 percent of all enterprises and 75 percent of GDP but received only 35 percent of all bank loans (Pitsilis et al. 2004).

Some restructuring of the state-owned sector has occurred. The introduction of a managerial responsibility system has brought a closer link between managerial performance and compensation. A number of state managers are now employed on three-year contracts, which can be terminated in the face of underperformance. The relaxation of labor protections saw the layoff of 26 million workers from SOEs between 1998 and 2002 (Smyth et al. 2005). Over the same period, new jobs created in non-state enterprises exceeded 16 million. While a small number of SOEs, such as PetroChina, ChinaMobile, and ChinaTelecom, have become very profitable, consistent with a gradual reformist strategy, the principal focus has been on the encouragement of alternatives to SOEs. Privatization has overwhelmingly concentrated on small and medium SOEs. This strategy has provided employment alternatives for laid-off workers but has increased competition and depressed prices obtained by SOEs. This has exacerbated losses incurred in the state-owned sector. While it appears that China can sustain lay-offs of some three to five million workers per year without the danger of widespread social unrest (Fan 2003), a concern is the fact that many of the largest layoffs are geographically concentrated in areas such as northeast China (Orr 2004).

The problems facing the Chinese banking industry are considerable. The sector lacks effective leadership. The central bank, the People's Bank of China, lacks the autonomy or the relevant policy instruments to operate effectively as an independent bank. Furthermore, interest rates are directly controlled by the authorities and do not accurately reflect risk levels. Commercial banks are in a poor state. Banking is the dominant sector within the Chinese financial system, accounting for 96 percent of total financial assets. The banking system is highly concentrated with four state-owned banks playing the key role. Collectively they account for 90 percent of all loans to state-owned enterprises and almost 60 percent of total bank assets. The problem for these banks is that they perform a dual function—they are both instruments of government policy (primarily in financing SOEs) and commercial financial intermediaries. Unfortunately, in many ways these two roles are inconsistent. Sound commercial lending practices are unlikely when the authorities are directing lending. A number of China's leading banks are technically insolvent, burdened with more nonperforming loans than equity. Official figures suggest that at the end of 2004, nonperforming loans (NPLs) amounted to $205 billion,

13 percent of total assets. Within the four major state-owned banks, NPLs constitute somewhere between 26 and 35 percent of total loans. If anything, these figures probably represent a considerable underestimate of the problem (Lardy 1998). The declining performance of state-owned enterprises is the main cause of the burden of NPLs. SOE performance has been declining since 1978 and the start of liberalization. In 1997 almost 40 percent of industrial SOEs incurred losses compared with 19 percent in 1978. Indeed, total losses in 1997 far exceeded the earnings of profitable SOEs (Wolf et al. 2003). The sources of this poor performance include poor management and price controls on the output of SOEs.

The authorities have been willing to ensure liquidity levels at the leading banks providing them with huge cash injections. In 2003 Chinese banks received $45 billion in foreign reserves. In addition, the creation in 1999 of four asset management companies relieved the banks of $169 billion in NPLs. By 2003 only about one-third of this had been sold, at a discount of almost 80 percent (Deloitte Research 2004b). Foreign investors are not permitted to purchase NPLs. Government support has been financed by the accumulation and mediation of foreign reserves, which are in part the result of the undervaluation of the Chinese currency. The combination of low interest rates and considerable cash reserves has encouraged very high rates of bank lending. While this may appear to assist the NPL problem, by spreading these loans over a greater volume of lending, the opposite is more likely. High lending levels mean that marginally profitable projects could be funded and excessive capacity built up, depressing product prices. The net result is likely to be further NPLs.

The banks themselves appear reluctant to force repayment, perhaps because of a fear that such actions will make transparent their poor credit assessment practices. The government is reluctant to pursue the bankruptcy option and has never put into place effective bankruptcy procedures. It also failed to ensure an adequate level of competition between banks.

The first step in reform is to lift the burden of NPLs, which hamper the banks. But this in itself is not enough. Without reform of the Chinese banking culture, the absence of sound governance, coupled with ongoing state influence, means that NPLs will continue to be created.

Reform measures have been targeted toward a small number of the largest banks, a number of which are being groomed for foreign participation, and have not really impacted on the more than 100 smaller regional and local banks or the more than 3,000 credit cooperatives, which control almost half of all banking assets in China (Bekier et al. 2005). While there are more than 60 foreign banks operating in China, they control only 1.4 percent of banking assets (Deloitte Research 2004b). The concentration of savings and bank deposits constitutes a further constraint to bank reform. About 2 percent of Chinese households control more than half of all deposits, creating a potential liquidity crisis if reforms are not handled carefully (Pitsilis et al. 2004). Other measures that seem necessary include improvements in banking transparency, particularly around bad debts, and the provision of lending guidelines that would go some way toward overcoming poor credit-risk management practices. In turn, these measures would require institutions and mechanisms to ensure compliance. In combination, these are formidable challenges.

Financial reform in China needs to go beyond the banking system. The stockmarket is also fraught with problems, including its inability to attract funds sitting idly in banks; the burden of nontradeable shares held by SOEs, which account for two-thirds of total market value; restrictions on listing for companies lacking political connections; and limits on foreign investment (*Economist* 2005f). The importance of financial reform is considerable. Even in the absence of a financial crisis, the underlying weaknesses of the system have a negative effect on the control of inflation, the effective mobilization of savings, and the efficient use of financial resources, all of which could retard growth.

Excessive and inequitable regulation is a major impediment to higher growth within India. The World Bank estimates that senior Indian managers spend an average of 14 percent of their time dealing with regulatory matters, twice as much as their Chinese counterparts. The difficulties of starting or closing a business are also considerable; starting a new business takes 88 days on average, nearly twice as long as in China (see Table 3.1) (Sinha 2005a). One study suggests that the elimination of distortional regulations could add more than 3.5 percentage points to India's annual growth (Di Lodovico et al. 2001). In part, the problem is not simply the existence of these regulations;

rather, it arises because of their ambiguity, uneven application and enforcement, and susceptibility to government influence. Nevertheless, the elimination of such regulations is the most effective way to raise India's growth rate. While the two major political parties, the Bhartiya Janta Party (BJP) and the Congress Party, appear committed to further reform, they face immense difficulties in persuading their coalition parties of the value of this approach. The difficulties faced by Western retailers keen to participate in India's rapid growth are encapsulated in Box 4.1.

Box 4.1 Wal-Mart Seeks to Enter India

When President Bush visited India in March 2006 he was accompanied by a number of leading U.S. executives, including representatives of Wal-Mart. The world's largest retailer is strongly attracted to India's billion-plus consumer markets but is stymied by India's restrictions on foreign retailers. Foreign retailers can operate only as wholesalers.

Wal-Mart has been sourcing goods from India since 2001. In December 2005 it applied to open a liaison office in New Delhi. Wal-Mart says that its purpose is market research, but local retailers believe it will be used to lobby the government to relax rules on foreign retailers.

Local retailers are determined to make it difficult for Wal-Mart. Pantaloon Retail (India) Ltd., the country's top chain with some $450 million in annual revenue, has been pressing New Delhi to keep Wal-Mart out. Reliance is planning an initial investment of $750 million to set up 1,000 hypermarkets.

Source: *BusinessWeek* 2006j

It is apparent that there are strong linkages between the individual areas of required reform. Close relationships among the principal banks and state-owned enterprises in China have created a serious misallocation of capital. The amount of loans going to collective and private businesses does not reflect their importance to the economy. If the lack of capital restricts growth of the private sector, it also denies opportunities for the creation of new jobs for workers laid off by restructuring SOEs, reducing the incentive for further restructuring.

Sustainable Growth   The high rates of growth achieved by both China and India have raised concerns about the sustainability of development. The size of both countries means that their industrialization efforts will have huge implications for both resource demand and the global environment. Increased demand for energy resources from these two emerging economies has, at least in part, been blamed for record oil prices during 2006. Both are actively pursuing new supply sources of fossil fuels and are capable of utilizing nuclear energy. China, in particular, has a serious misdistribution of water supplies. Northern China, accounting for one-third of the country's population and output, has only 7.5 percent of naturally available water supplies. South China, in contrast, is prone to recurrent floods. Massive investments, such as the Three Gorges Project, are being used to better manage such resources. Wastewater management is an increasing problem with rapid industrialization and urbanization (Wolf et al. 2003). India is massively dependent on the burning of coal, creating significant air pollution. Neither country has yet reached a significant level of car ownership with the obvious implications for pollution and energy demand. China is an inefficient resource user; while it accounts for only 5 percent of global GDP, it accounts for nearly 9 percent of oil consumption, 25 percent of steel consumption, 30 percent of coal, and 13 percent of electricity (Deloitte Research 2004b). One estimate suggests that China is three times less efficient than the world average in converting energy to output (*BusinessWeek* 2005g). Neither India nor China has effective environmental laws and regulations, nor is enforcement at a satisfactory level. This carries a considerable price. The World Bank suggests that inefficient energy use costs China $120 billion per year in terms of lost output and pollution (*BusinessWeek* 2005g). However, moving to a more sustainable development model is likely to include additional charges for power, fuel, and water, all of which could trigger further social unrest. It is also likely to require a slowing of the growth rate, which would make it difficult to create the 17 million new jobs required each year. In this way China is in a bind; high growth designed to minimize social unrest probably means a continuation of wasteful energy usage.

Health and the Threat of HIV and AIDS　Both China and India have significant HIV- and AIDS-infected populations. Official figures suggest that in China between one and two million people are infected, with a 20 to 30 percent rate of increase in recent years. The United Nations estimates the total of infected Chinese could reach 10 million by 2010. Indian estimates suggest that at the end of 2003 some five million people were living with HIV or AIDS. Again, the United Nations believes this could reach 20 million by 2010. The causes of the epidemic appear similar for both countries, with extramarital heterosexual contact and intravenous drug use being the principal sources of transmission. In addition, China has a significant problem with the sale of contaminated blood products. While both countries recognize the severity of the problem, neither has in place an effective strategy to contain the spread of the disease. China's policy of segregating and prosecuting carriers is likely to encourage avoidance of the authorities and misrepresentation of one's health status. The evidence from countries such as Thailand, which is seen as a success case in combating the problem, is that a concerted response takes a number of years and is accompanied by rising infection rates for a considerable period. The economic costs of HIV and AIDS are likely to be considerable. In the case of India, the direct costs of treatment have been estimated at 1 percent of GDP (Anand et al. 1999). Such estimates do not include other impacts, such as the loss of output, savings, or labor and the negative impact on investment decisions. If widespread HIV and AIDS epidemics were to significantly shorten adult lifespan, this would seriously impact on the cost–benefit decision regarding investment in education and training. A shorter working life reduces the period available to recoup the costs of, and earn returns on, education. A decline in human capital investment would throw into jeopardy the ability of an emerging economy to move into more technologically sophisticated and higher-value activities. Furthermore, it is likely that international investment, technology transfer, and management secondment would all fall as international businesses perceived the local economy as carrying high health risks.

China, because of its one-child policy, will face a more general health-cost burden in the near future *(Economist* 2005a). There are expected to be more than 300 million Chinese aged 60 or over by the year 2025. Fewer than 17 percent of Chinese workers are currently enrolled in pension plans, and fewer than 1 in 20 have secure medical benefits. While the extended family remains a characteristic of Chinese society, the costs of building a broader social security system and caring for a large aging population will be considerable.

Improving the Business Climate   India faces an immense challenge in improving its business climate. Changes will be necessary if the country is to attract more international investment and ensure effective performance from its own firms. Inadequate infrastructure expenditure over a long period has created high costs for business in India. Infrastructure expenditure in 2003 was $21 billion, just 3.5 percent of GDP. This was one-seventh the amount spent by China in the same year; China's expenditure was also three times higher as a percentage of GDP. To a considerable extent, the low level of expenditure is a reflection of a low savings level; India's savings level between 1997 and 2004 was half that of China's. When this is added to the difficulty of attracting FDI, the demands on domestic savings from continuing government deficits, and the fact that much saving remains outside the financial system, the low level of infrastructure spending is not surprising. Like China, many Indian banks are state owned and are encouraged to direct lending to priority areas.

India's infrastructure needs range across roads, railways, communications, and airports. Past underinvestment means that most infrastructure services in India cost considerably more than those in China (see Table 3.1) (Ahya and Sheth 2005). There is little doubt that underinvestment in infrastructure is imposing huge costs on business and is impeding India's ability to reach its growth potential (Ahya and Sheth 2005). For example, more than 60 percent of Indian businesses have their own power generators to compensate for frequent power disruptions (Sinha 2005a). In part, the lack of investment appears to be related to the coalition political structure that has existed since the mid-1990s. Coalition politics makes it difficult to undertake significant shifts in expenditure patterns. The Indian authorities also show only limited ability to handle large infrastructure projects. Private-sector participation has also been low in Indian infrastructure investments. The electricity distribution network is more than 90 percent government owned. Investors are concerned about the setting of infrastructure service prices, policy inconsistency, and high rates of theft and corruption.

Within the transport sector, India's railways struggle to compete with road use. The railway system is overstaffed, requires government allocation approval for any investment, and subsidizes passenger transport at the expense of freight business. The roading network suffers from a neglect of maintenance and extensive overuse. The major ports in India are state owned and fall far below the efficiency levels of neighboring alternatives such as Singapore and Columbo. Ports, like the railways, are overstaffed and have failed to invest in modern equipment. They add significantly to the cost of undertaking international trade.

However, the past few years have seen a renewed commitment from the central government to improve infrastructure investment. The National Highway Authority of India has ambitious plans for extending and upgrading the national road network. Attempts are also being made to make such projects more attractive to the private sector. Similar initiatives are under way in the power sector. India has a daily power shortfall of 13,000 megawatts. All but 1 of the 29 state electricity boards loses money (*BusinessWeek* 2005h). The government has recognized that weaknesses in the transmission and distribution systems are discouraging private investors. An estimated 40 percent of electricity output is lost through leakage, theft, or free provision to favored groups such as farmers. The 2003 Electricity Act is an attempt to address some of these problems and has created state regulatory commissions, increased competition, and increased penalties for theft. A major project involving foreign participation is attempting to create a national transmission grid. A number of states have begun to unbundle utilities into separate generation, transmission, and distribution entities to improve efficiency and their attractiveness to the private sector. A continuing weakness is government ownership of both the major producers and the regulators. This is an unattractive scenario for private investors. Furthermore, because of political difficulties, progress in reforming the power sector has been slow.

The one area of infrastructure where India is internationally competitive is telecommunications, where extensive liberalization, considerable competition, and appropriate regulation have resulted in a strong and cost-efficient industry, which has underpinned much of the spectacular growth in business services.

India also faces challenges in ensuring the future availability of suitably qualified and competitively priced workers. While the size of the labor force would suggest that this should not be a problem in the immediate future, it appears to be a concern to Indian executives, particularly in the IT industries (Bever et al. 2005). More generally, the Indian labor market is in desperate need of reform. A statute from 1947, the Industrial Disputes Act, requires employers with a workforce of 100 or more to obtain state government approval of any layoffs. The result has been stagnation of employment growth within large manufacturing firms but dynamic growth, with 25 million new jobs created over the past decade, in small and service firms, which are exempt from this legislation. This provision is a major disincentive to investment by large manufacturing multinationals.

Conclusions

This chapter has argued that it is possible to draw some general, but nevertheless useful, conclusions about the evolution of large emerging economies. We suggest a generic growth process that is driven by both external and internal factors. Externally, both China and India have achieved rapid growth during the global era and are subject to the influence of a range of international organizations and agreements, as well as the globalization of trade and investment. At the same time, once economic stabilization has been achieved, there is a role for discretionary industrial policy, and this helps shape the growth of markets, institutions, and competition. Furthermore, discretionary policy creates the idiosyncrasies that are present in all economies. The fact that China and India have pursued quite different paths to development suggests that there is no single or simple formula.

However, the evolutionary path outlined here is by no means inevitable or programmable. There exist many obstacles to continued high growth. We have classified these as external or internal, and they may be shared by the two countries or unique. Externally, both China and India are subject to a protectionist backlash as a result of the pace and impact of their development. At the same time, both remain vulnerable to vexing external entanglements that could trigger serious repercussions. Internally, both are struggling to contain growing inequality, to maintain the reform process, and to overcome domestic weaknesses.

Implications for Management

1. While it is possible to make some generalizations regarding the development of emerging markets, this is still an idiosyncratic process. This means that market assessment is a unique process.
2. Both China and India have pursued a gradualist approach to development, and this is unlikely to change in the future. Variations in development are largely a result of discretionary industrial policy.
3. We may expect to see institutional development but not convergence. Relationship-based business systems can coexist with an increasingly rules-based system.
4. Economic evolution in both China and India has placed heavy reliance on external resources possessed by international businesses. In the case of China, this has been predominantly in the form of foreign direct investment. For India the outsourcing of work has been more important.
5. For both countries there is a range of external and internal factors that could threaten the evolution process. In combination, these factors could trigger collapse (Chang 2001). However, these problems are more likely to slow than to stop economic progress (Shenkar 2005).

Discussion Questions

1. Compare and contrast the development paths followed by Japan and the Asian Tigers and those of China and India. Identify the key elements for sustained development.
2. What lessons does the development experience of China and India provide for developing countries in other parts of the world?

5

CHINA AND INDIA

Competition, Complementarities, Collaboration, Innovation?

Introduction

The renaissance of China and India represents the most important trend in the world economy today. Indeed, it may prove to be the most significant economic event of this century. Its significance stems from not just the scale of these countries, but in part from the almost simultaneous take-off of their two economies and the extent of potential complementarities between them. Their scale is not disputed. Between them, China and India account for one-third of the world's population and more importantly 40 percent of the world's working population. By 2010 they are expected to add a further 140 million to their populations, ten times the number for Europe and the United States. The combined income of China and India, in purchasing power parity terms, is 20 percent of the global total, up from 10 percent in 1990. The fact that the two countries have accounted for an average of 30 percent of world income growth in recent years suggests that they are likely to be a key factor in future business cycles.

The timing and origins of economic reform and the subsequent take-off of India and China stem from both a desire to regain lost power and prestige as well as concern with the demise of the Soviet economic model. The last decade of the twentieth century and the adoption of new development models are seen within both countries as the most promising path to regaining the glory of the past, something that both strongly desire. The timing of reform in China and India is not coincidental. Being heavily influenced by the Soviet model in the second half of the past century both were rightly concerned in witnessing the collapse of the Soviet bloc in 1989. China's reforms, particularly agricultural reforms, were already well under way, but it is perhaps not surprising that 1991 saw the monumental decision to open the Chinese economy to the rest of the world. Similarly, the Indian currency crisis of 1991 and 1992 provided an opportunity to radically alter the country's development strategy and to move away from pervasive regulation and state planning. Furthermore, insights gained from the dramatic failure of radical reform in the Soviet Union have strengthened the case for incremental change pursued by both China and India. While both countries have adopted incremental development models, the emphasis within these has differed. India has focused on developing its already well-established market-supporting institutional framework, while China has followed its East Asian neighbors with the move to a more open and market-based economy.

Because China has enjoyed a decade lead over India in reform and the fact that the two countries seem to have pursued quite different development paths (China's focus has been manufacturing, India's most dynamic sector is services), the two appear complementary. However, the reality is much more complex. In many areas (energy, the attraction of foreign investment) the two appear to be strong competitors. Furthermore, analysis suggests that if both countries are to maintain their recent strong growth, they are likely to increasingly encroach upon one another's strengths. Thus we may expect greater competition if the structures of the two economies converge.

This chapter examines the myriad economic relationships between these two big emerging markets. We consider first the structure of the two economies and how these have evolved.

The section titled "Competition" examines sectors such as offshore sourcing where the two appear to be in direct competition. Areas of complementarity and collaboration are highlighted in "Complementarities" and "Collaboration." The ability of China and India to move up the value chain through innovation and economic upgrading is then discussed. "Internationalization of Domestic Firms" considers the internationalization of Chinese and Indian firms and whether these countries will produce major global businesses of their own.

"Challenges That Each Country Faces" summarizes the key challenges that each country faces in the future evolution of their economies, followed by brief conclusions. Supporting data for the discussion is provided in Table 5.1.

Structure of the Chinese and Indian Economies

At first glance, the structure of the economies of China and India suggests considerable complementarities between the two countries. China is now recognized as a key global manufacturing center, the "workshop of the world," while India is a leader in business services. This popular view is borne out by the data. In 2003, industry accounted for 52.3 percent of China's GDP and services accounted for 33.1 percent. For India, industry was just 26.8 percent of GDP, but services accounted for a sizable 51.0 percent (see Table 2.1). Growth patterns in recent years have reinforced these structural differences. In India, the services sector has grown much faster than manufacturing; in China the opposite has occurred. Trade patterns also reflect these differences. India's leading exports are found in sectors of high labor and low capital intensity, such as commercial services, gems and jewelry, engineering goods, agricultural goods, and textiles. China's trade growth has been more broadly based across the manufacturing sector. It enjoys comparative advantage in segments with high labor and capital or infrastructure intensity, such as electronics, computers and telecommunications, machinery, and garments.

Even within sectors there are notable differences between the two economies. India's strength in manufacturing is in small-scale batch production (see Box 5.1). This is apparent in pharmaceutical production, for example, where India is an important contract manufacturer for the major multinationals. India is well suited to pharmaceutical production, which has high knowledge content and a low weight-to-value ratio, meaning that such products are not overly dependent on India's ailing infrastructure. Companies such as Matrix operate in the niche business of producing ingredients for global pharmaceutical firms. In 2003, pharmaceutical products accounted for 4 percent of India's total exports.

Table 5.1   China and India: Competitiveness Indicators

	CHINA	INDIA
Economic structure 2002 (% share of production)		
Food and commodities	7.9	21.7
Chemicals	4.5	11.2
Textiles, clothing, and footwear	21.0	24.2
Metals and minerals manufacture	7.5	23.7
Machinery	8.7	5.5
Office machines and electronics	34.2	2.9
Other machinery	16.2	10.8
Total	100.0	100.0
Energy dependency		
Oil imports as a % of consumption 2003	33	70
Oil as a % of total imports	10	33
Oil demanded as a % of global oil demand 2003	7.5	3
Productivity (CAGR[compound annual growth rate]) of labor productivity 1990–2003 %)	7.3	3.3
Growth competitiveness index 2003 (rank)	44th	56th
Human Capital Indicators		
Total labor force (millions)	744	378
Female (% of total)	41.5	32.0
Agricultural workforce (% of total)	45.2	58.0
Unemployment rate (%)	3.6	9.2
Gross enrollment ratio		
Primary schools (%)	114	102
Secondary schools (%)	68	49
Tertiary education (%)	13	10
Literacy (%)		
Male	92	68
Female	78	45
Total public expenditure on education (% of GDP)	2.2	4.0
Total public expenditure on education (per capita $)	19.5	18.4
Tertiary educated (population over 25 with completed tertiary education) (millions)	17.5	16.1
Graduates per 1,000 people	14	16
Annual production of graduate engineers	490,000	400,000
U.S. FDA-approved pharmaceutical plants	20	65
U.S. pharmaceutical patents 1997–2001	54	126

Table 5.1   China and India: Competitiveness Indicators (continued)

CMM-rated software firms (population)		
Level 5	2	50 (50% fully local)
Level 4	0	27 (75% fully local)
Number of firms in the *BusinessWeek* largest emerging market companies	20/200	11/200
Forbes listing of the world's best small companies	4/200	13/200
Health Indicators		
Physicians (per 1,000 people)	2	0.4
Health expenditure (as % of GDP)	5.0	5.0
Health expenditure per capita ($)	45	23
Infant mortality per 1,000 live births	27	61
Life expectancy at birth (years)	71	63
Population in poverty (%)	10	25

Source: Ahya and Xie 2004.

Box 5.1 Balkrishna Tires

Balkrishna Tires is a Bombay-based tire manufacturer. It started as a producer of scooter tires but struggled to remain competitive after industry deregulation in the early 1990s. In response, it sought export niche markets and moved into the highly specialized business of off-highway tires, primarily tires for agricultural and construction use. Ninety-five percent of production is exported to 75 markets around the world. Sales grew from $7.5 million to $85 million between 2000 and 2005 within a global market that is worth some $3.75 billion per year. About 65 percent of products are sold in Europe where farms are small and methods scientific, requiring tractors with different tire types for agribusiness like grapevine cultivation and orchid farming. The bigger tire manufacturers such as Bridgestone and Michelin see the off-highway business as too low volume, too fragmented, and too labor intensive.

Balkrishna Tires is able to overcome these obstacles by drawing on India's comparative advantages. It has developed flexible production systems that allow it to produce 1,500 styles.

By drawing on India's considerable engineering skills, it spends 4 percent of revenue on R&D and has the capacity to change 25 molds per day, five times that of competitors, allowing it to make 150 different types of tires. Second, it exploits India's low labor and production costs. Balkrishna's labor costs are just 4 percent of sales compared with 33 percent for Western producers. Third, it has access to cheap raw materials because India is the world's third largest producer of rubber.

However, the company still struggles with India's infrastructure deficiencies and in seeking to expand capacity is looking at building plants in other Indian states, closer to seaports.

Source: BusinessWeek Online 2005l.

China's broader base in manufacturing has enabled it to be far more integrated into the world economy than India. Perhaps two in every five Chinese are linked to the world economy, some 450 million people, while the comparable figure for India is closer to one in five. On almost any measure, the Chinese economy is more open than that of India. A striking difference is apparent in tariff levels, which as a percentage of import value now average around 3 percent in China but 15 percent in India.

Developments in the export structure of both countries show that China has been much more responsive to changing market opportunities than India. For India, exports of food, metal ore, and petroleum products still account for over one-fifth of total exports, while in China the share of food and primary commodities has fallen rapidly and now accounts for less than 8 percent of total exports. On the other hand, machinery, office machines, and electronics account for more than 40 percent of China's exports but less than 10 percent for India. Import figures support the belief that China's structural adjustment has been much greater than that of India. China is far more likely than India to import components and resources for further processing. Basic commodities, including food, raw materials, energy, and basic metal manufactures, still account for two-thirds of India's imports, while the comparable figure for China is 40 percent (Rautava 2005).

The mix of China's exports has changed dramatically in a short period of time. While machinery and electrical appliances were just 2.8 percent of Chinese exports in 1986, they made up 23.7 percent by 1998. Similarly, China has rapidly increased its share of world output of items such as personal computers and keyboards at the same time that the share of ASEAN (Association of Southeast Asian Nations) producers has fallen (Deloitte Research 2003).

Because of differences in resource endowments and quality of infrastructure, India has the potential to be more competitive than China in resource-based sectors such as aluminum, steel, paper, and agricultural products, but achieving the necessary scale to be cost efficient is very difficult with India's current infrastructure. Infrastructure weaknesses limit firm scale and are particularly onerous for small firms, which cannot make the huge investments necessary to achieve a degree of self-sufficiency in critical areas such as power provision. The result is that India's largest steel company has an annual capacity just 11 percent of that of China's top two producers. Because of its considerably higher savings rate and ability to attract international capital, China is likely to remain the stronger of the two countries in infrastructure- and capital-intensive industries.

A unique feature of both China and India, and in marked contrast to the earlier high-growth Asian economies of Taiwan, South Korea, Hong Kong, and Singapore, is that the former should be able to maintain their low-cost positions while upgrading their economies. This is primarily because of the vast supplies of labor that both enjoy. There will certainly be considerable opportunities to continue to produce low-technology, labor-intensive products. Surveys suggest that the amount spent on components and materials sourced from low-cost countries will increase significantly over the next few years, and that most of the increased supply will come from China (Quint and Shorten 2005). Furthermore, many Chinese manufacturing firms are linked into the global economy in a shallow manner and are trapped in the production of cost-sensitive undifferentiated commodities (Rosen 2003a; Steinfeld 2004).

However, the future may see a growing convergence of the development models of China and India. This could occur as both increase their share of world trade to perhaps 20 percent by 2010 (Ahya and Xie

2004). In particular, India can be expected to emphasize the development of its manufacturing sector, and China can be expected to focus on increasing the international competitiveness of its service sector.

There are several reasons to expect India to seek to develop its manufacturing industry. One is the need to create employment opportunities for the vast numbers of relatively unskilled who will enter the Indian labor market in future decades. It would be hard to imagine that the service sector could provide jobs for all of these. In addition, manufacturing offers far more attractive trading opportunities than services. Currently, 80 percent of total world trade (goods and services) is in goods.

At the same time, emerging opportunities for China are likely to be found in services. China is already a significant player in world service markets. However, to develop its market share in services, China will need to overcome several obstacles, particularly in ensuring an adequate supply of appropriately skilled graduates (MGI [McKinsey Global Institute] 2005). Equally, India will need to make considerable investments in schooling, in lowering trade barriers, and in continuing economic reform if it is to develop an internationally competitive manufacturing sector.

The huge pressures on both countries to maintain growth rates, to deepen and broaden their economies, and to tackle underlying constraints may set them on a path of increasingly direct economic competition.

Competition

While the above discussion suggests that China and India may be set to experience greater direct competition in the future, it is important to recognize that there already exist areas where they are in direct conflict. Currently, both China and India compete for low-end manufacturing and service jobs that are leaving the high-wage economies. While part of this competition is with other potential locations, much of it is now between the two economies. The high rates of growth enjoyed by both countries mean that they also compete for energy and raw materials.

In terms of the offshore sourcing of services, India has a substantial lead over China and enjoys a strong competitive advantage. This is apparent from the fact that India has approximately 60 percent of the global market for offshore services (Sheshabalya 2005) and China has perhaps 5 percent (*Economist* 2006b). However, China has ambitious plans to develop the service side of its economy, and part of that involves competing for outsourced services, bringing it into direct competition with India. The market is an attractive one, expected to be worth almost $75 billion by 2007, and growing at a rapid rate (*Economist* 2006b). Market growth is driven by two key factors: more firms seeking to reduce costs by outsourcing service tasks and a growing ability to outsource more of any activity. For example, the offshore component of IT services is expected to grow from 5 percent in 2003 to possibly 23 percent by 2007 (Sheshabalya 2005).

China starts from a modest foundation in competing for international services. Cities such as Dalian, with its geographic and linguistic links with Japan and South Korea, undertake back-office services for companies from these countries. Chinese wages for engineers, particularly away from the coastal cities, are extremely competitive and labor turnover rates are lower than those in India. China offers excellent infrastructure and a viable alternative location for international businesses fearing overdependency on India. It also makes sense for China to provide business services that support their attractiveness as a global manufacturing center. Many international businesses, and some local firms, are seeking such services to support their growing Chinese operations.

However, to compete successfully in this market, China will need to overcome a number of limitations. Studies question the suitability of many of China's graduates for employment in the service sector. Many of those who would be suitable are absorbed by the booming domestic economy. Fewer than 10 percent of all Chinese graduates may be suitable for employment in international services, compared with perhaps 25 percent in India (Farrell and Grant 2005). Employers have expressed concerns about the strong theoretical bias in the education of Chinese graduate engineers. Often employers have to make considerable investments in developing vocational and commercial capability (*Economist* 2006b). This is not a cost that is incurred in India. Furthermore, Chinese graduates are far less capable than their Indian counterparts in the use of English, particularly written and spoken English. This limits the ability of Chinese firms to capture work in the very large English-language segment of the industry. However, it is important to note that China doubled the number of English-speaking graduates it produced between 2000 and 2004 (Filippo et al. 2005). It has also spawned a small number of highly creative software firms that are managed more along Western than Chinese lines (Levy 2006).

The fragmentation of Chinese service firms is a further problem. None are as large as their Indian competitors, and there are few incentives for consolidation. Indeed, the regional focus of Chinese officials and the absence of an effective industry body make it unlikely that world-class Chinese service providers will emerge in the foreseeable future. The top ten IT-services companies in China have only 20 percent of the market compared with 45 percent for India's leading ten firms. Only five Chinese software providers have more than 2,000 employees (Filippo et al. 2005). International clients see small companies as risky partners subject to damaging losses of key staff, liquidity difficulties, and limited project management skills. Similarly, Chinese firms have not achieved the international quality certification levels that have boosted overseas confidence in Indian service producers. Meanwhile, large American, European, and even Indian business service providers are now well established in the Chinese market. The likely outcome is that China may capture a growing share of the lower-level business services, such as data entry, while India emphasizes the higher-order services such as research, design, and testing, where creativity and strong linguistic and cultural skills are of paramount importance.

In fact, India has already spawned a number of small, specialized, high-value service providers. MarketRx provides knowledge process outsourcing for sales teams from global pharmaceutical companies including GlaxoSmithKline, Johnson and Johnson, and Eli Lilley. Huge opportunities are also to be found in the health care business where unlimited demand and increasingly expensive technology in the West are triggering the search for cost savings (Sheshabalya 2005).

India is also using its complementary strengths to create a competitive advantage in emerging fields. The combination of IT and pharmaceutical expertise has created Indian firms that are world leaders in areas such as clinical data management and in-silico modeling. In some cases, highly complex customized service products have been created for specific customers. For example, Infosys produced a distributor management application package (DMAP) for Reebok. India's i-Flex produces the most widely used banking software products. The upgrading of Indian software firms has been facilitated by their pursuit of international quality accreditation. There are more ISO-9000 accredited software companies in India than there are in the United States. India also has more capability maturity model (CMM) certified firms than any other emerging economy (see Table 5.1) (Sheshabalya 2005).

However, it is by no means obvious that India will be able to maintain its lead in IT and business processing services. India's cost advantage in services has been eroded by rising wage costs and the need to provide perks. To some degree, this has been offset to date by falling costs elsewhere, for example, falling telecommunications costs as a result of deregulation and increased competition. But rising costs and high rates of labor turnover are forcing firms to become increasingly creative. Wipro has a company-sponsored match-making service—the "Cupid section" on Channel W, Wipro's intranet. A number of single staff have signed up with a few marriages resulting. Wipro believes that such arrangements increase the emotional bond between employees and the company (*Fortune* 2005).

More generally, for India to retain its competitive advantage it will need to find ways to overcome wage growth pressures and labor shortages. One solution is to expand the number of centers that can attract service firms, beyond already congested locations such as Bangalore. Another would be to expand service provision beyond basic business services and IT and into high-value areas such as design and R&D. This would enable higher-value creation with a given amount of resources. However, such a strategy would be dependent on ensuring adequate supplies of labor, encouraging more students to take specialist degrees such as engineering rather than generalist programs, and upgrading infrastructure and lifestyle if the appropriate people are to be attracted and retained (Farrell, Kaka, and Sturze 2005).

Indian software firms may also seek to move further afield in an attempt to protect their competitive advantage. One option is to form alliances within Latin America where service providers are emphasizing *near sourcing*, exploiting their proximity to the North American market and shared time zone. Countries including Mexico, Argentina, and Chile could be potential partners. One advantage of such arrangements is that they could give Indian firms access to projects involving sensitive aviation and energy technology, which for reasons of trade preferences and legislative restrictions are more likely to go to Mexico (*BusinessWeek* 2006a).

When we consider the competitive position of China and India in the distant future, demographic trends become the key factor. India's population is growing at twice the rate of China's, and India's working population is likely to exceed that of China's in 2040. Because of its one-child policy, China's population is, on average, older than that of India's, and the country is likely to experience a sharp rise in its age dependency ratio (the ratio of the nonworking to the working population) beginning about 2025. This means that India is likely to be able to maintain higher growth rates in the long term, while China may be constrained by labor shortages and rising welfare costs.

Complementarities

While strong competition between China and India is evident in a number of sectors, there also exist significant complementarities between the two that businesses may seek to exploit.

One area is the growth of consumer markets in India and China. Rising income levels in both China and India have created increasingly attractive markets for many international businesses. For industries such as automobiles, these markets represent the next frontier. Higher incomes and lower prices mean that the Chinese market is the larger and more developed of the two. For example, the average Indian is able to spend about 48 percent of disposable income on products other than food, beverages, and tobacco, while the average

Chinese has 62 percent (of a higher disposable income) (Ahya and Xie 2004). The Indian market is some 5 to 20 years behind China, depending on the particular item. Because of China's higher income levels, savings rates, and lower product prices, the lag is highest for durable consumer goods. China's market development is now creating elements rarely seen in the poorest economies, such as targeted advertising (see Box 5.2).

Box 5.2 Focus Media Holding Ltd

The growth of consumer markets in China has brought increased competition for the attention of potential buyers. Part of this has been a rapid growth in advertising. Focus Media Holding Ltd was created to replace the simple posters found on elevator doors with video screens. Because elevators in China are slow, and people spend an average of five minutes per day waiting for them, there is a sizable captive audience. In a six-month trial of 50 Shanghai buildings, Focus Media secured contracts from Hennessy Cognac, Fujifilm, TAG Heuer watches, ChinaTelecom, and others. The concept proved popular and the company has moved into supermarkets and airport shuttle buses. It now operates more than 35,000 screens in 52 Chinese cities.

Source: BusinessWeek Online 2005l.

Complementarities are also apparent in the educational reforms that both countries have pursued. China's focus has been on schooling, where increased expenditure and the requirement of a nine-year compulsory education period have dramatically reduced illiteracy. In 2000, China's literacy rate was 94 percent. In contrast, India has focused on tertiary education, producing in world-class institutions the engineers, scientists, and managers who have fueled its dynamic IT, software, and business services sectors. At the same time, the country has an overall literacy rate of just 65 percent. These contrasting strategies in human capital development play to the competitive strengths of each: China has the vast number of economically literate necessary for its factories; India has the elite graduates who staff its service centers. Clearly, companies that are able to bridge the two, perhaps basing

R&D or design in India and manufacturing in China, can profitably exploit these complementarities.

Chinese and Indian firms are now starting to exploit the opportunities that exist in one another's economies. India has facilitated China's economic development by exporting raw materials and semi-finished goods, as well as shipping Chinese cargo overseas. Chinese companies have begun to tap into India's consumer market by exporting electrical machinery, home appliances, and consumer electronics. Trade between the two countries has grown from $300 million in 1994 to $13.6 billion in 2005.

Indian service firms are also looking increasingly toward China. A number of opportunities present themselves. First, because China is the preferred location for Japanese and Korean outsourcers, Indian firms need to have a presence in China to get access to this work. Second, the demand for business service providers in China appears to exceed the capacity of local firms, so there are attractive prospects for Indian investors. Third, the business services model pioneered by Indian firms is based on skills and scale, and apart from India, China is the only other Asian market that offers this combination. Thus, as a market it is compatible with the competencies of Indian service firms. Finally, a presence in China may be an effective way for Indian firms to deter Chinese providers from driving the IT services market down and commoditizing such services.

Collaboration

Perhaps not surprisingly, the existence of competition and recognition of complementarities is encouraging collaboration between Chinese and Indian business in a number of areas. The most developed of these is in the energy field. Cooperative arrangements between China and India have emerged in the oil industry after a January 2006 agreement. This follows a period of strong competition between the two that saw China outbid India in deals in Nigeria, Kazakhstan, Ecuador, Angola, and Myanmar. China National Petroleum had to offer a $600 million premium to outbid India's OMEL (ONGC Mittal Energy Ltd), a joint venture between state-owned ONGC (Oil and Natural

Gas Corporation) and the private Mittal Group, to acquire Canadian independent PetroKazakhstan in August 2005. More recently, India's OVL (ONGC Videsh Ltd) and CNPC (China National Petroleum Corporation) submitted a 50-50 joint bid for PetroCanada's stake in Syrian oil-producing assets held in a consortium with Royal Dutch Shell and Syrian Petroleum.

A further benefit of collaboration could be the development of a more open and efficient energy market in Asia. Energy markets in the Asian region are far less sophisticated than those in Europe or North America. Asian oil importers would benefit from the development of pricing and benchmarking standards, strategic reserves, opportunities for hedging, and shared investments in infrastructure (Bozon et al. 2005).

Cooperation may also be initiated from outside. This appears to be the case in the global information technology industry where the United States is driving a new international division of labor, to the exclusion of European and Japanese competitors. Lenovo's acquisition of IBM's personal computer business has highlighted an emerging vertical structure. Under this arrangement, the United States plays the lead role as the center for innovation, with U.S. firms such as Intel, IBM, Motorola, and Dell responsible for half of all R&D spending in the IT industry. This is then aligned with India's software prowess and China's huge advantage in hardware production. The United States appears to be the strongest placed to drive this global production model because its firms are at the forefront of innovation (in both technology and business models) and the country's openness to migration helps offset the unfavorable demographics facing the wealthy economies. The U.S. initiative appears to be at the expense of Europe and Japan (Lehmann 2005). We may expect to see industries such as automobile manufacturing moving increasingly in this direction.

Innovation and Economic Upgrading

The phenomenal growth of both China and India means that inevitably, over time, they will seek to upgrade their economies and to develop their innovative capability. Their size and expected future economic position means that both will seek to reduce their dependence on imported and older technologies. Economic upgrading is necessary to both broaden their economies and avoid direct competition with other low-cost emerging economies, such as Indonesia, Vietnam, and parts of Latin America and Eastern Europe. At the present time, both China and India are considered to have medium innovation levels (UNCTAD [United Nations Conference on Trade and Development] 2005).

Upgrading of production has been occurring for a number of years, particularly in China. One factor responsible for this is that foreign investors have brought more advanced technologies to China. The attraction of its domestic market has enabled China to obtain foreign technology and management skills at an unprecedented rate. A number of state-owned banks and car manufacturers have been able to attract multiple foreign partners. Each of China's top three automobile manufacturers—Shanghai Automotive Industry Corporation (SAIC), China FAW (First Automotive Works), and Dong Feng Motor Corporation—has two or three foreign partners. In late 2005 the Bank of China was engaged in negotiations with four banks seeking to take a stake in its business. These included two European banks (Royal Bank of Scotland and UBS); the Asian Development Bank; and Temasek, the Singaporean government's investment arm. While spreading risk for individual investors, such an arrangement would also give China access to an unusually wide range of expertise. This is likely to accelerate the pace of upgrading within Chinese industry. Regional investors, particularly from Taiwan, have brought considerable manufacturing expertise, which is now disseminating to local Chinese firms. China is also able to utilize its growing pool of scientific and engineering personnel, both locally educated and overseas returnees. Excellent infrastructure makes it possible to source components and move final products easily and cheaply. It also facilitates the development of clusters of specialist suppliers enabling firms to move up their industry value chain as they accumulate experience.

Similar upgrading is occurring within some areas of Indian business. For example, while to date much of India's pharmaceutical production has been contract manufacturing, there are considerable opportunities to produce products that are going off patent. The number of patent filings by Indian companies is significantly higher than that of Chinese firms (see Table 5.1) (Ahya and Xie 2004). To make the transition into new products, Dr. Reddy's, for example, has formed partnerships with global giants such as Novartis while bolstering its generic business by acquiring British generic maker BMS Laboratories. One assessment suggests that India also has the potential to become a global hub in the education and financial services industries (Rajan 2005).

However, the level of spending on R&D in both China and India means that neither country is likely to become a major technological power in the short term. While China's expenditure on R&D increased during the 1990s, this was largely the result of economic growth. Absolute spending rose from $21 billion in 1996 to $70 billion in 2002, behind only the United States and Japan in absolute terms. By 2004 China's R&D spending as a percentage of GDP reached 1.3 percent, far in excess of India's 0.77 percent but well below the United States at 2.7 percent or the OECD (Organization for Economic Cooperation and Development) average of 2.26 percent. The growth in research activities has seen Chinese firms upgrading their R&D capabilities. In large- and medium-sized firms the proportion of R&D personnel to total employees has grown from 2.6 percent in 1987 to 3.9 percent in 1998, and the share of scientists and engineers among R&D personnel rose from 28.2 percent in 1987 to 54.4 percent in 1998 (OECD 2002). National brand leaders such as TCL, Haier, and Lenovo in consumer electronics and Pearl River, which manufactures pianos, all commit a significant share of revenue to research and development.

Emerging economies such as China and India enjoy an advantage in that they have not had to make investments in second-generation technologies, allowing them to move swiftly into attractive emerging areas such as mobile phone technology, agricultural genetics, biotechnology, and nanotechnology. An example is provided by China's commitment to the development of the hydrogen-powered car. The Chinese authorities have put $200 million into fuel-cell research in the past couple of years. The development of such a vehicle would not only revolutionize the industry, it would also greatly reduce China's dependence on oil and the production of greenhouse gas emissions. Because the Chinese car market is still comparatively small (about

20 million cars or eight cars per 1,000 persons compared with 940 in the United States), China might be able to avoid the massive costs involved in building a conventional vehicle fleet.

Reliance on Foreign Technology

However, because of the time it takes to build technological capability, both China and India look to foreign investment and technology to upgrade their capability (Chen and Dean 2006). In 2003 about 23.7 percent of business R&D in China was undertaken by foreign affiliates. In India in 1999, because of much lower levels of foreign investment, the comparable figure was just 3.4 percent (UNCTAD 2005). Foreign investors contribute to upgrading local technological capability in two main ways. The first is through the production and export of high-technology products from the host economy. The second is through the placement of R&D activities in an emerging economy (R&D outsourcing).

Because of its advantage in manufacturing, it is China that has benefited most from the establishment of higher-technology manufacturing activities by foreign investors. More than half of China's exports are made by foreign-owned firms that use China as a major sourcing and production base. In 2000, 55 percent of China's exports were processed and 41 percent of imports were destined for export processing (Deloitte Research 2003). Foreign firms account for three-quarters of China's technology exports and even more of what are termed high-technology exports. Exports from these firms are also growing more rapidly than average. Between 1996 and 2000, exports by foreign-invested firms increased 94 percent, twice the rate for all other exports (Deloitte Research 2003). However, many of the products that China classifies as high technology are more accurately described as mature commodities, such as DVD players and laser printers. The key components incorporated in these products, such as computer chips, are imported. In the early 1990s this resulted in a sizable high-technology trade deficit for China, particularly in regard to the United States. However, China's spectacular export growth has seen this deficit turned into a sizable surplus.

There is now significant economic interdependence between China and the United States in the trade and production of high-tech products. In 2004 China was the sixth largest market for U.S. high-tech exports. U.S. exports to China of such products trebled between 1998 and 2004 to reach $8.7 billion. However, at the same time, high-tech exports from China to the United States more than quadrupled from $16.2 billion to $68.2 billion (AeA [American Electronics Association] 2005b). The result is that China now enjoys a considerable surplus in the trade of high-tech products. However, this is largely attributable to the activities of international firms who use China as a major processing and exporting base for such products.

The second major way in which technological capability is upgraded in emerging markets is through the outsourcing of innovation activity. In exactly the same way that manufacturing and business services have been outsourced, recent years have seen a similar trend in R&D activities. Innovation outsourcing is prompted by three main factors. The first is a recognition that innovation will continue to be a key source of competitive advantage for many firms and that the pace of innovation is rising. Firms that wish to stay at the forefront of technological change increasingly search globally for new sources and locations for innovation. Second, the rising costs of innovation encourage a search for lower-cost locations, particularly locations such as China and India, which offer highly skilled labor at comparatively low wage rates. Third, the continuing fall in international communication and control costs has enabled firms to rethink their boundaries in an attempt to improve costs, speed, and flexibility. It is no longer the case that all R&D activities are best undertaken in the home country, or even within the one organization. The growing demand for strategic partnerships between firms is reflected in this new assessment of the boundaries of the enterprise.

Of the many possible locations where R&D might be undertaken, China and India are two of the most popular. This is reflected both in the number of R&D ventures that have already been established and from surveys of company intentions on the location of innovation activities (Jaruzelski et al. 2005). There were more than 700 foreign-affiliated R&D centers in China in 2004 (UNCTAD 2005). These tend to be concentrated in technology-intensive industries such as ICT (*information and communications technologies*), automobiles, and chemicals. They are particularly likely to be present in large cities with strong established technological bases and plentiful supplies of skilled people. In India, more than 100 international businesses have established R&D centers, many in the pharmaceutical industry (UNCTAD 2005). Survey evidence confirms that potential investors rate China and India as by far the most attractive locations for future R&D investments (Booz Allen Hamilton and INSEAD 2006).

The motives for locating innovative activities in China and India reflect the cost and availability of R&D resources. Studies for China highlight the availability of skilled staff, opportunities for entering into research agreements with local universities and research institutes, the existence of science parks and innovation clusters, the provision of financial incentives, and the possibility of lowering costs across all stages of the R&D process (UNCTAD 2005). The interesting feature of China is that while cost savings are a strong incentive for foreign firms, foreign placement of R&D activities increasingly forms part of global strategy. This suggests not only that China will attract further R&D investment, but that such investment will move beyond support and adaptation work to full-scale and globally applicable R&D.

Studies of India reveal similar attractions (Reddy 2000). India provides a plentiful supply of well-qualified scientists and engineers. It also has a number of highly regarded scientific institutes, which often work with foreign R&D centers. Furthermore, Indian firms in software and pharmaceuticals have begun the process of building strategic alliances with multinational competitors and are increasing the attractiveness of India as a business location in these industries.

Both China and India are moving to take advantage of the opportunities offered by outsourcing of innovation. They are attempting to move into new industries and to build sufficient critical mass to enhance absorption. For example, in the aircraft industry India's HCL Technologies is codeveloping software for the new Boeing 787 Dreamliner while China undertakes lower-level assembly work for planes such as the Airbus A320 but does not yet have the technological sophistication to produce components in the composite materials that the 787 will require. China is upgrading its electronics industry and has created the basis of an outsourcing hub in automobiles. It has also just begun to export automobiles. China enjoys a huge cost advantage over Western manufacturers in such industries. For example, Volkswagen's labor costs are about fifty times higher in West Germany than in China. Box 5.3 illustrates the way that foreign R&D has evolved in the mobile telecommunications industry in China.

Box 5.3 Foreign R&D in the Chinese Mobile Telecommunications Industry

Rapid growth in China's telecommunications market has seen it emerge as the largest mobile market in terms of capacity and number of subscribers. The major telecommunications equipment producers have established a strong presence in China, including R&D centers. In 2004, Motorola had 15 such centers in China with 1,300 employees; Nokia had 5 centers, Ericsson had 9, and Siemens had 4.

Initially the main function of these R&D centers was to adapt technology developed by the parent company to the specific market requirements in China. However, because mobile telecommunications products are highly standardized and the size and sophistication of the Chinese market has been rapidly increasing, local adaptive R&D has evolved into global innovative R&D. Every tenth mobile handset sold globally by Nokia has been designed in Beijing.

Many of the R&D centers have capabilities in the area of 3G (third generation) technologies and now develop products for both the Chinese and global markets. Nine cities in China host 3G-related R&D centers owned by foreign firms or domestic companies (Huawei and ZTE). 3G equipment developed and manufactured locally by both foreign and domestic firms has begun to supply the global market. In this way the R&D activities in China have helped the firms concerned with expanding their business in other locations as well, which in turn has had positive effects on their respective home countries.

Source: UNCTAD 2005, 196.

Policy Initiatives

To make the most of the opportunities for upgrading economic activity and increasing innovation, governments in both China and India have introduced a number of relevant policy initiatives.

One set of policies are designed to improve the efficiency of domestic firms and to prepare them for increased competition. Consolidation is occurring in the Chinese steel industry as the number two steel firm, Angang, merged in 2005 with the number five firm Bengang. This has created another sizable producer with capacity similar to that of South Korea's POSCO or China's leading steel producer Baosteel Group. This is the first step in the consolidation of China's 800 steel mills and part of a government blueprint for the industry that foresees two industry leaders and envisages the country's 10 largest mills accounting for 50 percent of steel output by 2010. Consolidation is also occurring in other sectors. In Chinese retailing, the Bailian Group, itself the result of a seven-way merger in 2003, merged two department store chains—Hualian and Number One Department Store—to create the largest listed Chinese retailer. The Indian government is seeking to merge Air India and Indian Airlines, the country's two largest airlines. Independently, both airlines are unprofitable and have lost market share to private carriers. Neither has managed to gain acceptance to the international airline alliances (*Economist* 2006c). There are a number of industries in both countries that would benefit from rationalization and consolidation if they are to upgrade in the future.

It is possible to identify a number of industry sectors in which India could achieve a strong competitive position in the future. These build on existing strengths and include financial analysis, industrial engineering, analytics (using Indian mathematicians to devise models for risk analysis, consumer behavior, and industrial processes), and drug research. Moreover, there are important synergies between traditional industries and the application of ideas from newer sectors. For example, Cummins uses its new R&D center in Pune to develop the sophisticated computer models needed to electronically design upgrades and prototypes for its engine technology.

A second policy initiative, one particularly emphasized in China, is the setting of technology standards. Technology standards that focus on the demand side of upgrading are used to complement supply-side improvements to infrastructure, education, and intellectual property protection. Here China is able to use the size and importance of its domestic market to set or influence international technology standards in a range of information technology, media, and telecommunications industries. The advantage of such a strategy to China is twofold. First, such standards provide a strong competitive impetus to its own firms, which may enjoy significant advantages when they are involved in the early determination, adoption, and proliferation of technology standards. Second, at the same time, China's dependence on foreign technology and the burden of royalty payments is reduced.

The strategy of technology standard adoption is an attractive one for China. Its huge and rapidly growing market, particularly for electronic and information products, means that it must be included in any decision on standards. The acceptance of standards occurs because they can be proliferated at low cost. Adoption in a market as significant as China is increasingly a critical determinant of global cost effectiveness. Furthermore, technology standards are dependent on government–industry cooperation, and this is an area where China has well-recognized skills. Chinese businesses are moving forward on a number of standards including computer operating systems, radio frequency identification tags, audio and visual compression, cellular networks, and satellite positioning systems (Deloitte Research 2004a).

Third, both China and India need to undertake a range of improvements to their innovative capability or, more generally, the creation of an effective national innovation system. A national innovation system describes an institutional framework that is effective in fostering innovation. The key elements of such a system include human resources, intellectual property rights systems, competition policy, and the creation of appropriate forms of funding. In addition, an emerging economy that targets foreign investment in R&D will also need to consider how to encourage such investment and how to maximize the positive spillovers for local firms.

Human Resources

As indicated elsewhere in this book, China and India are major sources of scientific and technical manpower. In absolute numbers, both countries are among the leading producers, although there is some question over the proportion of these workers who are suitable for employment in international businesses (Farrell, Kaka, and Sturze 2005). China has made significant improvements in its education system and has the benefit of many of its foreign-educated students now seeking to return to work on the mainland. The return rate is thought to be around 25 to 30 percent (Shenkar 2005). One area where controls are needed is in minimizing the likelihood of scientific fraud (*Economist* 2006d). The improvements China has made come after the Cultural Revolution, a period of massive disruption to human capital formation when schools closed for three to four years and universities for even longer. Both China and India were ranked as being low in terms of the 2001 Human Capital Index (UNCTAD 2005).

Intellectual Property

A sound intellectual property rights system is important in fostering innovative activity. The ability to assign property rights in knowledge assets facilitates both the creation and exchange of such assets. It can also assist domestic firms and institutions in their negotiations with foreign investors. China, in particular, needs to strengthen its intellectual property laws if it is to encourage innovation among its own firms. Indeed, in one extreme case, General Motors has accused Chery, a Chinese car manufacturer, of pirating two of its models. Because of their concerns with existing legislation and its inconsistent enforcement, foreign firms in China are moving to protect their intellectual property by setting up wholly owned ventures and may attempt to bypass intermediaries in the supply chain whom they do not fully trust. They are being extremely cautious in staff selection and may even monitor the activities of their Chinese partners (Dietz et al. 2005). One effect could be to impede the development of supply clusters. Asia has yet to develop world-class knowledge-based innovation clusters. According to the 2005 World Knowledge Competitiveness Index, the top 20 places were dominated by U.S. locales (Robert Huggins Associates 2005).

Competition Policy

Effective competition policies complement more direct initiatives to stimulate innovation by ensuring a general incentive for all firms to seek a competitive edge, often through innovation. Research evidence supports the idea that competitive pressure does encourage higher levels of innovative activity (Boone 2001). Competition policy needs to focus not simply on the specific industry in which innovation is desired, but also on related and supporting industries. The reality is that very few industries are innovative and competitive in isolation; most draw upon the contribution of related and supporting industries. For this reason, policy needs to acknowledge the interdependencies that exist among industries. At the same time, it is critical for the competition authorities to strike the appropriate balance between encouraging competition and facilitating cooperation and interaction.

Some clusters are beginning to appear in Chinese and Indian industries. China's many science and technology parks are playing an important role as incubators for new clusters (Walcott 2003). Some 140,000 information technology professionals now work in Bangalore. That is 20,000 more than in Silicon Valley. For SAP, the German software company, there is an emerging cluster around Bangalore that contains many of its customers, its global partners, and some 3,000 engineers trained in SAP software within the large Indian IT services firms. The range of skills available is also deepening. In 2004 Reuters announced that it would eliminate up to 20 editorial positions in the United States and Europe and hire up to 60 replacements in India based at their Bangalore facility. Reuters has been seeking to cut costs as a result of strong competition from rival Bloomberg.

Competition policy needs to encompass merger control. Growth by acquisition or merger may have both positive and negative impacts on the incentive to innovate. The positive effects include the opportunities for spreading the costs of innovation across a larger (merged) sales or distribution network, as well as access to additional R&D

resources. On the other hand, the consolidation of market power may impact negatively on the incentive to innovate. Where there is a significant foreign-owned business sector, it is important to ensure coherence and consistency between competition and investment attraction policies. It would, for example, be counterproductive to attract foreign investors by promising them shelter from competition in the form of imports or the entry of domestic firms, both of which reduce competitive pressure and hence the incentive to innovate. India is badly in need of a more comprehensive and coherent competition policy. Regulations that restrict a wide range of products to small, inefficient producers or that protect state-owned corporations detract from both efficiency and innovation (Padhi et al. 2004). While levels of competition are increasing in China, in part because of WTO obligations, many state-controlled firms face little real competitive pressure.

Funding

The encouragement of innovation, and in particular its commercialization, requires appropriate levels and types of funding. The funding of innovation is by no means straightforward, in part because of the associated risks. The risks associated with innovation fall into two groups. The first are the risks that the invention will be a failure in the technical sense, that is, it does not achieve what is claimed for it. This might occur in the case of a new drug that does not have the desired effects. Related to this is the problem of buyer uncertainty, where it is difficult to attract funding to an intangible idea. To obtain funding, the inventor needs to disclose the technology; once this is done the buyer has obtained the idea without paying. At the same time, there is a second set of risks, those related to commercialization. Even if the technology works, there is no guarantee that it will be commercially successful. Of course it is commercialization that recoups the costs of development. Because of these risks and aspects of market failure, innovation requires appropriate funding at different stages. Much of the early development and prototyping is funded by personal savings or, in the case of corporate research, retained profits. Government grants and cooperation with publicly funded bodies such as science parks also plays a critical role at this stage.

At the commercialization stage there is a need for a significant injection of additional funding. Innovation and new product development within large corporations can be funded internally, and there is ready access to the necessary skills, experience, and resources needed to take the product to market. However, much innovation occurs within small, and often new, businesses. In such cases, external funds are generally needed. Perhaps the most common form of such funding is provided by the venture capital industry. Venture capital involves the investment of equity to support the creation and development of new and generally high-growth businesses. Venture capital has played a particularly important role within high-technology sectors such as electronics, medical instruments, and biotechnology. However, more generally, American companies originally funded with venture capital now account for 11 percent of annual U.S. GDP. Such businesses include FedEx, Intel, Apple, Amazon, and Starbucks. The attraction of venture capital is much more than simply the cash it brings. Rather, many new small businesses also benefit from the expertise, experience, and network contacts that venture capitalists can contribute.

Innovation funding is not well developed in China and India. Much of India's industry remains in the hands of family-owned conglomerates. Within such conglomerates, less profitable activities are cross-subsidized. Lenders face a challenging environment with high levels of corruption and embezzlement. As discussed in previous chapters, China's financial markets are underdeveloped and truncated. Financial institutions, particularly the key banks, face directed lending policies and offer little to small, private-sector firms. This undoubtedly restricts the most innovative sector of the economy.

Other Obstacles to the Creation of an
Effective National Innovation System

China faces other significant challenges in developing a national innovation system. Time has not been kind to Chinese innovation since the eighteenth century (Shenkar 2005). While China has a long and distinguished history of invention (paper, gunpowder, the cannon, navigation aids, etc.), this was eclipsed by the rise of the West and the Industrial Revolution. For the past 200 years, China has been more concerned with maintaining stability than moving forward. Furthermore, the Chinese strength was in invention and not necessarily in innovation (the commercialization of invention). While the military defeats and occupations of the past two centuries have made Chinese leaders well aware of the significance of technology, they inherited a poor innovation system. Fifty years of centralized planning have led to a highly compartmentalized system with poor integration between universities, research institutes, and businesses. The dispersion of research facilities across the country for strategic reasons means that few innovative clusters exist. Restrictions on knowledge sharing and a lack of transparency also inhibit the inquisitive processes that underpin innovation. Furthermore, the existence of a massive reserve of low-cost labor reduces the incentive to upgrade into more capital- or knowledge-intensive activities. While the constraint of scarce labor provided a powerful incentive for countries like Singapore, Japan, and South Korea to upgrade, estimates suggest that China may be able to maintain low wages for perhaps four more decades.

How Much of a Threat Do China and India Pose?

While both China and India are eager to upgrade their economies and to become stronger players in the market for innovation, this is not likely to happen in the short term. Over the next 5 to 10 years we can expect both countries to concentrate on building scale and consolidating their positions in the mass production of goods and services. In the area of innovation they are both likely to be "fast followers," adopting innovations in the same way that Japan did. There is little doubt that China is some years in front of India in the technological race. Despite its weak national innovation system, China has benefited immensely from the presence of many large multinational enterprises. In the medium term (10 to 20 years) we might expect both countries to develop strengths in process technologies. Local firms may provide a very serious competitive threat in the development of new business models. These firms will find new ways to combine low costs, locally sourced resources, and unique market knowledge to develop ways of delivering value that Western firms will find difficult to match. This is already occurring in the Indian automobile industry, Chinese electronics, and business services in both countries.

In terms of the adjustments that the advanced countries will have to make, India may have a greater impact than China because of the importance of services to the wealthiest economies. For example, manufacturing accounts for just 14 percent of U.S. output and 11 percent of jobs; services, on the other hand, account for 60 percent of output and two-thirds of all jobs. If China is successful in building a strong position in basic business services (Luo 2001) and India responds by moving up the service value chain, the disruption could be considerable.

It would also be dangerous for advanced countries to believe that the challenge they face is simply that existing jobs are being transferred or that new jobs are being created elsewhere. Rather, the problem that emerges is the fragmentation of the apprenticeship path within affected industries. Even if the work being outsourced is at a basic level, it is still the first rung in the career ladder, which the most sophisticated professionals need to work through if they are to acquire the skills and experience that are needed in higher-level positions. An obvious risk is that the basic work being undertaken by Chinese and Indian workers now provides them with the foundation on which to upgrade in the future. If significant wage disparities persist, then much of this work may be undertaken in the emerging economies. This would occur if higher-level work was outsourced by multinational enterprises, which could effectively transfer the entire value chain, or if domestic firms began to move into these industry segments.

Internationalization of Domestic Firms

Further evidence of economic upgrading may be provided by the emergence of successful international businesses from China and India. Conceptualization of the development process, and in particular the idea of the *investment development path* (Dunning and Narula 1996), suggests that as a nation's income levels rise it is likely to experience an improvement in its net outward investment position. This means that outward investment by its domestic firms begins to exceed the value of inward investment. Thus, rising outward investment levels might be interpreted as a sign of growth and increasing economic sophistication. Given the massive inflow of foreign investment into China in particular, it is unlikely that the country will experience a shift from a net inflow to net outflow in the near future. However, there are definite signs that both Chinese and Indian firms are beginning to enter overseas markets.

The Chinese authorities have supported a strategy of internationalization of Chinese business since the early 1990s. They targeted around 120 state-owned enterprises in a range of sectors including automobiles, electronics, machinery, chemicals, and pharmaceuticals, which were seen as being at the forefront of the country's internationalization efforts. The development of these firms was supported in a number of ways, including financial support, protection from competition, and the granting of greater autonomy in management decision making. The result was an increase in outward investment from the end of the 1990s and a cumulative stock of overseas investment of US$37 billion by the end of 2003, more than seven times the amount of Indian overseas investment (Wu 2005). This investment is widely dispersed geographically and is the result of the multiple motives that are driving Chinese firms to internationalize (Keller and Zhou 2003).

Different industries appear to be driven by different motives. The primary driver is the desire to access new markets, particularly in industries such as whiteware and electronics where there is excess capacity, declining demand, and massive competition in the home market. A second key motivation is to secure resources, which helps explain the presence of Chinese investors in resource-rich economies such as Australia, Canada, and Indonesia. This motive accounts for more than one-quarter of overseas investment. A third motive may be a desire to achieve long-term access to markets that could be closed to exports. Baosteel's determination to set up a major steel plant in Brazil, primarily to serve the Brazilian car industry, is an example. The fourth motive is a desire to obtain foreign technology and brand names and explains deals such as Lenovo's acquisition of IBM's PC division and TCL's purchase of Thomson. Part of this strategy is to buy "troubled" companies in the developed countries and use China's lower costs to nurse them back to profitability. Shanghai Electronic Group's purchase of the bankrupt Japanese Akiyama Publishing Machinery Company is an example. This same motive appeared to be behind Haier's aborted attempt to acquire the U.S. manufacturer Maytag. With growing consolidation and internationalization, Chinese companies are now beginning to make international rankings such as *BusinessWeek*'s Top 200 Emerging-Market Companies and the *Forbes* listing of the best small firms (see Table 5.1). Lenovo is now the world's third largest computer manufacturer with a global market share of 7.2 percent in 2005.

While the outward investment of Chinese firms to date has been modest, we may expect to see further internationalization. Chinese acquisitions went from $2 billion to $3 billion in 2003 and 2004 to more than $23 billion in the first half of 2005. Recent government policy changes, including the relaxation of outward investment approvals and further financial support to the Export-Import Bank of China, demonstrate a strong political desire for internationalization. However, in the developed markets Chinese firms are comparatively late entrants and as a result are likely to face considerable challenges. Recent events highlight the political sensitivity toward investment by what are seen as politically supported and favored firms. It is also unclear how effective investors from emerging markets will be in integrating and developing acquired businesses, particularly where those firms are competitively weak. TCL's acquisition of Alcatel's mobile handset operation has not reached expected sales and profitability levels. D'Long, a Chinese conglomerate, collapsed in 2004 after acquiring troubled U.S. firm Murray lawnmowers and parts of the bankrupt aircraft maker Fairchild Dornier. In many cases the Chinese acquirer may have plenty of cash as a result of directed bank loans but is often suffering as a result of ferocious competition in the home market.

Indian businesses are also seeking to expand into overseas markets. Some of the large business service providers are moving into the markets of Europe and North America to be closer to their clients (Bever et al. 2005). At the same time, to remain competitive Indian service firms such as Wipro are adapting Toyota's production methods to improve the quality and efficiency of its operations. They use the *kaizen* system to elicit employee suggestions and are automating processes to skip manual steps and improve quality (*BusinessWeek* 2005i).

There is evidence that Chinese firms are routinely overpaying for the assets they acquire (*Economist* 2005g). Furthermore, they cannot exploit the opportunity to cut costs by relocating production back to China in the case of resource-based investments. It is also unclear what the benefits of introducing an acquired brand into the domestic market are, given the persistence of overcapacity and the presence of most global brands already. A strategy of internationalization based primarily on a desire to avoid cutthroat competition in the home market does not build from a position of sustainable advantage.

The reality is that Chinese managers have little experience of building global businesses. Even building a strong domestic brand at home is difficult. In many industries persistent overcapacity puts pressure on margins. When brands such as Tsingtao beer and Li-Ning shoes are successful they attract the attention of counterfeiters. Furthermore, recent liberalization of retailing coupled with the growing power of multinational retailers such as Wal-Mart and Carrefour may reduce the value of domestic brands and will certainly weaken existing distribution arrangements. However, Chinese businesses are learning to find ways to overcome these challenges. The Chinese water bottler Wahaha has built a strong domestic market position by concentrating on second-tier cities and avoiding head-on competition.

Others are tapping into experienced staff by hiring senior marketing personnel from Western multinationals, as Li-Ning did in hiring from P&G (Proctor and Gamble). Chinese firms are also learning from the international expansion of South Korean firms and are entering other developing markets first. This is the strategy of car manufacturer Geely in entering Middle Eastern markets and Haier in India (*BusinessWeek* 2004c).

Inward foreign direct investment has played an important role in the internationalization of domestic firms, certainly in the case of China. The impact of inward investment depends, to a considerable degree, on the terms on which investment is made and the host country's underlying regulatory framework. In the case of China's consumer electronics industry, foreign investment has increased competition, lowered prices, improved quality, and encouraged internationally competitive firms such as Galanz and TCL. Indeed, a number of studies have reported the incentive to internationalize provided by thin profits in the home market (Keller and Zhou 2003; Wu 2005). In contrast, until recently, Chinese automobile producers were sheltered by high tariffs, joint venture requirements, and local content requirements. The result was the creation of excess profits within multinational investors (Farrell et al. 2004).

For these reasons, international expansion by greenfield investment is the preferred strategy of Chinese firms (Keller and Zhou 2003). However, the high level of competitive pressure faced by Chinese businesses in their home market means that the desire to internationalize will continue to be strong. Such pressures are likely to be of increasing importance in the service sector as these industries experience full liberalization under the terms of China's WTO accession (Luo 2001). The difficulties facing Chinese firms in their efforts to internationalize are illustrated in Box 5.4, which examines the experience of Haier.

Box 5.4 The Internationalization of Haier

Haier is China's leading seller of home appliances. Efforts to internationalize have seen it enjoy overseas sales of $1 billion and 22 overseas factories. However, there appear to be few synergies between domestic and international business, with the possible exception that both are driven by opportunism. While the company has strong domestic market shares in washing machines, refrigerators, and dishwashers, overseas it concentrates on smaller niches including minifridges and wine coolers. However, compared with its global rivals, it lacks R&D, design skills, and distribution and service networks. Haier has just 10 researchers in the United States. It struggles with the dilemma of wanting to produce overseas to be close to customers but then losing the huge cost advantage of Chinese labor.

It appears to have difficulties encouraging and managing creativity. Granting freedom to its engineers has given Haier 96 categories of goods in 15,100 specifications. This probably adds more to costs and complexity than to sales. Furthermore, the company has moved beyond white goods into computers, mobile phones, and pharmaceuticals, products that share little with its core business. The result is a firm that is broad but shallow, thinly spread, and managerially stretched. It appears to be a long way from the focused global brand that underpins success in the global white ware industry. Its business strategy, the so-called three-in-one strategy of putting design, production, and sales all in one country, is characteristic of a multidomestic strategy, which most major appliance manufacturers critically reassessed almost 20 years ago.

Source: Economist 2004c.

However, it may be wrong to think of China's failure to produce the large, integrated enterprises that are characteristic of Western markets as a major weakness (Nolan 2001).

These enterprises have, in most cases, developed over a considerable period of time within a business environment that until recently encouraged scale, size, and vertical integration. While size continues to be an important characteristic of leading firms in many industries (Bryan and Zanini 2005), the future may change this. The increasing use and sophistication of information technology, coupled with the ability to empower and coordinate individual efforts, means that the future organization may look dramatically different to the global competitor of today. In a way analogous to the ability of an emerging economy to leapfrog certain technologies, enterprises from these markets may also be able to bypass conventional organizational forms. If this is the case, and it is by no means a compelling case, then we may be looking in the wrong places for the future global businesses that could emerge from China and India.

Challenges That Each Country Faces

If China and India are to successfully upgrade their economies and emerge as technological leaders, they will have to overcome a number of challenges.

For India the key challenge is to broaden the base of economic growth beyond services. This is necessary both to broaden and sustain economic development and to ensure social stability. India's demographic trends make it clear that employment creation must be a priority. The Indian economy will need to accommodate 83 million new labor market entrants by 2010. Official unemployment is currently running at 9.2 percent. Without a broadening of the economic base, and in particular more rapid growth within manufacturing, rising unemployment could threaten social stability and continuing growth. There is also some tentative evidence that economic concerns are driving political voting patterns. Rising unemployment has been correlated with political fragmentation, with an increasing emphasis on local economic conditions and policies. This has contributed to the challenge of further economic reform through complex coalition political arrangements.

Any broadening of the Indian manufacturing sector will necessitate a number of major reforms. The first is the need to invest in education and training, particularly at the schooling level. As mentioned above, while India is able to produce world-class graduates in a number of areas, there persists a very high level of illiteracy. Many of the new labor market entrants of the future will be drawn from this group, and gainful employment for them will require a higher level of basic literacy. Second, the creation of a larger and competitive manufacturing sector will necessitate considerable investment. This could be achieved in a number of ways, including further privatization, increased inward investment, and stimulating domestic saving. Augmenting savings will almost certainly imply extensive taxation reform (Ahya and Xie 2004). Third, continuing economic reform will also be required. For the manufacturing sector, the key changes are increased labor market flexibility, further investment in infrastructure, and increased decentralization of public expenditure to the state level. For the latter to be achieved a reduction in state deficits will have to occur.

The challenges facing China are no less daunting. In summary, China will need to sustain its position in manufacturing industries where it is already competitive, support the upgrading of economic activity, and strengthen its fledgling service sector. To achieve this, a number of generic economic initiatives are recommended. The first is the need to strengthen China's market-supporting institutions. The country has the opportunity to devise institutional arrangements that are both consistent with its economic aspirations and not burdened by history. Second, future growth of the economy will be driven largely by the private sector. Government policies should ensure, at the very least, that this sector is in no way disadvantaged in comparison with the public sector. This raises a third policy need—the continuing reform of China's troubled banking sector. The opening up of the financial sector to foreign investment and international standards of governance may be the best assurance of improvement. Fourth, if China is to provide employees suitable for more complex and technologically advanced manufacturing and for a growing service sector, there must be an increased focus on tertiary education. Despite its much larger population than countries such as Russia and India, China's graduate numbers are only marginally higher. On a per capita basis, China produces just 14 graduates per 1,000 people, well below the United States with 192 per 1,000. While the focus of education spending has been on ensuring widespread literacy, and this has been largely achieved, further commitment to specialized tertiary training will be necessary in the future. For an internationally attractive service sector, more English-speaking graduates will be necessary. China is already moving in this direction. Some estimates suggest that up to one-fifth of all Chinese are learning English at some level. More formally, the government has lowered the age from 12 to 9 at which primary school pupils begin to learn English; at many schools in the more commercially open eastern cities, English-language study begins at the age of 6.

A more general concern for the Chinese authorities is the need to foster creativity. In part this will require greater freedom of ideas and the exchange of information. The authorities seem to find it very difficult to reconcile this need with the equally compelling desire to maintain control. The result is a regular crackdown on the exchange of ideas and the media. As might be expected with economic development, there is a growing desire for more freedom and new avenues of expression are emerging. Officially there are about 280,000 registered nongovernment organizations (NGOs) in China, but the real total may be much higher. Many of these are now seeking to provide redress for social injustices, which have traditionally been suppressed (French 2006). The authorities appear unclear about how to respond. On the one hand, such organizations provide valuable input into government decision making in the most far-reaching economic and social transformation the world has ever seen. On the other hand, such organizations are seen as potentially subversive.

When criticism is clearly directed at the political leadership, intervention is swift and absolute. In recent years, two newspapers have been closed indefinitely. In addition, a popular book highlighting the difficulties faced by peasant farmers has been banned and its authors face a lawsuit (Mooney 2004). More recently a moratorium was placed on all new foreign magazines on topics other than science and technology (Fowler and Qin 2006). At the same time, the Internet is strictly regulated in China, with estimates suggesting that some 40,000 "officials" may be involved in its control. Control is increasingly sophisticated with the use of keyword searching, the blocking of "sensitive" e-mails, and filtering technology. Managing this balance between control and demands for increasing freedom, and ultimately, perhaps, political democracy, may be the key challenge facing China's leadership.

Conclusions

In this chapter we have examined the economic positions of China and India and how the two countries relate to one another. For the next few years we can confidently conclude that China and India will be regarded as complementary locations within the international business environment. China is firmly established as the global manufacturing factory while India is the global services workshop. This means that for most business investors the key to understanding these two countries is to recognize the importance of China *and* India, not China *or* India. While the overall relationship is complementary, considerable competition already exists between the two countries in attracting foreign investment and securing energy supplies. As they both seek to broaden and upgrade their economies (as China moves further into service industries and India deepens its manufacturing sector), the two could compete directly across a wide range of industries. At the same time, economic ties between China and India are deepening. They are collaborating in energy exploration, and in 2004 bilateral trade reached $13 billion; while only 1 percent of China's total trade, this was a full 9 percent for India. Increasingly, we may expect to see the development of a competitive partnership between Asia's emerging economic powers.

In the long term it is likely that demographics will largely determine competitive success. Demographic trends favor India, which has a younger average population and will enjoy positive employment growth for longer than China. However, for the foreseeable future it is clear that both countries are following distinctive development paths, and it would be wrong to argue that it is one generic development model or that either India or China offer evidence of a clearly superior model (Huang and Khanna 2003). That simply is not the case. Furthermore, both countries face considerable challenges if they are to enjoy sustained growth and to successfully upgrade their economies.

Implications for Management

1. For Western businesses, China and India offer complementary production locations—in essence, China for hardware and India for software.
2. Within both economies there are focused niches of expertise, such as batch manufacturing and resource-based processing in India.
3. Both economies offer unique opportunities in that they appear able to maintain their cost competitiveness for at least the next decade while upgrading their economies.
4. In upgrading, both economies will rely heavily on the transfer of technology from multinational enterprises.
5. The internationalization of Chinese and Indian firms will add significantly to competition in a number of industries.

Discussion Questions

1. Examine the following statement: The apparent complementarities of the Chinese and Indian economies mean that
international businesses should focus on China and India, not
China or India.
2. Is it possible to foster creativity in a society that strictly controls the exchange of information and ideas? If so, how can
this be done?

6

THE POLITICAL ECONOMY OF
THE RISE OF CHINA AND INDIA

Introduction

It would be shortsighted to believe that the rise of China and India will have only an economic impact on the rest of the world. The size and strategic importance of both countries mean that they also have significant implications for international relations in the broadest sense. In this chapter we will consider some of the international issues that have been associated with the rise of China and India. Some of these issues are predominantly economic, others are more strategic or political in nature. We begin by looking at the broad implications of the rise of these two countries. This is followed by consideration of how they are likely to affect the regional economies of Asia. In the section titled "China, India, and Developing Countries," we look at relationships among China, India, and the least developed countries. Both China and India have shown strong interest in Africa and Latin America, areas that have been seen as of only marginal interest by other major powers. "China, India, and Developed Countries" examines some of the issues facing developed countries as their relationships with China and India deepen. The integration of China and India within the strategies of international businesses has dramatically changed the nature of global production systems. The difficulties many advanced economies have experienced in adjusting to the rise of China and India have triggered a variety of protectionist responses and may threaten the process of globalization. Concluding comments are contained in the last section.

171

Emerging Markets and the World Economy

Seismic changes in the world economy are relatively rare but have happened before. In the past four centuries, three major shifts are discernible. The first was the rise of Europe from around the end of the seventeenth century, culminating in the Industrial Revolution, which brought a massive transfer of economic power from Asia (primarily India and China) to Europe. The second great shift occurred with the emergence of the continental United States in the late nineteenth and early twentieth centuries. The United States went on to be the dominant economic, political, and military power of the past century. The third great change has been the rise of Asia, first with Japan in the second half of the twentieth century and accelerating with the recent reemergence of China and India. Predictions suggest that by the middle of this century, China and India could account for half of all global output (Wilson and Purushothaman 2003).

Prestowitz (2004) argues that four factors have triggered this third great shift. The first was China's decision to open its economy and to commit to international capitalism. The second, taken in the light of China's early success and the demise of the Soviet Union, was India's decision to abandon socialist protectionism and liberalize its economy. Third, the success of the World Trade Organization and China's subsequent membership have eliminated many of the traditional barriers to trade and investment, increasing the attraction of the large Asian emerging economies. Finally, the rapid development of the Internet has significantly lowered the costs of managing global production systems encouraging a more rational global division of labor encompassing much of the Asian region. In the same way that the twentieth century is seen as the American century, the twenty-first century appears to be one that will be dominated by emerging markets, particularly China and India.

The size, openness, and early start that China enjoyed means that in the short to medium term it is likely to have the greatest economic impact on the rest of the world (Lardy 2002). Indeed, its future impact is likely to be much greater than at any time in history. Even when China was a major manufacturer, this was primarily intended for domestic markets. Prior to 1949, China's peak share of world trade was reached in the late 1920s at a comparatively low 2.2 percent. This figure was achieved again in 1993 (Ash 2002) and in 2005 reached 6.8 percent. Forecasts suggest that by 2020 China's share of world trade will be 10 percent, but in light of recent growth rates this seems conservative.

The extent and form of the impact of China and India depends on the sector or issue being considered. India's primary impact has been on internationally tradable business services and recently has threatened the job security of many professionals in the advanced economies. China's principal effect has been on commodities and manufactured products. However, the *Economist* (2005h) has recently argued that China now drives almost all aspects of the world economy.

First, in a positive way, the reentry of China and India into the world economy has increased specialization, the so-called international division of labor. As emerging economies have become major producers of labor-intensive manufactures and services, the developed countries have increasingly concentrated on higher-value activities.

Second, the growing importance of China and India has changed relative prices. Falling prices of labor-intensive manufactured goods such as shoes and clothing and of information technology–related services have more than offset rapid rises in the price of raw materials such as oil. China's integration boosted the global labor market by 25 percent. Given that the global capital stock has not increased at the same rate, this has reduced returns to labor, particularly the least skilled (Enderwick 2005), and boosted returns to capital. Profits as a share of national income have been at a historically high level in recent years.

Third, China now exercises a major influence on global inflation. It has pushed down prices of many products and its massive labor force has curtailed wage claims in the advanced economies. This has allowed the authorities to hold interest rates down, contributing to global liquidity bubbles, including rapid rises in house prices in many countries. The growth in global productive capacity has eased inflationary pressures. At the same time, strong demand for commodities such as oil will not only push up average prices, but could also increase price volatility. However, China's willingness to recycle its vast trade surplus back into U.S. bonds has kept U.S. (and world) interest rates down and maintained consumer spending. From a policy perspective, the nature of desirable inflation targets and the effective conduct of monetary policy will have to be reconsidered (*Economist* 2005h).

Fourth, China has encouraged further specialization, particularly within Asia where it has displaced some of the newly industrialized economies in the production of products such as toys, shoes, and sporting goods, much of which has now moved to the mainland. At the same time, these countries now ship more sophisticated components to China for reprocessing.

Fifth, China is a major driver of globally integrated value chains, and much of the growth of Chinese exports has been produced by foreign firms operating in China. A considerable amount of this growth is the result of decisions made by multinational enterprises on the relocation of production, rather than any increase in the competitiveness of Chinese firms.

China has also been important as an engine of growth in the Asian region, facilitating Japan's economic recovery.

While this discussion suggests that globalization has played an important part in facilitating the growth of China and India, both countries are beginning to see globalization as more than just an economic process. They increasingly recognize that globalization has strong political and security dimensions that must be addressed (Deng and Moore 2004). Effectively combating the new global threats—terrorism, unregulated capital flows, epidemics, and cross-border criminal activities—requires cooperative security rather than traditional competitive politics. By transforming the context of interstate competition to emphasize economic power, globalization has created powerful incentives for emerging markets to participate in transnational economic structures and multilateral institutions. In recognizing this, China and India have responded in three main ways.

First, they have increased their involvement in both regional and international bodies and institutions. China joined the Pacific Economic Cooperation Council (PECC) in September 1986 and Asia-Pacific Economic Cooperation (APEC) in 1991. WTO (World Trade Organization) mechanisms are one means by which China can defend its interests against European and American trade disputes with steel tariffs, textiles quotas, and allegations of dumping. Similarly, India has been fighting U.S. protectionism in the form of restrictions on outsourcing. Furthermore, growing involvement in a wide range of forums, including the WTO and APEC, could allow China and India to begin to actually influence the direction of globalization.

Second, in recent years both countries have attempted to improve relations with the "great powers," including Russia, Germany, France, and the European Union. Both China and India have worked closely with the United States, and India–U.S. relations are seen as markedly warmer in the past year. In 2003 China attended the G8 summit in France. The principal exception to these improvements has been Japan, where relations with China in particular have not gone well.

Third, while recent emphasis has been placed on growing participation in multilateral institutions, similar arguments can be made concerning how informal mechanisms of interdependence, particularly commercial ties, have consolidated relations with other great powers. China is a major exporter, one of the most important destinations for foreign investment, and a key purchaser of U.S. debt. India is one of the world's leading sources of business services and increasingly a key node in global innovation systems. It is hoped that such ties will reduce the perception that India and China are problem rivals that need to be contained. The rise of China provides a unique opportunity to test the value of such interdependencies because at no time in the past has a new potential superpower emerged while it was so intertwined economically with those countries that it appeared to threaten (Garten 2005). While growing interdependence may be effective in containing strategic intentions, it comes at the price of economic tensions. Recent examples include the backlash against outsourcing, pressures for revaluation of the yuan, concern over the U.S. trade deficit, and the imposition of temporary trade restrictions.

International Institutions

The growing economic and strategic power of China and India throws up the important issue of the appropriateness of existing institutions of international economic and political management. Our current institutions, encompassing trade, finance, development, and security, are a product of the late 1940s and were designed for a world recovering from the last world war. Their membership reflects the distribution of power at that time, and they seem ill equipped to deal with some of the more recent global problems. Asia holds more than half of the world's foreign reserves but has only 15 percent of the votes on the International Monetary Fund (IMF) executive board. While Asia accounts for 60 percent of the world's population and one-quarter of global GDP, it has only one of the five permanent seats on the U.N. Security Council. China has the world's largest army, some 2.5 million men, and the fourth largest defense budget. It has also been suggested that China in particular should be involved in the important economic policy group of the G7 or G8. Existing members may be reluctant to include China in the group because this would give China considerable powers to discourage protectionism. Another proposal has been for the creation of a G4 group comprising the United States, the Euro zone, China, and Japan to oversee financial and balance of payments issues (Kenen et al. 2004).

There is, however, some doubt about the commitment and ability of China and India to play a greater role in world affairs. While China's current leadership is seen as more technically competent and less ideologically rigid than in the past, it is still thought to have limited understanding of the West (Sutter 1999). Historically, China has displayed a strong preference for conducting its foreign relations in bilateral rather than multilateral forums (Yahuda 2002). China also faces a number of challenges in coordinating with others within such forums. A communist ideology, huge size, and autonomy of its domestic political system all contrast with other leading nations. China also has to balance the paradox that although it is most firmly integrated into the Asian region, its long-term interests in terms of technology acquisition and market access depend much more on the United States and the European Union (Yahuda 2002).

A more strident criticism is that China, India, and Japan have all been reluctant to take a lead in reshaping the institutions that manage the world order, largely because they are major beneficiaries of the existing order. According to Mahbubani (2005) these countries are happy to have a free ride on the efforts of others and to focus on domestic issues. While historically China has never been a particularly imperialistic nation, and in fact has often isolated itself from the rest of the world, there is concern that it could use external confrontation to distract attention from internal problems, such as rising social discontent. Many of India's elite have considerable experience, and perhaps a vested interest, in seeing the world from the perspective of a poor, ineffectual developing country with a detached and neutral foreign policy. They may be less comfortable assuming a partnership with the major powers (Zakaria 2006a).

The Danger of Containment

There is considerable agreement that the rise of China creates the greatest challenges for the United States. Historically, when the world's leading power is challenged by a rising one, the two have a difficult relationship. The experiences of Britain and Germany, as well as on a more limited economic dimension the United States and Japan, would support this concern. Some U.S. commentators clearly see the rise of China as signaling the demise of the United States (Prestowitz 2005a). However, the reality is probably that China wishes to create a more multipolar world and to offset what it sees as American hegemony. Indeed, it may see itself as filling the position that Russia once held.

There is a real danger that the United States will use its strategic power and relationships in an attempt to contain China. One concern is that India could play a key role in such a process. India's strategic value to the United States is considerable. It appears as a friendly democracy sitting between the two places that concern Americans the most: China and the Middle East. While relationships between India and the United States have warmed considerably in recent years, for India nonalignment is integral to its independence and is unlikely to be diminished. As Kissinger (2006) recognizes, India, with no desire to force its culture or institutions on others, makes for a poor partner for global ideological missions. However, for the United States it could be a useful ally in the containment of China.

The demise of Russia, the growing assertiveness of Japan, and China's closer ties with the United States mean that India must be careful to ensure that independence does not simply become isolation. India's best hope may lie with the cooperative pressures that globalization has brought. India offers an attractive offshore base for intellectual capital that the United States, constrained by an aging population and the growing number of international students now returning home, might wish to tap. The key issue is to accept that the challenge with China is not how best to contain it, but rather how best to make the necessary trade and production adjustments in light of its growing importance as a globally integrated economy. This is important because another lesson of history is that the rise of a new economic power can help lift the entire global economy. From 1820 to 1913, the average income growth in Western Europe was almost as fast as the United States (Mandel 2004). It is entirely plausible that the continued high growth of China and India could provide a similar engine of global growth in the twenty-first century.

China, India, and the Regional Economy

The rise of China and India has huge implications for the Asian regional economy. China in particular, with 15 neighbors by land and sea, has borders with more countries than any other. In recent times it has experienced problems with many of these. In the last 50 years, China has intervened militarily in the Korean peninsula as well as in Indochina. It has also fought border wars with India (1962) and the former Soviet Union (1969). In 1996 China tested missiles off the coast of Taiwan just before the island's first presidential election. During Mao Zedong's era, China alienated a number of governments in Southeast Asia in its support for communist insurgents. Japan, which brings most of its oil imports through the Straits of Taiwan, is concerned with China's intentions in this area. Russia is also concerned about China. The divergent growth pattern of the two economies over the past 15 years has left Russia feeling vulnerable. China has also made threats to its regional neighbors as occurred in 2004 when Singapore's deputy prime minister visited Taiwan.

Countries in Southeast Asia have recognized the dramatic economic and strategic shifts they now face. While Southeast Asia's role as the bridge between China and India was distorted by more than a century of colonialism and an alignment with Europe, the natural course of history has now been restored. There is growing acceptance that China will be the new economic engine of growth for the entire region, filling the role that Japan played between 1960 and 1990. The region's historical economic, political, and military dependence on the United States is giving way to a period when the nature of Sino–Indian relations will be the key determinant of the region's success and stability.

The regional effects are complex and in some ways contradictory. Economically, while some Asian economies appear to be competing directly with China, the increasingly sophisticated regional vertical integration of production means that this is not necessarily the case. A number of Asian economies are heavily involved in exports to China that are subject to further processing and re-export. This is apparent in industries such as office machinery, telecommunications equipment, and electronic components. However, in the longer term as China increases its production of components, it may become more of a threat to the Asian newly industrializing economies and ASEAN (Association of Southeast Asian Nations) countries (Shafaeddin 2004). In economic terms it is China and the ASEAN 4 (Indonesia, Malaysia, Philippines, and Thailand) that have the closest economic structures (Ahearne et al. 2003). There is little evidence that China has taken FDI that could have gone to the ASEAN or other neighboring countries (Wu and Keong 2003; Zhou and Lall 2005). While India is seeking to attract more FDI, there is little to suggest that this would be at the expense of other regional competitors; indeed, India's major rival for international investment is China (Srivastava and Sen 2004). However, it has been suggested that the most effective response for other Southeast Asian economies lies in further integration and the replacement of declining individual locational advantages by regional inducements (Buckley et al. 2005).

Evidence that the economies of China and its Southeast Asian neighbors are complementary is provided by the emergence of a complex regional international division of labor (Lall and Albaladejo 2004) and attempts at economic upgrading within the region. Both Singapore and Malaysia are attempting to move away from electronics, chemicals, and other labor-intensive manufacturing vulnerable to competition from China. In Taiwan, some manufacturers have shifted operations to China; others have attempted to remain competitive by bringing in cheap labor from places like the Philippines. The Taiwanese authorities have introduced some restrictions on investment, so that now every Taiwanese investment of more than $50 million must be approved on a case-by-case basis. Companies wanting to build chip plants on the mainland must agree to build more advanced ones in Taiwan first. Hong Kong in particular appears to be struggling in response to China. Its container ports face a threat from Xiamen, Shenzhen, and Shanghai, where costs are substantially lower and goods can be shipped directly. Shanghai's growing financial status is also a threat to the Hong Kong economy (Chandler 2003).

Japan remains vulnerable to the rise of China because its competitive advantage lies in manufacturing, and its economy, which has stagnated for a decade, is slow in responding to changes in the world economy (Shenkar 2005). The threat is significant only to the bottom end of Japanese manufactured products. Japan's economy has not been as immediately or as adversely affected as the United States's as a result of China's surge. This is probably the result of Japan's relative price insensitivity, high level of brand awareness, and fragmented distribution and retail sector (Shenkar 2005). Increasingly, however, major Japanese brands are being manufactured in China. While threatened by the rise of China, Japan is shifting its Asian economic interests from the southeast to the northeast, especially China. The rapid aging of the Japanese population means that the country will continue to move production overseas and that China will continue to be a prime location.

India has also strengthened links with the ASEAN grouping with the first ASEAN-Indian summit occurring in 2002. Since then India has signed a comprehensive economic cooperative agreement with Singapore and is close to finalizing a similar agreement with Thailand. India also has a functioning free trade agreement with Sri Lanka and a common market with Nepal. Also proposed is an Asian Economic Community (AEC), which would comprise Japan, ASEAN, China, India, and South Korea (JACIK). These JACIK countries account for about one-fifth of world merchandise trade and more than half of all foreign reserves. As mentioned above, it is quite possible that as India's economy grows, governments in Southeast Asia may choose to move closer to India in an attempt to build a potential geopolitical counterweight to China (National Intelligence Council 2004).

Strength in Diversity?

A major strength of the Asian region is its considerable diversity in terms of resources, skills, and levels of development. This creates tremendous opportunities for complementary economic relations. There are very strong economic complementarities between East Asia and India. India's strengths in computer software complement East Asia's considerable IT hardware and electronics sectors. While East Asia has strengths in product development, India has well-developed process development skills. Mutually beneficial R&D activities between the two areas are also possible (Kumar 2002).

The very ambitious plans that both China and India have could bring major changes in relative economic power and opportunity into the future. India's decision to invest in a shipping canal project between the Palk Bay and Gulf of Mannar will allow much of its trade to bypass Sri Lanka, causing major dislocations to an economy that has made major infrastructure investments in ports to handle Indian traffic.

The relevant economic region for China and India has been extended by the race to access energy and raw materials in areas of Central Asia. China's interest in Central Asia is largely the result of its need for additional energy resources. However, in the longer term, China will benefit from having supportive and successful neighbors. The opportunity for China to extend its sphere of influence in Central Asia is, in part, the result of Russia's waning control over the region. In addition, China has moved to formalize relations and to offer mutual benefits. The Shanghai Cooperation Organization (SCO) established in June 2001 involves China, Russia, Kazakhstan, Tajikistan, Kyrgyzstan, and Uzbekistan and is designed to achieve a more institutionalized form of cooperation on issues ranging from antiterrorism to trade.

How other Asian economies will be impacted by the rapid development of China and India is unclear. History suggests that when a new great power rises the implications for its weaker neighbors are rarely good. Ireland's experience with Britain, Latin America's experience with the United States, and East Asia's experience with Japan all suggest concerns. China's tendency to stoke the fires of nationalism in an attempt to legitimize its internal authoritarianism has created problems with Japan and Taiwan. China and Japan have been rivals for the better part of a millennium, and that tension has evolved in recent years to encompass historical grievances as well as conflict over gas and oil reserves in the East China Sea. China's rise has also robbed Japan of its identity as the world's economic miracle (Tamamoto 2006). However, there is a very fine line between mutual cooperation with, and domination of, neighboring economies. The very agreements and linkages with Southeast Asia that China interprets as evidence of its benevolent intentions may also be seen as a snare designed to capture the very same countries. It is hard to see Myanmar as much more than a client state of China.

However, it is important not to lose sight of the fact that both China and India place considerable reliance on the other economies of Asia. For example, neither China nor India possess what have been termed global cities (Friedmann 1995)—centers that play a critical role in facilitating trade and investment with the rest of the world. Tokyo, Singapore, and Hong Kong continue to perform these roles for the regional economy.

China, India, and Developing Countries

The effects of China and India on developing countries beyond the Asian region depend very much on the economic structure and position of those countries. Where such countries compete directly with China and India, they are likely to face considerable challenges. On the other hand, if they supply raw materials or sophisticated components, they are likely to experience strong growth from relationships with China and India. Thus, Latin America, Argentina, Chile, and Brazil, all major commodity exporters, have enjoyed considerable export benefits, while Mexico, an important manufacturing center, has faced crippling competition from China (*BusinessWeek* 2003c; Goldman Sachs 2003; Jenkins and Peters 2006; Rosen 2003b). India and China are attractive markets for countries such as Brazil, which wants to diversify exports beyond its traditional markets such as the United States and Europe, which currently account for about 70 percent of Latin America's exports.

India has also shown increased interest in Latin America, although China's exports to the region in 2004 were nine times those of India. India's exports to Latin America include auto parts, machinery, pharmaceutical products, and textiles. The Indian software services giant Tata Consultancy Services has a presence in Uruguay, Mexico, Brazil, Chile, and Argentina. India has also made some oil-related investments in Venezuela and Ecuador. The ability of China and India to penetrate the markets of Africa and Latin America coincides with a diminished presence in these areas of powers such as Russia and the United States.

The experience of Mexico highlights the considerable competitive strengths that the large emerging economies of Asia enjoy (see Box 6.1). Despite the advantages of proximity and NAFTA (North American Free Trade Agreement) agreement with the United States, Mexico has lost significant market share in the clothing industry. The success of China in particular may suggest that it may not be possible for other Latin American economies to successfully pursue export-led growth. Given the importance of the North American market and the fact that proximity and trade preference have not been enough to counteract the threat from Asia, it is difficult to see how later-developing Latin American economies could make the necessary breakthrough (Farrell, Puron, and Remes 2005).

Box 6.1 How China is Eating Mexico's Lunch

Mexico's comparative advantage lies in lower labor costs than the United States; proximity to developed North America; and, for some industries, somewhat lower costs due to different regulations on areas associated with high per capita income economies such as environmental protection. On the other hand, comparative disadvantages include an intrusive bureaucracy that is sometimes corrupt, sometimes simply hostile to the private sector; poor utilities and transportation infrastructure; underinvestment in human development; and a less-than-dynamic industrial structure reflecting imperfect financial intermediation and residual statism.

China's reforms challenge Mexico's comparative advantages head on, and make the disadvantages starker. China wins on low labor costs and many other costs of doing business, while quality control, technology diffusion, mid-level management skills, and physical infrastructure are improving fast enough to impress even skeptics and make Mexico's shortcomings in these areas more apparent.

What's left? Mexico's proximity to the U.S. market is the remaining hope. Proximity as salvation presupposes either the criticality of just-in-time timetables or else prohibitively high costs for shipping weightier goods. Looking at the comparative advantage data post-1996, there are a handful of sectors where Mexico stayed ahead of both the world and China: television receivers, engines, various vehicle categories, vehicle parts, meters and control systems, and medical instruments. In several of these (the automobile cluster) and a number of others where Mexico's lead is far slimmer, recent Chinese advances portend steep export gains in coming years. Heavy items more expensive to ship may be more important, although Chinese multinationals like Haier have set up manufacturing in North America precisely to compete in segments (such as refrigerators) where long-distance shipping is too costly. With the phase out of global textile and apparel constraints, as much as 85 percent of global manufacturing in that sector may end up in China, according to U.S. government estimates: for the 27 percent of *maquiladoras* and 226,000 workers still in that sector, there is serious trouble ahead.

Source: Rosen 2003b.

It is the newly liberalized clothing and textiles industry that perhaps best illustrates the competitive threat that developing countries face. China's combination of size, low costs, skilled workers, superior infrastructure, access to raw materials, and links to major retailers makes it a formidable challenger that has gained global market share at the expense of smaller rivals such as Vietnam, Lesotho, Haiti, Mauritius, Cambodia, the Dominican Republic, and Bangladesh. As a result, the jobs of some 30 million workers in dozens of developing countries are threatened. The United States is concerned that the losses could be destabilizing in neighboring countries in the Caribbean, Central America, and the Andean nations (*BusinessWeek* 2003c).

The experience of resource-rich commodity exporters resulting from the rapid growth of China and India has been quite different. This is well illustrated in the case of oil. Despite the trend toward more efficient energy use, total energy consumed is expected to rise by about 50 percent in the next two decades compared with a 34 percent expansion between 1980 and 2000, with an increasing share provided by petroleum (National Intelligence Council 2004). Experts believe China will need to boost its energy consumption by about 150 percent, while India will need to nearly double its consumption by 2020 to maintain a steady rate of economic growth (National Intelligence Council 2004). China and India prefer to secure future oil supplies through their firms investing overseas rather than by purchasing imports on the international market.

Both China and India have been aggressive in seeking new sources of supply from developing countries. Both have made major investments in Russia, Latin America, and the Middle East. In Africa, Chad, Niger, Ghana, and Congo have been targeted (Mitra 2005). However, interest in Africa extends beyond oil. China has sourced minerals and tobacco from Zimbabwe and copper from Zambia. It has also made major investments in telecommunications and agriculture in countries like Kenya and Botswana, which are not mineral rich. China has also aggressively courted smaller, low-profile groupings such as the Community of Portuguese Language Countries, which has provided supporters in both Europe and Africa (Horta and Storey 2006).

There is considerable concern with the types of resource deals that China and India are making. Neither is hesitant about contracts with so-called pariah states, such as Sudan and Myanmar. India also has plans for a pipeline from Iran to India through Pakistan and has provided considerable economic assistance to Iran. China's strategy in Africa, in contrast to those of earlier colonizing nations, is based on coordinating all elements of national influence, linking trade, investment, aid, and military assistance. China describes this as a strategic partnership. It appears to have brought some success. China has gained some valuable concessions at the expense of Western firms by offering soft loans or combining oil deals with non-oil investments. In Sudan, which is threatened with United Nations sanctions over Darfur, Chinese officials have secured valuable oil rights. American efforts to impose United Nations sanctions on Sudan were met with the threat of veto by China. Both China and India will need to carefully balance such agreements with the need to maintain relations with the rest of the major powers on whom they depend for capital, technology, and markets.

While the concept of a strategic partnership may sound appealing, the experience of some developing countries has not been positive. China's closer involvement with Brazil helped the latter recover from an earlier recession through the export of soybeans and iron ore, but since then Brazil has been overwhelmed by low-cost imports from China and promised investment deals have not materialized (Moffett and Samor 2005). Brazil's failure to get China to impose voluntary export restrictions in industries such as shoes, toys, and textiles led to it granting safeguards to Brazilian competitors. Brazil's decision to recognize China as a market economy made the imposition of anti-dumping penalties very difficult. Brazilian industry has also become divided in their view of China. Large commodity exporters are concerned that relations with China could deteriorate; smaller competing manufacturers are struggling to survive both at home and in third markets against Chinese producers. Argentina has had a similar experience, which in August 2005 led the government to place licensing requirements on imports of Chinese shoes and toys.

Another important way in which China and India have affected the developing countries is as a role model for those seeking to modernize. Inspired by the success of India, countries as diverse as Russia, Morocco, Nicaragua, the Philippines, and Botswana are seeking to attract outsourcing work (Beshouri et al. 2005; Tetrault et al. 2005). China's influence has led to the development of the so-called *Beijing consensus* (Ramo 2004), which promotes a pragmatic approach within a developmental state, and an alternative to the Washington consensus promoted by Western aid and development institutions.

China, India, and Developed Countries

The rapid rise of China and India has created significant adjustment costs for a number of firms and industries in the developed countries. The problems have resulted from the speed with which China and India have moved into world markets as well as the size of their economies. As has been observed, even if all U.S. jobs were moved to China, there would still be surplus labor in China. China's impact on manufacturing has been much greater in the United States than Europe because European governments offer higher levels of protection to their industries and tend to support their firms in export markets. India's impact is likely to be felt perhaps a decade later than China's, being most significant beginning in 2015. The welfare and employment effects of outsourcing depend to a large extent on the adjustment capacity of the source country concerned. Studies suggest that while the United States gains from outsourcing (MGI [McKinsey Global Institute] 2003b), Germany may not (MGI 2004). Furthermore, we may expect the balance of power in a number of technologies to move from the West to the East.

China's penetration of the U.S. market has created a division among firms, particularly the large retailers who clearly gain from ties with China, and smaller producers who struggle to remain competitive in clothing, footwear, furniture, and similar industries. Concerns over job security have triggered growing protectionism. However, not all of the effects resulting from the rise of China and India are negative. Both also provide huge opportunities. For example, developing such large countries within the constraints of energy and environmental challenges is something that will require the technological know-how of the developed countries as well as changes in lifestyle and consumption, which are likely to be pioneered by Western economies.

China, India, and Global Restructuring

The participation of China and India in the world economy has created new opportunities for the global restructuring of industries. Some of the most advanced developments are seen in the information technology industry.

The IT industry is being restructured as higher-end R&D activities are moving from their traditional bases in countries like the United States to emerging markets including India. The geographical center of the industry is no longer solely the Silicon Valley. New centers have been created in cities such as Austin, Texas; Richmond, Virginia; Armonk, New York; and Walldorf (Germany), the home bases of leading producers Dell, Microsoft, IBM, and SAP. As large parts of the business migrate overseas to India, China, and Eastern Europe, the IT industry has developed a sophisticated and complex globally integrated supply chain. The growing maturity of the industry means that it is no longer dominated by innovation and the nurturing of start-ups. Increasingly, customers and investors are valuing consolidation, integration, and effective execution.

It is not just IT hardware that has shifted offshore; increasingly other industry segments have become more mobile as the boundaries among software, IT services, and business processes have become indistinct. While the Silicon Valley may retain its leading role as the center of innovation, profit from other stages in the industry value chain will be increasingly captured in other parts of the world (*Economist* 2003c).

IBM's recently announced restructuring of its global IT services workforce, making clear the centrality of India in this process, is a further example. The company's emerging strategy, involving global integration of operations, is based on a recognition that low-cost skilled labor may be a necessary condition for success but is unlikely to be sufficient. Rather, to better meet the needs of customers, IBM is organizing its 200,000-member workforce along skill rather than geographical lines. In the future, employees will be clustered into competency centers, offering a combination of lower cost and proximity to customers. India plays a critical role in this process, with IBM's Indian workforce rising by 34,000 in the past 2.5 years. India is now IBM's second-largest workforce behind the United States. This has not been a painless process, with IBM cutting 15,000 positions in higher-cost economies in 2005 alone (*BusinessWeek* 2006b).

The Revival of Protectionism?

Growing competition, the deepening of offshore sourcing, and global rationalization of industries once seen as the exclusive province of the developed countries have triggered widespread concern. This concern is shared by workers, smaller producers, and now government officials.

There are several factors behind the mounting calls for protectionism. One is the concern that recent trade patterns, particularly the growth of white-collar offshoring, challenges conventional trade theory. Trade theory finds it difficult to explain the large number of increasingly skilled activities and jobs that have shifted overseas; these would be expected to be retained in the wealthy countries at least until emerging countries have achieved a higher level of productivity. Furthermore, many displaced workers who are subsequently reemployed are not upskilling; often they end up on lower wage levels. Those who remain in jobs subject to direct competition from China and India face depressed wages. They may also experience work intensification, where increased output is expected for a given level of input or rewards. These changes are not what are predicted in the relatively costless adjustment processes of traditional economics.

A second factor is the difficulty of balancing an open economy with the levels of security characteristic of the post-911 world. Recent U.S. opposition to the attempt by UAE-based DP World to take over management at six U.S. ports, an industry already characterized by a high level of foreign ownership, is an example of selective protectionism (Meckler and Machalaba 2006). Recent concerns expressed about a possible security risk of the 16,000 Lenovo personal computers intended for the U.S. State Department are a further example of such sentiment.

Despite evidence that protectionism carries very high costs and does little to prevent job losses (Rivoli 2005), the Bush administration, which has been under considerable pressure to protect U.S. workers, has responded with limited protectionism. The measures have focused on selected industries and markets—steel, clothing, furniture, and consumer goods. The European Union has followed a similar path with temporary restrictions on a number of clothing and textile products from China. It is recognized that outright protectionism would have effects well beyond the aim of protecting workers and could threaten capital inflows, currency values, and the willingness to hold government stocks.

More generally, there are signs of rising dissatisfaction with the processes of globalization and growing nationalism. The French controls on Italian energy firms seeking to acquire French companies, the public rejection of attempts to inject more flexibility into the French labor markets, EU tariffs on Chinese shoes, and U.S. attempts to restrict public sector offshore sourcing all reflect concern with the uneven distribution of the costs and benefits of globalization. The irony is that governments most supportive of globalization have been the least active in intervening to ensure a fairer distribution of the effects through progressive taxes and public investments in education and training. Similar dissatisfaction is also apparent within economies such as India, which have been major beneficiaries of globalization. Einhorn (2005) argues that if India were to switch its focus from regional trade agreements to multilateral initiatives, the benefits of globalization would be enjoyed by a larger share of the Indian population. A concern with India is that opposition to globalization is historically rooted in attitudes of public officials, unions, and businesses long wedded to the supposed benefits of self-sufficiency.

Some commentators believe that protectionist pressures have been contained because the world economy has been growing strongly in recent years. Any slowdown, and subsequent rise in unemployment or stagnation of wages, could heighten pressures. Both China and India have strong incentives to attempt to counter these concerns. Indian IT companies have responded to the growing protectionist backlash by placing offshore contracts with American firms. Both China and India have a vested interest in opposing protectionist sentiment and facilitating the Doha trade round.

One characteristic of the present protectionist debate differs substantially from earlier calls during the 1980s when the wave of Japanese competition appeared unstoppable. In the 1980s it was large firms in the steel, automobile, and consumer electronics industries that demanded protection. Today, many such firms are heavily involved in producing in, or outsourcing to, China and India, and it is the smaller firms that are the most vocal (*Economist* 2005i). However, not all firms or industries are banking on government protection. Italy, for example, faces considerable competition from Asia. Italy's textile and clothing industries lost 10,000 workers in 2005 as 2,000 companies were forced to close. Today the Italian textile and clothing industry employs 580,000 people, down from 670,000 a few years ago. However, successful survivors such as footwear maker Tod and the sunglasses manufacturer Safilo have moved upmarket to avoid head-on competition with China. Tod has invested heavily in its own brand and has moved to the very top of the market (Clark 2006).

Conclusions

This chapter has considered some of the political economy issues that have arisen as a result of China and India's rapid growth. The reemergence of these two countries as major powers is likely to be the most significant economic and political event in the first half of this century. Their size and relative openness mean that China and India will have an impact on the rest of the world that goes far beyond that of Japan and the newly industrializing Asian economies. To date, the primary impacts have been economic and have involved changes in relative prices, particularly higher commodity prices and returns on capital, as well as declining real wages for the least skilled. However, over the medium term, we may expect both China and India to play a greater role in international politics, and they may be pivotal in a restructuring of the international institutional arrangements that have prevailed since 1945.

The effect on particular countries depends to a significant extent on the structure and responsiveness of their economies. Developing countries that will do best in the face of competition from the Asian large emerging economies will be those that can avoid direct competition with them. Within the Asian region there is evidence of closer economic integration along with political fragmentation. Relations between Japan and China are particularly worrisome. The developed economies need to adapt to the competitive threat of China and India and avoid a level of protectionism that could endanger the global economy.

Implications for Management

1. The changes in relative prices that China and India have brought about encourage a reconsideration of ideal production processes and locations. This is already occurring with offshore sourcing of manufacturing, business services, and research and development. For many businesses this represents a considerable opportunity.
2. For firms competing with China and India there is a need to adjust and preferably to upgrade to avoid or minimize the impact of direct competition. The competitive threat from Asia will not disappear.
3. Firms need to recognize the limited effectiveness of protectionism and to see its purpose as providing breathing space for facilitating adjustment. Support should be offered to adjustment programs—new capital investment, increased innovation, brand building, and education and training.
4. In the longer term, as China and India begin to play a significant role in international relations, firms may expect to see a restructuring of international institutions and the business environment. Anticipating these changes provides considerable opportunities for business.

Discussion Questions

1. Is it likely that growing protectionism will hinder globalization? What arguments are there for and against continuing globalization?
2. How should the international institutions responsible for management of the world economy be restructured to reflect the rise of China and India? What sort of opposition would such restructuring be likely to face?

7

LESSONS FOR BUSINESS AND GOVERNMENT

Introduction

Earlier chapters have provided brief summaries of some of the implications for business resulting from our analysis of China and India. In this chapter these are developed in more detail to examine a number of important and recurring themes. We also look at the role that government policy could play in both fostering development in China and India and facilitating economic adjustment in the more developed nations.

The Attraction of China and India

We have identified four principal motives for entering large emerging markets such as China and India: to serve markets, to lower costs, to gain access to resources, and for the purpose of learning. These motives are not exclusive and over time may converge. For example, Motorola is to begin manufacturing cell phones and telecommunications equipment in India, where it also maintains six research and development centers which have developed leading-edge software for global products (*BusinessWeek* 2006c).

Markets

China is a major market for many products. It is already the world's largest market for mobile phones and in 2005 became the world's second largest market for new automobiles, with sales of almost six million. Forecasts suggest that India could be one of the world's top five consumer markets by 2010 (Bharadwaj et al. 2005). Both markets are developing fast and in a number of segments offer incredible growth prospects. For example, Airbus and Boeing are fighting over the Indian air travel market, which is growing at 25 percent annually. The number of passengers is expected to grow from 19 million annually today to 50 million by 2010, and a number of new airlines are expected to be established. Industry estimates suggest that India has the potential to buy at least 280 new planes by 2010. With an estimated value of $15 billion, India is the key market for both producers (*BusinessWeek* 2005j).

Rapid development also creates huge opportunities for infrastructure specialists. China plans to build more than 300 new cities over the next five years, bringing the total number of Chinese cities with populations over 200,000 to 1,000. Similar dynamics are apparent in India, which is building some 450 new shopping malls (*Economist* 2006e). Many of the key construction challenges likely to be encountered will be in areas such as power generation, waste disposal, and water management, areas in which Western firms are world leaders (Young and Riera 2006). Urban redevelopment will bring huge opportunities for service companies and for the development of public–private partnerships (Lane et al. 2004). One downstream effect of urbanization is the demand for household furnishings. IKEA recently opened a mega store in China in response to the millions of new home buyers and a vast new market that has been promoted by government policy encouraging both home ownership and increased consumer spending (*BusinessWeek* 2005k). In other industries liberalization is providing market stimulus. For example, the planned opening of China's publishing industry encouraged the entry of Bertelsmann in 2005.

The low average income and considerable inequalities in the distribution of income mean that markets in China and India are highly fragmented. The wealthiest households may enjoy very high levels of discretionary spending, but numerically they are small. In India the top of the distribution, *global Indians*, represent just 1.2 million households (Bharadwaj et al. 2005). At the same time some 260 millions Indians live on less than $1 a day. India has perhaps 150 million people with discretionary income. International businesses have focused at the top end of the market and not surprisingly are strongly represented in the premium market segments for products such as shampoo, laundry detergent, and biscuits (Chen and Penhirin 2004). Harley Davidson recently opened an official Beijing dealership. This is clearly a limited sales niche in a country where the average annual income is still only $1,200 (*BusinessWeek* 2006d).

However, in the future, international businesses will need to consider some of the lower-income groups. Not only are these numerically more important segments allowing economies of scale to be achieved, they are also the consumers who offer the most interesting challenges (Prahalad 2005). It is the 40 million households that have been termed *aspiring Indians* with incomes of $4,000 to $10,000 that are driving demand for consumer goods (Bharadwaj et al. 2005). In China the middle-class consumers of the future are currently dispersed and are likely to move increasingly from blue collar to service and knowledge industries. They offer huge opportunities (Farrell, Gersch, and Stephenson 2006).

The key challenge of these market segments is the need to develop low-cost value offerings and new business models. In essence, they provide the learning opportunities that international businesses will need to master if they are to compete successfully with local firms and to tackle the vast markets in emerging markets. At its simplest, product adaptation will be necessary. For example, in selling to those on lower incomes, motorcycle companies in India redesign bikes to sacrifice speed for mileage. In some cases this adaptation is required to meet the specific needs of a particular market and its unique characteristics. Nokia's best-selling GSM handset in India featured a torch, dust-resistant keypad, and an antislip grip for humid conditions as well as the ability to support Hindu. Given India's intermittent power supply, LG appliances built for a 220-volt supply system incorporate a power fluctuation tolerance range some five times higher than the norm.

More demanding is the need to develop new business models in an attempt to reach underdeveloped market segments. Hindustan Lever's Project Shakti is an innovative consumer education and distribution model that creates income-generating capabilities for underprivileged rural women by providing sustainable microenterprise opportunities to improve rural living standards through health and hygiene awareness. The model has now been extended onto an electronic platform as i-Shakti.

Low Costs

The opportunity to reduce costs is a second primary motive for entering emerging markets. In many cases the key attraction has been low-cost skilled labor. For many products and services, the savings have been considerable. Furthermore, lower labor costs have allowed activities to be undertaken that would not be feasible elsewhere. For example, a major U.S. bank saved $100 million by using low-cost offshore staff to detect fraud in low-value transactions that could not be scrutinized profitably at home (Chakrabarty et al. 2006). Companies that have been slow to establish themselves in lower-cost markets such as India find themselves at a competitive disadvantage and may be forced to make significant new investments to catch up (Bremner 2006).

It is, however, not clear how long China and India will be able to retain their cost advantage. The market for offshored information technology and business processes has nearly tripled since 2001 (Chakrabarty et al. 2006), and yet estimates suggest that this is perhaps just 10 percent of the potential market (Nasscom/McKinsey 2005). Further major growth is expected in the areas of banking and insurance. According to the Nasscom/McKinsey study, India has 28 percent of the suitably qualified people in low-cost countries, yet it is expected to face a shortfall in 2010 of 500,000 people. Estimates by international consultancy Everest Consultants suggest that India's advantage could last at least another 30 years (Everest Consultants 2006).

There is growing recognition of this looming shortage. Indian executives see the costs and availability of talent as the biggest constraint on business over the next five years (Bever et al. 2005). The Indian IT industry is already diversifying geographically to incorporate second-tier cities such as Hyderabad, Chennai, Pune, and Kolkata. Rising costs and very high rates of labor turnover are affecting investment decisions. Apple has recently shelved plans for a technical support center in Bangalore. Estimates suggest that in the Indian IT industry entry-level wages rose by as much as 13 percent annually between 2000 and 2004 while mid-level managers have enjoyed increases closer to 30 percent per annum over the same period (*BusinessWeek* 2006e).

Major cities in China are also experiencing shortages. The causes of this seem to be multifaceted. On the one hand, there has been a slowdown in those leaving the agricultural sector. In January 2004 the authorities extended the land contract time for farmers, which provided incentives to improve productivity. Farmers have also received additional subsidies and tax reductions. The effect has been to improve farmers' incomes relative to those of migrant workers. On the other hand, there is a sizable mismatch between those seeking work and the type of worker in demand. In general, those seeking work are older and less skilled than the ideal for employers. Labor market dualism has resulted in a continuing negative wage differential against migrant workers when compared with the average urban worker. The result of rising wages is a predictable one; it is encouraging an upgrading of industrial activity toward more capital- and technologically intensive processes. While labor costs in emerging economies will remain below those of the advanced economies, the differential may shrink. Rising labor costs may threaten the growth of offshoring because sourcing from countries such as China and India involves significant setup costs, particularly in quality assurance, control, and logistics (Bergmann et al. 2004; Campbell et al. 2004).

Specialist Resources and Learning Opportunities

A third motive for investing in emerging markets is to gain access to specialist resources and opportunities for learning. Both China and India possess pockets of highly skilled specialist labor. International businesses see Indian manufacturing focusing on batch and skill-intensive industries. In industries such as automotive components and pharmaceuticals, India has low costs, process skills, and capabilities in product and capital engineering. India has 75 pharmaceutical plants approved by the U.S. Food and Drug Administration, more than any country outside the United States. As discussed earlier, car companies such as General Motors are increasingly sourcing from India and China in an attempt to cut costs and improve quality. Businesses can also learn important lessons from tapping into new consumer segments in emerging markets. Similarly, the competitive strengths of domestic companies can provide interesting strategic lessons for Western business (Sinha 2005b).

Accessing specialist resources comes at a price. International businesses need to make investments to develop suppliers, create a dialogue with the authorities to help build goodwill and provide input on regulatory issues, and develop local management talent (Luthra et al. 2005). The following box, which summarizes the contributions of Suzuki and Toyota to the Indian automotive sector, highlights the need for market-making expenditures.

Box 7.1 Suzuki and Toyota in the Indian Automobile Industry

It is now widely agreed that India, along with China, Thailand, and Mexico, could become one of the leading developing country suppliers of automobile components. India's automobile component exports, including those from multinational parts suppliers, grew at an annual rate of 25 percent in the five years to 2003 and are now worth more than $1 billion per year.

Suzuki's 1983 collaboration with the Indian government led to the formation of Maruti Udyog Limited (MUL). By sourcing cars entirely locally, MUL aimed to maintain low prices and to increase its production volume. With almost no vendor base in India, MUL rose to the challenge of establishing one by helping create joint ventures between its Japanese suppliers and Indian partners.

MUL not only arranged for collaboration between Indian and foreign companies, but also helped Indian suppliers grow by implementing manufacturing and quality standards. It even provided technical support by bringing in experts from Japan to train personnel for key suppliers. The implementation of the Japanese production system, which helped local suppliers raise their productivity while cutting costs, was an overarching benefit of these efforts.

Toyota was the first automaker (in 2001) to see India as a source of components. After concluding that the advantages outweighed any near-term shortcomings, the company invested almost $200 million in six joint ventures to help local suppliers develop scale in their manufacturing operations. Toyota also focused on localizing the content of its Qualis and Corolla models. Local content now accounts for 74 percent and 55 percent of the cost of the Qualis and Corolla, respectively. Through economies of scale in manufacturing, Toyota then turned India into a regional sourcing hub. It now exports transmission assemblies (one of the most complex parts of any automobile) from India; other automakers limit themselves to importing only simple Indian components. Toyota has also invested significant amounts to bring Indian suppliers up to its global standards.

Source: Luthra et al. 2005.

The Challenges of Doing Business with China and India

The previous chapters have highlighted a significant number of challenges that international businesses face when doing business with China and India. For convenience we can divide these into those challenges that are shared by all or most emerging markets and those more specific to China and India.

Challenges of Emerging Markets

As Chapters 3 and 4 in particular make clear, emerging markets bring considerable managerial and strategic challenges for international businesses. Rather than reiterate these, we focus on those that are likely to be particularly novel. One is risk, particularly informational risk. The paucity of information in emerging markets encourages investors to seek local partners who can help manage risk, emulate other successful investors or competitors, and cultivate strong relationships with relevant stakeholders. Gathering sound data rather than making decisions based purely on intuition is a major responsibility of senior management in an emerging economy.

Second, our discussion suggests that investors will face higher levels of competition than might be expected. Competition comes from both other investors and increasingly strong local firms. In some cases local firms may enjoy preferential access to funds, the best foreign partners, and trade protection. Such firms are also capable of innovative strategic moves. When eBay entered the Chinese market, local rival Alibaba sold a 40 percent stake to Yahoo!, considerably strengthening its competitive position (*Time* 2005). Many investors have experienced debilitating competition in the Chinese market. While the profitability of foreign firms in China has improved since 1990, profits often have to be reinvested to maintain a strong market position (Woetzel 2004a). High-technology companies competing in China face limited demand growth in high-end product segments, severe pricing pressure, industry overinvestment and overcapacity, high turnover of qualified local management talent, and difficulty in managing joint venture partners.

Third, the strategies available to international firms are constrained by the existence of significant market failures. Many industries in India are stifled by product market restrictions and labor market distortions. Domestic firms, long familiar with such failures, develop close government relations or utilize structures, such as the conglomerate business, to counteract these malfunctions. Limited experience with widespread market failures may place international businesses at a comparative disadvantage. Despite their obvious attractions in terms of size and growth, both China and India have relatively poor business environments. The 2006 Economist Intelligence Unit ranking of 82 economies placed China at 50th and India at 58th in terms of the attractiveness of their business environments. Some markets are difficult simply because they are underdeveloped. Within sports marketing, for example, there is little understanding of the business by sports teams and officials, fans are fickle, corruption is rife, and media market research is poor (*BusinessWeek* 2003d). These markets are not sufficiently mature to justify involvement at the present time.

Fourth, in contrast to what are often long-established domestic market positions, the timing of entry matters in an emerging market. However, it is not readily apparent that either early or later entry is invariably the best path (Luo and Peng 1998). Our discussion has also highlighted a related point that there may be a significant cost to early entry, namely the need to undertake market-making expenditures. Such expenditures may be necessary to educate the consumer, to build effective distribution, and to develop local suppliers (see Box 7.1). The lower penetration rates of products such as beauty products, credit cards, and air conditioners in markets such as India may reflect a lack of understanding of what products and brands do, and generic consumer education becomes a prerequisite to sales (Bharadwaj et al. 2005). Effective distribution is both difficult and expensive in India where some 12 million mom-and-pop stores have long dominated retailing. The key seems to be to use third-party distribution because building a system is both expensive and time consuming (Bharadwaj et al. 2005).

Challenges of China and India

When we turn to the specific cases of the Chinese and Indian markets, other challenges become apparent. Within China we have seen the need for the authorities to tackle the massive inefficiencies that exist in the state-owned sector and in banking. A more general concern is the need to manage growing income inequality between the urban and rural sectors. In the longer term, the key challenge facing China may be demands for political democracy. In economic terms, greater democracy and freedom of expression may be necessary conditions for fostering creativity. International businesses need to be aware of the directions that policies are likely to take in countering these problems. For India, maintaining the reform process, boosting infrastructure, and reducing excessive levels of regulation are the priorities. In the medium term the authorities will also wish to broaden the growth engine of the economy beyond IT and software.

For international businesses there are five main lessons that should be learned. The first is the mistaken belief that entry by international firms is essentially passive in emerging markets. This is far from the truth; the reality is that such entrants trigger a competitive response from local businesses. Chinese and Indian firms are actively upgrading their activities. In some cases they are developing innovative production approaches that drive down costs and prices. Chinese motorcycle manufacturers now account for 50 percent of global production and in a decade have been able to cut prices from around $700 to under $200. As a result, Honda's share of the Vietnamese motorcycle market fell from 90 percent in 1997 to 30 percent in 2002 (Brown and Hagel 2005).

Second, emerging market companies are fast learners and should not be underestimated. They are knowledgeable about the low-income segments in developing markets, which represent the majority of consumers in the world. This is an area where few Western firms have experience and yet may be the key arena within which future international business competition takes place. Emerging market firms are learning to internationalize into relatively sheltered markets and to gradually build capability. As we noted, Chinese car exports are heading to Africa, South Asia, and the Middle East, not North America and Europe—yet, anyway. Mainland Chinese consumer electronics retailers such as Gnome Home Appliances and MKD are initially entering Hong Kong challenging culturally similar firms such as Fortress and Broadway. The Chinese car industry is recruiting global executives with the experience to drive brand and design strategies.

However, their attempts to internationalize are frustrated by a lack of competitive advantages and inappropriate structures. State-backed Chinese businesses are negatively perceived in the advanced economies. Indian family-owned conglomerates struggle to overcome internal conflict, as the recent problems of the Reliance Group highlight. Where they are successful in achieving international status, emerging market firms are prompting a competitive reaction. There is no doubt that the internationalization of Infosys, Tata, and Wipro has triggered strategic restructuring within Western firms such as IBM and EDS.

In many cases the strongest market positions are achieved by competitors from other developing economies. Thus, highly successful Samsung washing machines sold in India include memory backup to compensate for frequent power outages and a special rinse cycle for saris to prevent them from becoming twisted and knotted (Bharadwaj et al. 2005). Whether it is because of a greater affinity with emerging market demand patterns or a commitment to market research and adaptation, these firms are formidable competitors. Admittedly, some Western firms are catching on. They are pioneering smaller-sized, cheaper products in soft drinks, biscuits, and shampoo. They are experimenting with more flexible payment options, including financing, pay per use, and community use in the case of PC makers (Bharadwaj et al. 2005). More generally, the challenge will be to develop new products, price points, and business models that appeal to emerging markets and can match the strategies of local firms. Foreign firms will need to drop costs by 30 to 50 percent and leverage global brands and marketing know-how if they are to bring themselves into line with their Chinese competitors (Von Morgenstern 2006). Companies such as LG Electronics, Toyota, and Hyundai are the leaders in this at the present time (Jain et al. 2005).

Third, it is easy to underestimate the competitive capability of emerging market firms. This occurs for two main reasons. The first is that conventional measures of competitive success, such as firm internationalization, may not be the most appropriate measures. The limited internationalization of Chinese and Indian firms does not mean they are uncompetitive; rather, it suggests that with some exceptions, in technology and resource-seeking investments, they are currently focusing on their large and rapidly growing home markets. If we think back to the frenzy generated by the competitiveness of Japanese firms in the 1970s and 1980s, much of this was based on export penetration and predated most of the outward investment by Japanese firms. Given their considerable cost and market size advantages, the strategy of Chinese and Indian firms is even more likely to be domestically focused. A second reason is that some emerging market firms are disguising their capabilities. This is occurring as they move up the industry value chain but are still classed within the same general industry segment. For example, Indian BPO (business process outsourcing) firms are increasingly moving into knowledge process outsourcing, which is qualitatively different and involves real judgment and analysis from local workers. Increasing familiarity with outsourced processes will not only allow outsourcers to improve on these processes, but may also allow them to develop a better understanding of the processes than their clients, enabling them to capture more of the industry value chain (*Economist* 2006e). Furthermore, at the moment Indian firms are using such innovations to retain customers and maintain margins. Effectively, they are not charging for additional value.

Fourth, it is necessary for Western firms to see their business involvement in China and India in strategic terms because these markets will become increasingly important drivers of global strategy in many industries. Microsoft recognized early in its involvement in China the importance of the country's human resources and the value of transferring lessons to other emerging markets such as India (Buderi and Huang 2006). Nokia provides an illustrative example of such thinking. It is the number one brand in both China and India with a market share of 31 percent and 60 percent, respectively. China is now the world's largest cell phone market, and the Indian market is growing rapidly. While Nokia was an early entrant into both markets, it struggled in India under burdensome regulations. In China, Nokia lagged Motorola and faced strong domestic competition. In response, Nokia decentralized operations and introduced market-specific models. It was able to apply this experience in other emerging markets, including India. Nokia was also able to take advantage of the errors of competitors. Motorola, for example, was late in entering the Indian market and underestimated the threat of domestic rivals in China. Local Chinese cell phone manufacturers suffered quality problems (*BusinessWeek* 2006f). The experience of the cell phone industry is increasingly being replicated in other consumer electronics sectors and is likely to spread soon to other industries, including automobiles.

Fifth, as we suggested before, the question of entry timing is a critical one in emerging markets. In some sectors of Chinese manufacturing it may already be too late for many international firms contemplating entry. Market shaping and dominant positions are already evident in automobiles, consumer electronics, processed foods, and pharmaceuticals. Early movers such as Volkswagen, which entered its partnership with SAIC in the mid-1980s; HSBC in banking; Citibank in credit cards; AIG in insurance; and Carrefour in retailing have all benefited from taking an early position in China (Woetzel 2004b). However, later entry can be successful when major shifts in market demand or technology occur. Hyundai and Honda have both rapidly gained market share in the Chinese market as demand shifted from predominantly public to private purchasers of vehicles. It is also important for international investors to recognize that expansion strategies may be just as important as the initial entry mode in determining success in emerging markets (Van Den Bulcke et al. 1999).

However, when entry carries significant market-making or adaptation costs, the analysis of optimal timing becomes more complex. The Home Depot, for example, has shown considerable hesitancy with regard to the Chinese market despite the presence of its British rival B&Q and local players Homemart, Homeway, and Orient Home. B&Q has had a presence in China since 1999 and now has 49 stores. The Home Depot's rivals have spent years cultivating relationships with suppliers and occupy the prime retail locations in the big cities. The Home Depot's reluctance is largely the result of the considerable differences between Western and Chinese DIY (do-it-yourself) markets. In the United States, The Home Depot provides tools, parts, and advice to home improvers. In China, new houses and apartments are sold as simply a shell with the buyer responsible for all the finishing work. In such a market, The Home Depot would have to train all its staffers to do floor-to-ceiling installations, and it has not developed relationships with tradesmen and contractors (*BusinessWeek* 2006g). In the absence of a successful acquisition, the costs of entry facing The Home Depot appear extremely high.

The Contribution of Foreign Business to China and India

It should be clear from our discussion that foreign businesses have made a major contribution to the development of both China and India and will continue to do so. This suggests that foreign investment brings benefits to both the investing firms and the host country. The impact can be direct, for example, in the case of Suzuki and Maruti, summarized in Box 7.1, or indirect through its impact on productivity (Lui et al. 2001) or industry structure (Luo and Tan 1997). However, emerging markets are not identical, and international investors need to tailor strategies to the particular circumstances they face. Cummins, for example, uses China for mass production, whereas in India the company produces low-volume and more complex industrial goods (*BusinessWeek* 2005a).

Foreign investment may also play a key role in restructuring industries or facilitating infrastructure development. By November 2005, 18 foreign institutions had invested a total of about $13 billion in 16 Chinese banks, an industry that is likely to benefit considerably from an injection of outside management expertise. India's port privatization program has, since 1996, attracted investment from both domestic and foreign firms. The impact on productivity has been considerable, with average turnaround time declining from about eight days then to just over three days now. In other areas of infrastructure, the Indian authorities have put considerable emphasis both on private–public partnerships and in attracting foreign investment. Recently Delhi and Mumbai airports, in desperate need of upgrading, were handed over to private consortia.

Foreign investors need to recognize that the considerable attractions of access to the markets and resources of China and India mean that some concessions may need to be made. The power of multinational investors may be muted in such markets. Wal-Mart has ambitious plans to expand in China, but contrary to its North American policy stance it has agreed to establish officially sanctioned unions in its Chinese stores if workers request this (McGregor 2004).

An important implication for host-country governments is the recognition that the beneficial impacts of inward investment depend critically on absorptive capacity and the influence of government policy, particularly competition policy (Farrell et al. 2004). While we have discussed the desirability of increasing foreign investment levels in India, it is worth noting that foreign investment and offshore sourcing share a number of similarities when considering their contribution to economic development. Both bring additional external resources, and both offer technology and opportunities for upgrading. Both also facilitate overseas market access and the adoption of leading-edge management practices. In addition, both encourage the employment of complementary local and overseas resources and can generate strong spillovers. When we recognize the similarities between foreign direct investment and offshoring, it is apparent that the gap between China and India in terms of attracting external resources may not be as great as is often thought.

There is also a need to understand the complex interactions among inward investment, economic restructuring, and institutional develop-

ment. In the case of China, it has been suggested that foreign investment has allowed the authorities to restructure productive relations
between capital and labor (Gallagher 2005). The argument suggests
that foreign firms have placed competitive pressure on the state sector, necessitating the adoption of new, more flexible labor practices.
Acceptance of these changes in one sector has allowed difficult and
politically sensitive labor reforms to be extended to other parts of the
economy resulting in a stronger state; a weakened civil society, particularly organized labor; and the postponement of political reform.
Direct reform of the socialist labor contract (lifetime employment,
extensive welfare benefits, and little labor mobility) could have triggered social discontent. By channeling the efficiency benefits of such
reform from the foreign-funded sector to the rest of the economy, the
authorities have strengthened national sentiment and avoided responsibility (Gallagher 2005).

Role of Supportive Government Policy

Our discussion has highlighted the importance for India of reforming
public sector economic involvement and the efficiency of government
policy. As Joshi (1998) argues, the Indian state has been overly active
in areas outside its competence while at the time neglecting core areas
such as primary health care and education. It follows that the role
of the state must be redefined. A pressing need is the continuance
of further reforms. A study by the McKinsey Global Institute found
three principal barriers to faster growth in India: the multiplicity of
regulations governing product markets, distortions in the market for
land, and widespread government ownership of business. Together
these were estimated to inhibit Indian growth by 4 percent per annum
(Di Lodovico et al. 2001).

The *Economist* (2006e) has suggested that the reforms of the past
1.5 decades have been the easy part, and that India needs further
substantial reforms to increase competition, relax labor laws, increase
education expenditures, and improve infrastructure. The difficulty of
further reform is compounded by the fact that, unlike 1991, there is no
pressing economic crisis to propel further liberalization, and the types

of reforms needed do not lend themselves to the gradual and sur-
reptitious approaches that have been successful. Labor market reform
is likely to prove particularly problematic as the present government
depends for parliamentary support on Communist parties, which are
indebted to India's trade unions.

There are also significant obstacles to increased infrastructure
spending. Morgan Stanley estimates that India needs to spend $100
billion per year on infrastructure by 2010; in 2003 it spent just $21
billion. Increasing spending is hampered by the government's relatively low tax revenues and high fiscal deficits at the state level.

The policy challenges for the Chinese authorities lie in the financial and state-owned sectors. The Chinese authorities perhaps need
to accept the superiority of shifting from providing resources for
improving the efficiency of state-owned enterprises toward channeling
more resources to the private sector. At the same time, state-owned
enterprises should be allowed to fail (Garnaut and Song 2004). Both
countries face considerable policy tribulations in managing economic
upgrading. Poor understanding of the economics of the knowledge
economy creates difficulties in the design of effective policy. Both
China and India must also overcome the inertia of economic systems
that emphasize labor cost competitiveness rather than the application
of advanced knowledge.

Policy Implications for Developed Countries

The rise of China and India has raised considerable competitive and
adjustment issues for developed countries. While it is increasingly
accepted that blunt protectionism does little to maintain jobs, there is
a policy need to minimize the dislocations of adjustment.

In competitive terms, the key long-term issue may be the new global
competition that increasingly revolves around the ability to attract,
use, and retain creative people (Florida 2005). While such people were
once almost exclusively found in the large advanced economies such
as the United States, strong competition is now coming from other
developed economies facing unfavorable demographics and emerging markets eager to attract and employ their many talented people

living abroad. Cities including Bangalore, Beijing, and Shanghai are wooing foreign technology companies, upgrading their higher-education systems, investing heavily in innovation, and expanding cultural and lifestyle amenities. The lead long enjoyed by the United States in this area is declining as other countries compete for global talent and the United States tightens its immigration and visa regulations and increasingly fails to nurture domestic creativity (Florida 2005).

Part of the difficulty of devising effective adjustment policies is a result of the uneven impact of the resurgence of emerging economies. Numerically, the biggest winners are consumers. Farmers and commodity exporters also benefit. Large retailers are able to access lower-cost sources, strengthening their competitive positions and margins. The most obvious losers are manufacturing and service workers whose jobs come under threat. The most commonly used policies to tackle the threat from emerging economies are those based on education and training and broad economic upgrading and those that focus on improving the efficiency of market adjustment.

Education and Upgrading

A long-favored response to competition from lower-wage economies has been education and training. The idea behind such policies is to relinquish work that is no longer competitive in high-wage economies and retool released workers to undertake more skilled activities. Effectively, the aim is to avoid direct competition with the lower-wage economy. Implicit in such policies is the assumption that unemployed resources can be redeployed at low cost. While such a policy still has much to commend it, there is growing concern that education may no longer provide the assurance that it once did. Given the huge strides that countries like China and India have made in upgrading the quality of their education systems, it is possible for an employee in the developed world to be educationally competitive but not wage competitive. In essence, China and India are able to produce comparable graduates who are prepared to work for a fraction of developed country wages. Such developments are fueling a view that globalization may no longer be an unequivocally positive force for countries such as the United States (Bernstein 2004). As falling transport and communication costs increase the range of work that can be sent overseas, the critical distinction may no longer be the skill componen, but rather the issue of whether or not the work can be delivered electronically (Blinder 2006).

China now awards more than one-fifth of all engineering degrees worldwide; even India produces more than the United States. While high-tech industry employment in the United States expanded by 50 percent between 1990 and 2002, the number of U.S. engineering bachelor degrees fell by 6 percent over the same period (AeA 2005a). The effects of a shortage of skilled staff can be far-reaching. It is worth recalling that the origin of IT offshore sourcing to India was a shortage of staff to deal with the problems of Y2K.

Developed countries such as the United States face a number of threats to their leadership in high-technology industries. Other countries are making huge strides in developing their national innovation systems. As noted earlier, China now produces almost four times as many engineers as the United States. At the same time, U.S. federal support for R&D is declining. While the U.S. schooling system is not providing the number or quality of engineering graduates required, it is increasingly difficult in the post-911 environment to meet the shortfall through immigration or foreign student placements (AeA 2005a). However, it is worth noting that the number of graduates says little about their quality or about the effectiveness of the country's national innovation system in transferring ideas through to successful products. The United States still contains 18 of the world's top 20 universities (Zakaria 2006b).

Proposals to maintain competitiveness in high-tech industries imply a significant role for public authorities. These involve improvements in the education system, increased public support of R&D, a commitment to upgrading critical knowledge-based infrastructure such as broadband and cellular penetration, support for highly skilled immigration, and a general reduction in business compliance costs (AeA 2005a).

A number of industries are striking back at Asian competitors. For example, the small-sized, premium Italian furniture brands are seeking strength from collaboration. With annual average sales of just $600,000, Italy's small furniture companies have very limited resources to survive extreme price competition. Operating as a loose federation has provided savings in the areas of purchasing, transport, and logistics. Trying to offer the personalization of an artisan product within the framework of a global business is an attempt to sidestep direct price competition (*BusinessWeek* 2006h).

Labor Market Adjustment

For developed economies, growing competition and the futility of protectionism increase the need for efficient internal adjustment. Broadly, as low-skilled jobs are lost or such work is outsourced overseas, the maintenance of employment levels requires economic upgrading and an efficient labor market. The International Labor Organization estimates that the OECD (Organization for Economic Cooperation and Development) countries have around 40 million unemployed workers; worldwide the figure is in excess of 800 million. The wealthy countries must develop knowledge, R&D spending, and innovation to facilitate their shift into high-technology, higher-value-added products and services if they are to maintain and improve living standards. Similarly, if new technological opportunities are to be exploited, product markets should also be competitive. Adjustment programs need to be extended beyond manufacturing to include service industries, which are increasingly mobile.

Adjustment is far from costless. One study that focused on five U.S. import-competing industries reported that almost two-thirds of workers who lost their jobs between 1979 and 1999 as a result of import competition eventually found a new one (Kletzer 2001). However, on average they experienced wage cuts of 13 percent. While one-third of those displaced maintained or improved their earnings, one-quarter suffered a pay cut of at least 30 percent. Those suffering the most significant cuts were older, less educated, and less skilled and had benefited from tenure in their previous work. Labor adjustment policies are increasingly shifting from passive forms of income compensation to more active measures that assist job search, relocation, and retraining.

Tax policy can also be used to influence the nature of global business activity. While there is growing concern with the practice of offshore sourcing, it is currently treated benignly in tax terms. There may be a case for tax policy changes that could be used to alter the attractiveness of this option.

Conclusions

This chapter has developed some of the key implications for business and policy makers of the rise of China and India. There is little doubt that for many businesses China and India offer irresistible attractions as markets, low-cost supply bases, and sources of unique resources. At the same time, many smaller national firms are struggling to survive the competitive onslaught from Chinese and Indian exporters. One common denominator that all Western businesses face is the need to either match the price levels of these firms or avoid direct competition. The longer-term threat presented by China and India is perhaps the most significant. This is the opportunity to learn how best to serve the millions of low-income households that are experiencing rapid growth in discretionary income. Such consumers require new price and value offerings, in many cases in the guise of novel business models. A failure to acquire such knowledge may be the most serious competitive disadvantage for Western businesses over the next decade.

For policy makers in the emerging economies it is important to maintain the reform process and to address the infrastructure and market failures that we have alluded to in previous chapters. For the advanced economies the policy task is twofold. The first is investment and commitment to maintaining a lead in higher technology, innovative, and creative industries. Second, at the same time, efficient adjustment to the rise of China and India will facilitate orderly upgrading and restructuring.

8

FINAL THOUGHTS

Introduction

In considering the economic renaissance of China and India, we are in effect looking at the most significant change in the structure of the world economy this century. Rapid growth enjoyed by almost half of the world's population has altered relative prices, provided vast new markets, and threatened job security within wealthy countries. The rise of China and India appears to have reached a point where it is now likely to be irreversible: certainly some of the challenges we have discussed could delay the process but do not seem likely to derail it.

It is important to note the limitations of our discussion. Our focus has been on the economic and institutional development of large emerging economies; we have paid very little attention to the need for cultural awareness and adaptation to the unique business systems of these economies. Business success in any emerging market requires an understanding of culture and business relations as well as the economic opportunities and challenges they present.

Similarities and Contrasts

The development experience of China and India highlights a number of similarities as well as contrasts. In terms of similarities, both countries have adopted gradualist reform programs: neither has attempted the "big bang" adjustment pursued within parts of Eastern Europe. Gradualism has allowed experimentation, which has been critical to maintaining growth over a period of decades. Both countries have recognized the need for political stability but have achieved this in different ways. A centralized Chinese Communist Party has achieved remarkable growth and reform within an authoritarian political system. In contrast, India has attained slower growth within a highly resilient democracy capable of accommodating a vast array of demands. Development in both China and India has been driven, at least in part, by involvement with the rest of the world. China has attracted huge amounts of foreign investment; India has sought offshore sourcing. Both have relied on sales to the advanced markets. As a result, both countries have experienced unequal development and rising inequality, familiar products of global integration. For both countries, their major challenges are internal. For China it involves financial reform, further privatization, containing rising inequality, and freeing up the exchange of ideas and information. India faces major challenges in improving infrastructure, maintaining reform, and attracting external resources. At the same time a protectionist threat hangs over both countries. They may become victims of their own success.

While similarities are apparent, their development experience also highlights some significant contrasts. China is more open and internationally integrated than India. The Chinese authorities retain more direct controls over economic affairs with financing provisions, tariff protection, and controls on stock market listings. The economic structures of China and India are complementary, with China stronger in hardware and India a leader in software.

It is also appropriate to acknowledge the remarkable achievements that governments in both countries have achieved. The sheer complexity of reform in China, for example, would tax policy officials anywhere. China is effectively undergoing four simultaneous transitions: from a command to a market economy, from a rural to an urban society, from a centralized to a decentralized political system, and from an agricultural to an industrial society.

Opportunities and Threats

As we have stressed repeatedly, large emerging markets bring both opportunities and threats for international businesses. The opportunities include new markets, access to new sources of often low-cost resources, and opportunities for learning. At the same time they present considerable challenges. In the short term the key threat is the so-called China (or India) Price—the ability of these countries to produce products and services of comparable quality at far lower costs than is possible in Western economies. The threat is readily evident in industries such as clothing, footwear, wooden furniture, toys, sporting goods, consumer electronics, and business services and is adversely affecting a number of Western businesses and the job security of many relatively low- or medium-skilled employees. In the longer term the threat is that this competitive pressure will be extended into higher-value manufacturing activities, R&D, and a range of service businesses. The early signs of Chinese and Indian success in these areas are increasingly apparent. It would be a mistake to dismiss such a threat as unimportant simply because of the limited internationalization of Chinese and Indian firms. Rather, it is the considerable locational advantages of these countries that attract new investment and increased offshoring. Western policy makers seem to be poorly equipped to respond to this redistribution of activity.

Our discussion highlights the need for Western businesses to learn how to match the cost-to-value offerings from emerging markets and to successfully serve the massive lower-income consumer segments that are rapidly emerging. Over the next few decades, business models based on such segments are likely to become universal (Desvaux and Ramsay 2006).

Impact on the Rest of the World

Given their huge populations, rapid growth within China and India will create a fairer world overall. The many millions of low-income individuals who will enjoy rising wealth will fuel future demand, potentially benefiting much of the rest of the world economy. However, this will not be without cost. The adjustment problem for the advanced economies could create a new economic underclass in wealthy economies that experience difficulties in responding to the new competition. An equally worrisome concern is that the success of the large emerging markets could come at the price of further marginalization of developing economies in Latin America, the Middle East, and Africa. Our discussion highlights the way that Mexico, parts of developing Asia, and a wide range of textile exporters are struggling against Chinese competition.

Our analysis has some important implications for development more generally. It should be apparent that the experience of China and India does not indicate the existence of a clearly superior development model. While there are some shared commonalities, the overwhelming picture is one of experimentation and uniqueness. Clearly there are some fundamentals that must be attained before development can take place. The first is the creation of political and economic stability. Without this, the catalyst for development simply cannot take place. Similarly, research overwhelmingly supports the superiority of market forces in the efficient allocation of resources. Indeed, many of the chief failings apparent in both China and India are the result of excessive or misguided government intervention.

The experience of China and India also makes clear the importance of external resources in the development process. This is, however, more than simply a need for capital or aid. The most effective resource package entails capital, technology, management skills, and market access. As we have argued, this has been achieved in China through massive inflows of FDI and in India through offshore sourcing. The rapid growth achieved by both has been facilitated by the ability to quickly penetrate developed markets whether through contract manufacturing or through the processing of business services.

Similarly, size seems to matter for rapid development. Huge market opportunities and an expectation that low labor costs can be maintained well into the future have favored China and India, despite the fact that neither is seen as possessing a particularly attractive business environment.

The New Protectionism

The strains of adjustment to the rise of China and India are considerable. Already they are raising concerns of a new protectionist backlash, which is compounded by rising concerns regarding security. The stymieing of trade negotiations, imposition of social clauses within trade agreements, massive trade imbalances, calls for exchange rate adjustments, and targeted protectionist measures all raise the dangers of limiting the power of China and India to continue to serve as engines of world growth. Protectionism is certainly a potential problem recognized by the world's major international investors (UNCTAD [United Nations Conference on Trade and Development] 2004).

However, it may be erroneous to believe that China and India are the sole source of economic disruption. There are grounds for believing that technical change, particularly in the area of information technology, is biased toward foreign direct investment and offshoring, lowering the costs of managing and controlling such processes. Technological change that reduces jobs to a predetermined set of procedures encourages the shifting of such work. Similarly, both processes—foreign investment and offshoring—are now offering such levels of competitive advantage that they have achieved a virtuous circle whereby they offer more than just labor cost savings. Offshoring, for example, can allow new revenue opportunities that would not be profitable if handled by higher-cost employees (Daga and Kaka 2006; Goolsby 2006). At the same time, there may be early signs of growing resentment of foreign investors within China itself and a view that China no longer needs the volume of such investment (*BusinessWeek* 2006i).

However, the reality is that the continued success of China and India depends, to a very considerable degree, on the effectiveness of internal decisions and management. The key challenges faced by both countries are internal (*Economist* 2006f). China, in particular, faces daunting challenges in terms of land reform (*Economist* 2006g) and the relaxation of political controls if a truly creative society is to evolve. There is also a need for smarter policy interventions. Interventions that can target two or more desirable policy objectives will be increasingly important. For example, financial reforms could help achieve multiple objectives in both improving the efficiency of capital allocation and reducing inequality (Farrell, Lund, and Morin 2006).

In closing, it is worth observing that the significance of China and India is something that has been noted before. Napoleon's famous quote, "China is a sleeping giant, long may it sleep, for when it awakes it will shake the world," and Albert Einstein's observation that "[w]e owe a lot to the Indians, who taught us to count, without which no worthwhile scientific discovery could have been made" both highlight the likelihood of these countries shaking, and increasingly shaping, our world.

References

Acemoglu, D., S. Johnson, and J. Robinson. 2001. The colonial origins of comparative development: An empirical investigation. *American Economic Review* 91(5): 1369–1401.

AeA (American Electronics Association). 2005a. *Losing the Competitive Advantage? The Challenge for Science and Technology in the United States.* Washington, DC: American Electronics Association.

AeA (American Electronics Association). 2005b. Like it or not, China and the U.S. are intricately linked. *AeA Competitiveness Series* (Washington, DC), Vol. 4 (November): 1–4.

Ahearne, A. G., J. G. Fernald, P. Loungani, and J. W. Schindler. 2003. China and emerging Asia: Comrades or competitors? *Seoul Journal of Economics* 16(2): 183–213.

Ahya, C., and M. Sheth. 2005. *India Infrastructure: Changing Gear.* New York: Morgan Stanley.

Ahya, C., and A. Xie. 2004. *India and China: A Special Economic Analysis.* Shanghai: Morgan Stanley Asia/Pacific (July).

Aidt, T. S. 2003. Economic analysis of corruption: A survey. *Economic Journal* 113(491): F632–F652.

Anand, K., C. S. Pandav, and L. M. Nath. 1999. Impact of HIV/AIDs on the national economy of India. *Health Policy* 47(3): 195–205.

Aron, J. 2000. Growth and institutions: A review of the evidence. *World Bank Research Observer* 15(1): 99–135.

Ash, R. 2002. Does the Chinese economy matter? In *China's Place in Global Geopolitics*, ed. K. E. Brodsgaard and B. Heurlin. London: Routledge Curzon.

Asia Today International (Sydney). 2003. Growth of the Chinese Economy. *Asia Today International* 21(March):

Bachman, S. L. 2006. Anxious America—Part I. *YaleGlobal* 9(March). http://yaleglobal.yale.edu./display.article?id=7100.

Balfour, F. 2006. Pfizer's long march through China's courts. *BusinessWeek Online*, June 21.

Balu, R. 2001. Strategic innovation: Hindustan Lever Ltd., *FastCompany*, no. 47 (June 2001). http://www.fastcompany.com/magazine/47/hindustan.html.

Beck, T., A. Demirguc-Kunt, and R. Levine. 2003. Law and finance: Why does legal origin matter? *Journal of Comparative Economics* 31(4): 653–675.

Bekier, M., R. Huang, and G. P. Wilson. 2005. How to fix China's banking system. *McKinsey Quarterly*, no. 1, 110–119.

Berg, A., and A. Krueger. 2003. Trade, growth and poverty: A selective survey. IMF Working Paper 03/30, International Monetary Fund, Washington, DC.

Bergmann, M., R. Mangaleswaran, and G. A. Mercer. 2004. Global sourcing in the auto industry. *McKinsey Quarterly Special Edition: China Today*, 43–51.

Bernstein, A. 2004. Special report: Shaking up trade theory. *BusinessWeek*, December 6, 116–120.

Beshouri, C. P., D. Farrell, and F. Umezawa. 2005. Attracting more offshoring to the Philippines. *McKinsey Quarterly*, no. 4: 13–16.

Bever, E. J., E. Stephenson, and D. W. Tanner. 2005. How Indian executives see the world. *McKinsey Quarterly 2005 Special Edition: Fulfilling India's Promise*, 34–41.

Bharadwaj, V. T., G. M. Swaroop, and I. Vittal. 2005. Winning the Indian consumer. *McKinsey Quarterly 2005 Special Edition: Fulfilling India's Promise*, 43–51.

Blinder, A. S. 2006. Offshoring: The next industrial revolution. *Foreign Affairs* 85(March/April): 113–128.

Bolt, P. J. 1996. Looking at the diaspora: The overseas Chinese and China's economic development 1978-1994. *Diaspora: A Journal of Transnational Studies* 5(3): 467–496.

Bona, A. 2004. *Debunking the Myths of Contact Center Outsourcing*, Gartner Report Note, July 22.

Boone, J. 2001. Intensity of competition and the incentive to innovate. *International Journal of Industrial Organization* 19: 705–726.

Booz Allen Hamilton and INSEAD. 2006. *Innovation: Is Global the Way Forward?* Fontainebleau: Booz Allen Hamilton and INSEAD.

Boycko, M., A. Shleifer, and R. W. Vishny. 1996. A theory of privatisation. *Economic Journal* 106(435): 309–319.

Bozon, I. J. H., S. Narayanswamy, and V. Tuli. 2005. Securing Asia's energy future. *McKinsey Quarterly Online*, April.

Bransten, J. 2004. Central Asia: China's mounting influence. *EurasiaNet*, November 24.

Bremner, B. 2005. Japan's carmakers find China's fast lane. *BusinessWeek Online*, December 21.

Bremner, B. 2006. EDS: Getting out front in outsourcing. *BusinessWeek Online*, June 26.

Brown, D. H., and A. McBean. 2005. *Challenges for China's Development: An Enterprise Perspective*. London and New York: Routledge.

Brown, J. S., and J. Hagel III. 2005. Innovation blowback: Disruptive management practices from Asia. *McKinsey Quarterly*, no. 1, 35–45.

Bryan, L. L., and M. Zanini. 2005. Strategy in an era of global giants. *McKinsey Quarterly*, no. 4, 47–59.

Buck, T., R. Minder, and T. Barber. 2005. Chinese shoe sales strain EU trade ties. *Financial Times*, June 9.

Buckley, P. J., and M. C. Casson. 1975. *The Future of the Multinational Enterprise*. London: Macmillan.

Buckley, P. J., J. Clegg, A. R. Cross, and H. Tan. 2005. China's inward foreign direct investment success: Southeast Asia in the shadow of the dragon. *Multinational Business Review* 13(1): 3–31.

Buderi, R., and G. T. Huang. 2006. *Guanxi, Microsoft, China and Bill Gate's Plan to Win the Road Ahead*. New York: Simon and Schuster.

BusinessWeek. 2002a. Greater China. *BusinessWeek*, December 9, 20–34.

BusinessWeek. 2003a. Asia tech. *BusinessWeek*, April 14, 52–56.

BusinessWeek. 2003b. Where free trade hurts. *BusinessWeek*, December 15, 22–26.

BusinessWeek. 2003c. Wasting away. *BusinessWeek*, June 2, 26–27.

BusinessWeek. 2003d. Game plan B. *BusinessWeek*, September 15, 22–23.

BusinessWeek. 2004a. The China price. *BusinessWeek*, December 6, 102–112.

BusinessWeek. 2004b. Shaking up trade theory. *BusinessWeek*, December 6, 116–120.

BusinessWeek. 2004c. China's power brands. *BusinessWeek Online*, November 8.

BusinessWeek. 2004d. Big Blue's bold step into China. *BusinessWeek Online*, December 20.

BusinessWeek. 2004e. The beer wars come to a head. *BusinessWeek Online*, May 24.

BusinessWeek. 2005a. How Cummins does it. *BusinessWeek*, August 22.

BusinessWeek. 2005b. Fakes! *BusinessWeek Online*, February 7.

BusinessWeek. 2005c. Dell: Time for a new model? *BusinessWeek*, April 11.

BusinessWeek. 2005d. There's no holding back China's textile trade. *BusinessWeek Online*, May 9.

BusinessWeek. 2005e. China and India—The challenge expert roundtable 8: What could go wrong? *BusinessWeek Online*, August 22.

BusinessWeek. 2005f. The state's long apron strings. *BusinessWeek Online*, August 22.

BusinessWeek. 2005g. China's wasteful ways. *BusinessWeek Online*, April 11.

BusinessWeek. 2005h. Not enough power to the people. *BusinessWeek Online*, May 23.

BusinessWeek. 2005i. Taking a page from Toyota's playbook. *BusinessWeek Online,* August 22.

BusinessWeek. 2005j. Dogfight over India. *BusinessWeek Online,* May 2.

BusinessWeek. 2005k. IKEA races to cash in on China's market. *BusinessWeek Online,* April 10.

BusinessWeek. 2005l. *BusinessWeek Online,* November 14.

BusinessWeek. 2005m. GM and VW: How not to succeed in China. *BusinessWeek,* May 9.

BusinessWeek. 2006a. Can Latin America challenge India? *BusinessWeek Online,* January 30.

BusinessWeek. 2006b. Big Blue shift. *BusinessWeek Online,* June 5.

BusinessWeek. 2006c. Motorola: "Made in India" phones coming. *BusinessWeek Online,* June 12. ·

BusinessWeek. 2006d. Hog heaven in Beijing. *BusinessWeek Online,* March 29.

BusinessWeek. 2006e. Apple follows its instincts out of India. *BusinessWeek Online,* June 5.

BusinessWeek. 2006f. Nokia connects. *BusinessWeek Online,* March 27.

BusinessWeek. 2006g. The Home Depot: One foot in China. *BusinessWeek Online,* May 1.

BusinessWeek. 2006h. "Made in Italy" keeps its cachet. *BusinessWeek Online,* April 10.

BusinessWeek. 2006i. China rolls up the welcome mat. *BusinessWeek Online,* June 16.

BusinessWeek. 2006j. Wal-Mart: Rapping on India's door. *BusinessWeek Online,* May 1.

Campbell, R. M., J. Hexter, and K. Yin. 2004. Getting sourcing right in China. *McKinsey Quarterly Special Edition: China Today,* 35–41.

Carpenter, G. S., and K. Nakamoto. 1989. Consumer preference formation and pioneering advantage. *Journal of Marketing Research* 26: 285–298.

Cavusgil, T. S. 1997. Measuring the potential of emerging markets: An indexing approach. *Business Horizons* 40(1): 87–91.

Cavusgil, T. S., P. N. Ghauri, and M. R. Agarwal. 2002. *Doing Business in Emerging Markets: Entry and Negotiation Strategies.* Thousand Oaks, CA: Sage Publications.

Chakrabarty, S. K., P. Gandhi, and N. Kaka. 2006. The untapped market for offshore services. *McKinsey Quarterly,* no. 2, 16–19.

Chandler, C. 2003. Coping with China. *Fortune,* January 20, 46–52.

Chang, G. 2001. *The Coming Collapse of China.* New York: Random House.

Chang, H-J. 2002. *Kicking Away the Ladder—Development Strategy in Historical Perspective.* London: Anthem Press.

Chang, H-J. 2005. Globalization, global standards and the future of East Asia. *Global Economic Review* 34(4): 363–378.

Chase-Dunn, C. 1975. The effects of international economic dependence on development and inequality: A cross-national study. *American Sociological Review* 40(6): 720–738.

Chat, T., N. Tracy, and Z. Wenhui. 1999. *China's Export Miracle: Origins, Results and Prospects.* New York: St. Martins Press.

Chen, K., and J. Dean. 2006. Low costs, plentiful talent make China a global magnet for R&D. *Wall Street Journal*, March 14.

Chen, Y., and J. Penhirin. 2004. Marketing to China's consumers. *McKinsey Quarterly Special Edition: China Today*, 63–73.

Clark, J. 2006. Stitching labor change in Italy. *Wall Street Journal*, April 17.

Cohen, R. 1997. *Global Diasporas: An Introduction.* London: UCL Press.

Commonwealth of Australia. 2001. *India: New Economy Old Economy.* Economic Analytical Unit, Department of Foreign Affairs and Trade, Canberra.

Coonan, C. 2005. Chinese farmers riot over crop poisoning. *The Times* (UK), April 12.

Daga, V., and N. F. Kaka. 2006. Taking offshoring beyond labor cost savings. *McKinsey Quarterly Web Exclusive*, May.

Damon, F-Y. 2003. Corruption in mainland China today: Data and law in a dubious battle. In *Fighting Corruption in Asia: Causes, Effects and Remedies*, ed. J. Kidd and F. J. Richter. Hackensack, NJ: World Scientific, 175–202.

Dapice, D. 2006. Unpopular globalization: Why so many are opposed. *Yale-Global*, February 2.

Dauderstadt, M., and J. Stetten. 2005. China and globalization. *Intereconomics* 40(4): 226–234.

Dearden, S. 2003. The challenge to corruption and the international business environment. In *Corruption and Governance in Asia*, ed. J. B. Kidd and F. J. Richter. Basingstoke, U.K.: Palgrave Macmillan.

Deloitte Research. 2003. *The World's Factory: China Enters the 21st Century.* New York: Deloitte Research Economic Study, August.

Deloitte Research. 2004a. *Changing China: Will China's Technology Standards Reshape Your Industry?* New York: Deloitte Research, July.

Deloitte Research. 2004b. *China at a Crossroads: Seven Risks of Doing Business.* New York: Deloitte Research Economic Study, September.

Deng, Y., and T. G. Moore. 2004. China views globalization: Toward a new great-power politics? *Washington Quarterly* 27(3): 117–136.

Desvaux, G., and A. J. Ramsay. 2006. Shaping China's home-improvement market: An interview with B&Q's CEO for Asia. *McKinsey Quarterly 2006 Special Edition: Serving the New Chinese Consumer*, 82–91.

Dietz, M. C., S-T. Lin, and L. Yang. 2005. Protecting intellectual property in China. *McKinsey Quarterly*, no. 3, 6–8.

Di Lodovico, A. M., W. W. Lewis, V. Palmade, and S. Sankhe. 2001. India—From emerging to surging. *McKinsey Quarterly*, no. 4, 28–50.

DiMaggio, P. 1994. Culture and economy. In *The Handbook of Economic Sociology*, ed. N. Smelster and R. Swedberg. Princeton, NJ: Princeton University Press, 27–57.

Doh, J. P., P. Rodriguez, K. Uhlenbruck, J. Collins, and L. Eden. 2003. Coping with corruption in foreign markets. *Academy of Management Executive* 17(3): 114–127.

Dunning, J. H. 1992. *Multinational Enterprises and the Global Economy*. Wokingham, U.K.: Addison Wesley.

Dunning, J. H., and R. Narula. 1996. The investment development path revisited: Some emerging issues. In *Foreign Direct Investment and Governments*, ed. J. H. Dunning and R. Narula. London: Routledge, 1–41.

Easterly, W., and R. Levine. 2003. Tropics, germs and crops: How endowments influence economic development. *Journal of Monetary Economics* 50(1): 3–39.

Economist. 2003a. Tilting at dragons: China and the world economy. *Economist*, October 25, 69–70.

Economist. 2003b. Is the wakening giant a monster? Special report: China's economy. *Economist*, February 15, 63–65.

Economist. 2003c. Special report. Information technology: The new geography of the IT industry. *Economist*, July 19, 47–49.

Economist. 2003d. January 25, 65.

Economist. 2004a. The dragon and the eagle: A survey of the world economy. *Economist*, October 2.

Economist. 2004b. A new scramble. *Economist*, November 25.

Economist. 2004c. China and global branding—The case of Haier. *Economist*, March 20.

Economist. 2005a. The tiger in front. *Economist*, March 5.

Economist. 2005b. China and the world economy. *Economist*, July 30, 65–67.

Economist. 2005c. The cauldron boils. *Economist*, September 29.

Economist. 2005d. The myth of China Inc. *Economist*, September 1.

Economist. 2005e. What's to stop India and China? *Economist*, October 27.

Economist. 2005f. A marginalized market. *Economist*, February 24.

Economist. 2005g. The dragon tucks in. *Economist*, June 30.

Economist. 2005h. Special report. China and the world economy: From T-shirts to T-bonds. *Economist*, July 30, 65–67.

Economist. 2005i. Putting up the barricades. *Economist*, April 25.

Economist. 2006a. Emerging markets: Climbing back. *Economist*, January 21, 69–70.

Economist. 2006b. Outsourcing to China, watch out India. *Economist*, May 4.

Economist. 2006c. Can India's nationalised airlines be revived? *Economist*, May 18.

Economist. 2006d. Chinese science: Faking. *Economist*, May 18.

Economist. 2006e. Now for the hard part: A survey of business in India. *Economist*, June 3.

Economist. 2006f. Coming out. *Economist*, March 23.

Economist. 2006g. How to make China even richer. *Economist*, March 23.

Economist. 2006h. The new titans. *Economist*, September 14.

Einhorn, J. 2005. Millions of Indians await benefits of globalization. *Yale-Global*, February 25.

Elliot, L. 2005. Bra wars: Europe strikes back. *Guardian*, August 26.

Enderwick, P. 2005. *Globalization and Labor*. New York: Chelsea House Publishers.

Engerman, S. L., and K. L. Sokoloff. 1997. Factor endowments, institutions, and differential paths of growth among new world economies: A view from economic historians of the United States. In *How Latin America Fell Behind*, ed. S. Haber. Stanford, CA: Stanford University Press, 260–304.

Enright, M. J., E. E. Scott, and K. Chang. 2005. *Regional Powerhouse: The Greater Pearl River Delta and the Rise of China*. New York: John Wiley.

Ethiraj, S., P. Kale, M. S. Krishnan, and J. V. Singh. 2004. Determinants of price in custom software: A Hedonic analysis of offshore development projects. Unpublished paper, Wharton Business School.

Everest Consultants. 2006. *2006 Global Sourcing Market Update*. Beaverton, OR: Everest Consultants.

Fan, G. 2003. The dual transformation of China: Past 20 years and 50 years ahead. In *Emerging Market Economies. Globalization and Development*, ed. G. Kolodko. Aldershot: Ashgate, 169–185.

Farrell, D., P. Gao, and G. R. Orr. 2004. Making foreign investment work for China. *McKinsey Quarterly 2004 Special Edition: China Today*, 24–33.

Farrell, D., U. A. Gersch, and E. Stephenson. 2006. The value of China's emerging middle class. *McKinsey Quarterly 2006 Special Edition: Serving the New Chinese Consumer*, 60–69.

Farrell, D., and A. J. Grant. 2005. China's looming talent shortage. *McKinsey Quarterly*, no. 4, 70–79.

Farrell, D., N. Kaka, and S. Sturze. 2005. Ensuring India's offshore future. *McKinsey Quarterly 2005 Special Edition: Fulfilling India's Promise*, 75–83.

Farrell, D., and A. M. Key. 2005. India's lagging financial system. *McKinsey Quarterly*, no. 2, 11–13.

Farrell, D., M. A. Laboissiere, and J. Rosenfeld. 2005. Sizing the emerging global labor market. *McKinsey Quarterly*, no. 3, 93–103.

Farrell, D., and S. Lund. 2005. Reforming India's financial system. *McKinsey Quarterly 2005 Special Edition: Fulfilling India's Promise*, 103–111.

Farrell, D., S. Lund, and F. Morin. 2006. How financial-system reform could benefit China. *McKinsey Quarterly 2006 Special Edition: Serving the New Chinese Consumer*, 92–105.

Farrell, D., A. Puron, and J. K. Remes. 2005. Beyond cheap labor: Lessons for developing economies. *McKinsey Quarterly*, no. 1, 99–109.

Filippo, G. D., J. Hou, and C. Ip. 2005. Can China compete in IT services? *McKinsey Quarterly*, no. 1, 10–11.

Financial Times. 2005. China now No. 2 market. June 1.

Fioravante, J. 2006. Lenovo caught up in U.S. security panic. *Asia Times Online*, April 5.

Florida, R. 2005. *The Flight of the Creative Class: The New Global Competition for Talent*. New York: Harper Collins.

Foreign Policy and the Fund for Peace. 2005. The failed states index. *Foreign Policy* 84(July–August).

Fortune. 2005. Outsourcer plays Cupid. *Fortune*, May 30, 77.

Fowler, G. A., and J. Qin. 2006. China curbs magazines from foreign publishers. *Wall Street Journal*, April 10.

French, H. W. 2006. Chinese turn to civic power as a new tool. *New York Times*, April 11.

Friedmann, J. 1995. Where we stand: A decade of world city research. In *World Cities in a World-System*, ed. P. L. Knox and P. J. Taylor. Cambridge, UK: Cambridge University Press, 21–47.

Gallagher, M. E. 2005. *Contagious Capitalism: Globalization and the Politics of Labor in China*. Princeton, NJ: Princeton University Press.

Garnaut, R., and L. Song, eds. 2004. *China's Third Economic Transformation: The Rise of the Private Economy*. London: Routledge Curzon.

Garten, J. E. 2005. Can China be contained? *YaleGlobal*, May 19.

Gilboy, G. J. 2004. The myth behind China's miracle. *Foreign Affairs* 83 (July/August): 33–44.

GlobalEdge. 2005. *Market Potential Indicators for Emerging Markets—2005.* Available at http://globaledge.msu.edu/ibrd/marketpot.asp

Goldman Sachs. 2003. *The Sweet and Sour Effects of China in Latin America.* New York: Goldman Sachs, November 7.

Gomory, R. E., and W. J. Baumol. 2000. *Global Trade and Conflicting National Interests*. Cambridge, MA: MIT Press.

Goodman, D. S. G., and G. Segal. 1997. *China Rising: Nationalism and Interdependence*. London: Routledge.

Goolsby, K. 2006. *Trend Report: New Strategies for Outsourced R&D*. Mumbai, India: Wipro Technologies and Outsourcing Center.

Granovetter, M. 1985. Economic action and social structure: The problem of embeddedness. *American Journal of Sociology* 91(3): 481–510.

Gray, C. W., and D. Kaufmann. 1998. Corruption and development. *Finance and Development* (March): 7–10.

Greenspan, A. 2004. The great reverse part III. *YaleGlobal*, September 8.

Gupta, S., H. Davoodi, and R. Alonso-Terme. 2002. Does corruption affect income inequality and poverty? *Economics of Governance* 3(1): 23–45.

Gwartney, J., R. Lawson, C. Edwards, W. Park, V. de Rugy, and S. Wagh. 2002. *Economic Freedom of the World: 2002 Annual Report*. Vancouver: The Fraser Institute.

Haley, U. C. V. 2003. Assessing and controlling business risks in China. *Journal of International Management* 9: 237–252.

Hausmann, R., and D. Rodrik. 2003. Economic development as self-discovery. *Journal of Development Economics* 42(2): 603–633.

Holz, C. A. 2003. *China's Industrial State-Owned Enterprises: Between Profitability and Bankruptcy*. New Jersey: World Scientific.

Hoover, W. E. Jr. 2006. Making China your second home market: An interview with the CEO of Danfoss. *McKinsey Quarterly*, no. 1, 84–93.

Horta, L., and I. Storey. 2006. China's Portuguese connection. *YaleGlobal*, June 22.

Huang, JR-T., C-C. Kuo, and A-P. Kao. 2003. The inequality of regional economic development in China between 1991 and 2001. *Journal of Chinese Economic and Business Studies* 1(3): 273–285.

Huang, Y., and T. Khanna. 2003. Can India overtake China? *Foreign Policy* (July–August): 73–81.

Human Security Centre. 2005. *Human Security Report 2005: War and Peace in the 21st Century*. New York: Oxford University Press.

Imbs, J., and R. Wacziarg. 2003. Stages of diversification. *American Economic Review* 93(1): 63–86.

IMF (International Monetary Fund). 2003. *World Economic Outlook: Growth and Institutions*. Washington, DC: International Monetary Fund.

IMF (International Monetary Fund). 2005. *World Economic Outlook: Globalization and External Imbalances*. Washington, DC: International Monetary Fund.

Independent. 2006. March 8.

International Intellectual Property Alliance. 2004. *Special 301 Report: People's Republic of China*, Washington, DC: IIPA.

Jain, K. P., N. A. S. Manson, and S. Sankhe. 2005. The right passage to India. *McKinsey Quarterly Web Exclusive*, February.

Jamison, K. R. 1999. *Night Falls Fast: Understanding Suicide*. New York: Vintage Books.

Jaruzelski, B., K. Dehoff, and R. Bordia. 2005. Money isn't everything: The Booz Allen Hamilton global innovation 1000. *strategy+business*, no. 41, Special Report.

Jenkins, R., and E. D. Peters. 2006. The impact of China on Latin America and the Caribbean. Unpublished paper, University of East Anglia, Norwich, U.K., April.

Johansen, J., and J-E. Vahlne. 1977. The internationalization process of the firm: A model of knowledge development and increasing foreign market commitments. *Journal of International Business Studies* 8: 23–32.

Joshi, V. 1998. India's economic reforms: Progress, problems, prospects. *Oxford Development Studies* 26(3): 333–350.

Kanbur, R., and X. Zhang. 1999. Which regional inequality? The evolution of rural-urban and inland-coastal inequality in China from 1983 to 1995. *Journal of Comparative Economics* 27: 686–701.

Kapur, D., and R. Webber. 2000. Governance-related conditionalities of the international financial institutions. G-24 Discussion Paper Series No. 6, UNCTAD (United Nations Conference on Trade and Development), Geneva, Switzerland.

Keller, E., and W. Zhou. 2003. *From Middle Kingdom to Global Market: Expansion Strategies and Success Factors for China's Emerging Multinationals*. Shanghai: Roland Berger Strategy Consultants.

Kenen, P., J. Shafer, N. Wicks, and C. Wyplosz. 2004. *International Economic and Financial Cooperation: New Issues, New Actors, New Responses*. Geneva: International Centre for Monetary and Banking Studies, London: Centre for Economic Policy Research.

Khanna, T. 2004. India's entrepreneurial advantage. *McKinsey Quarterly 2004 Special Edition: China Today,* 111–114.

Kim, W. C., and R. Mauborgne. 2005. *Blue Ocean Strategy: How to Create Uncontested Market Space and Make Competition Irrelevant.* Boston, MA: Harvard Business School Press.

Kissinger, H. A. 2006. A win-win partnership. *Khaleej Times,* March 17.

Kletzer, L. 2001. *Job Loss from Imports: Measuring the Costs.* Washington, DC: Institute for International Economics.

Kose, M. A., E. S. Prasad, and M. E. Terrones. 2004. Taking the plunge without getting hurt. *Finance and Development* (December): 44–47.

Kostova, T., and K. Roth. 2002. Adoption of an organizational practice by subsidiaries of multinational corporations: Institutional and relational effects. *Academy of Management Journal* 45(1): 215–233.

Kostova, T., and S. Zaheer. 1999. Organizational legitimacy under conditions of complexity: The case of the multinational enterprise. *Academy of Management Review* 24(1): 64–81.

Kripalani, M. 2003. India: Manufacturers in shackles. *BusinessWeek,* October 20, 26.

Kumar, N. 2002. *Towards an Asian Economic Community: The Relevance of India.* Research and information system for non-aligned and other developing countries. RIS Discussion Paper 34, New Delhi.

Kurian, N. J. 2000. Widening regional disparities in India—Some indicators. *Economic and Political Weekly,* February 12, 538–550.

Kwan, C. H. 2004. *The Rise of China: Challenges and Opportunities for Japan and the World.* Tokyo: Nomura Institute of Capital Markets Research, November.

Lall, S. 2004. Reinventing industrial strategy: The role of government policy in building industrial competitiveness. G-24 Discussion Paper Series No. 28, UNCTAD (United Nations Conference on Trade and Development), Geneva, Switzerland.

Lall, S., and M. Albaladejo. 2004. China's competitive performance: A threat to East Asian manufactured exports? *World Development* 32(9): 1441–1466.

Lane, K., J., Penhirin, and J. R. Woetzel. 2004. China tackles urban planning. *McKinsey Quarterly 2004 Special Edition,* 6–9.

La Porta, R., F. Lopez-de-Silanes, A. Shleifer, and R. W. Vishny. 1999. The quality of government. *Journal of Law, Economics and Organization* 15(1): 222–279.

Lardy, N. R. 1998. *China's Unfinished Economic Revolution.* Washington, DC: Brookings Institution.

Lardy, N. R. 2002. *Integrating China into the Global Economy.* Washington, DC: Brookings Institution.

Laursen, T., and S. Mahajan. 2005. Volatility, income distribution, and poverty. In *Managing Economic Volatility and Crises: A Practitioners Guide,* ed. J. Aizenman and B. Pinto. Cambridge, UK: Cambridge University Press.

Lee, J. 2000. Changes in the source of China's regional inequality. *China Economic Review* 11(3): 232–245.

Lehmann, J-P. 2005. China-IBM computer deal marks a new era. *YaleGlobal*, April 1.

Levy, S. 2006. Shanghai start ups. *Newsweek*, June 26. http://www.msnbc.msn.com/id/13393358/site/newsweek/print/1/displaymode/1098.

Lieberman, M. B., and D. B. Montgomery. 1988. First-mover advantages. *Strategic Management Journal* 9(summer): 41–58.

Lim, L. 2005. China shows the way in a quota-free market. *YaleGlobal*, February 21.

Lingle, C. 2000. China's future still uncertain. *Taipei Times*, 7, December 31.

Lu, M., and E. Wang. 2002. Forging ahead and falling behind: Changing regional inequalities in post-reform China. *Growth and Change* 33(1): 42–71.

Lui, X., D. Parker, K. Vaughan, and Y. Wei. 2001. The impact of foreign direct investment on labor productivity in the Chinese electronics industry. *International Business Review* 10(4): 421–439.

Luo, Y. 2001. *China's Service Sector*. Copenhagen: Copenhagen Business School Press.

Luo, Y. 2002. *Multinational Enterprises in Emerging Markets*. Copenhagen: Copenhagen Business School Press.

Luo, Y., and M. W. Peng. 1998. First mover advantages in investing in transitional economies. *Thunderbird International Business Review* 40(2): 141–163.

Luo, Y., and J. J. Tan. 1997. How much does industry structure impact foreign direct investment in China? *International Business Review* 6(4): 337–359.

Luthra, S., R. Mangaleswaran, and A. Padhi. 2005. When to make India a manufacturing base. *McKinsey Quarterly 2005 Special Edition: Fulfilling India's Promise*, 63–73.

Maddison, A. 2001. *The World Economy: A Millennial Perspective*. Paris: Development Centre Studies OECD (Organization for Economic Cooperation and Development).

Mahbubani, K. 2005. A gaping silence. *Newsweek International Issues* 2005. http://www.msnbc.msn.com/id/6728154/site/newsweek.

Mandel, M. J. 2004. Does it matter if China catches up to the U.S.? *BusinessWeek*, December 6, 122–124.

Martin, P., and C. A. Rogers. 2000. Long-term growth and short-term economic instability *European Economic Review* 44(2): 359–381.

Mauro, P. 1995. Corruption and growth. *Quarterly Journal of Economics* 110(3): 681–712.

McGregor, R. 2004. Wal-Mart gives in to China's Union Federation. *Financial Times*, November 23.

Meckler, L., and D. Machalaba. 2006. Port deal: Not a foreign idea. *Wall Street Journal*, March 10.

Megginson, W. L., and J. M. Netter. 2001. From state to market: A survey of empirical studies on privatization. *Journal of Economic Literature* 39(2): 321–389.

MGI (McKinsey Global Institute). 2003a. *New Horizons: Multinational Company Investment in Developing Countries.* New York: McKinsey Global Institute, October.

MGI (McKinsey Global Institute). 2003b. *Offshoring: Is It a Win-Win Game?* San Francisco, CA: McKinsey Global Institute, August.

MGI (McKinsey Global Institute). 2004. *Can Germany Win from Offshoring?* San Francisco, CA: McKinsey Global Institute, July.

MGI (McKinsey Global Institute). 2005. *The Emerging Global Labor Market.* San Francisco, CA: McKinsey Global Institute, June.

Mitra, P. 2005. India diplomacy energized by search for oil. *YaleGlobal,* March 14.

Mo, P. H. 2001. Corruption and economic growth. *Journal of Comparative Economics* 29(1): 66–79.

Moffett, M., and G. Samor. 2005. Brazil regrets its China affair. *Wall Street Journal,* October 12.

Moisés, N. 2000. Washington consensus or confusion? *Foreign Policy* 118(spring): 86–103.

Montiel, P. J. 2002. *Macroeconomics in Emerging Markets.* Cambridge: Cambridge University Press.

Mooney, P. 2004. "Bad press" causing headaches for Beijing. *YaleGlobal,* July 22.

Nasscom/McKinsey. 2005. *Extending India's Leadership in the Global IT and BPO Industries.* Mumbai, India: Nasscom/McKinsey, December.

National Intelligence Council. 2004. *Mapping the Global Future.* Report of the National Intelligence Council's 2020 Project, Washington, DC: National Intelligence Council, December.

Naughton, K. 2006. Outsourcing: Silicon Valley East. *Newsweek,* March 6.

Nolan, P. 2001. *China and the Global Business Revolution.* New York: Palgrave.

North, D. C. 1990. *Institutions, Institutional Change and Economic Performance.* New York: Cambridge University Press.

Norton, R., and J. Miskel. 1997. Spotting trouble: Identifying faltering and failing states. *Naval War College Review* 50(2): 79–91.

OECD (Organization for Economic Cooperation and Development). 2002. *China in the World Economy: The Domestic Policy Challenges.* Paris: OECD.

Orr, G. R. 2004. What executives are asking about China. *McKinsey Quarterly 2004 Special Edition: China Today,* 17–23.

Padhi, A., G. Pauwels, and C. Taylor. 2004. Freeing India's textile industry. *McKinsey Quarterly 2004 Special Edition,* 9–11.

Pallage, S., and M. Robe. 2003. On the welfare costs of economic fluctuations in developing countries. *International Economic Review* 44(May): 677–698.

Palmier, L. 1985. *The Control of Bureaucratic Corruption: Case Studies in Asia.* New Delhi: Allied.

Palmier, L. 2003. Corruption in context. In *Fighting Corruption in Asia: Causes, Effects and Remedies*, ed. J. Kidd and F. J. Richter. Hackensack, NJ: World Scientific, 73–90.

Panagariya, A. 2001. The Indian diaspora in the United States. *Economic Times*, May 23.

Park, J. D. 1997. *China in the 21st Century*. Seoul: Korea Economic Daily Publishing.

Patel, B. 2005. National employment guarantee scheme—Remedy worse than disease? *The Hindu Business Line*, October 4.

Phelps, E. S. 2004. Effects of China's recent development in the rest of the world with special attention to Latin America. *Journal of Policy Modelling* 26: 903–910.

Pitsilis, E. V., J. R. Woetzel, and J. Wong. 2004. Checking China's vital signs. *McKinsey Quarterly 2004 Special Edition: China Today*, 7–15.

Prahalad, C. K. 2005. *The Fortune at the Bottom of the Pyramid*. Upper Saddle River, NJ: Wharton School/Pearson Education.

Prestowitz, C. 2004. The great reverse—Part I. *YaleGlobal*, September 2.

Prestowitz, C. 2005a. *Three Billion New Capitalists: The Great Shift of Wealth and Power to the East*. New York: Basic Books.

Prestowitz, C. 2005b. China-India entente shifts global balance. *YaleGlobal*, April 15.

PricewaterhouseCoopers. 2001. *The Opacity Index*. Paris: Pricewaterhouse-Coopers, January.

PricewaterhouseCoopers. 2006. *9th Annual Global CEO Survey. Globalization and Complexity: Inevitable Forces in a Changing Economy*. New York: PricewaterhouseCoopers.

Quint, M., and D. Shorten. 2005. The China syndrome. Resilience report, Booz Allen and Hamilton. *strategy+business*, issue 38, Spring: 1–6.

Rajan, R. G. 2005. Making India a global hub. *McKinsey Quarterly 2005 Special Edition: Fulfilling India's Promise*, 112–121.

Ramey, G., and V. Ramey. 1995. Cross-country evidence on the link between volatility and growth. *American Economic Review* 85(5): 1138–1151.

Ramo, J. C. 2004. *The Beijing Consensus*. London: Foreign Policy Centre, May.

Rautava, J. 2005. Is India emerging as a global economic powerhouse equal to China? Bank of Finland Institute for Economies in Transition Paper No 2., Helsinki.

Rawski, T. G. 2001. What's happening to China's GDP statistics? Unpublished paper, Department of Economics, University of Pittsburgh, Pittsburgh, PA, September.

Reddy, P. 2000. *Globalization of Corporate R&D: Implications for Innovation Systems in Host Countries*. London and New York: Routledge.

Rivoli, P. 2005. Tangled threads of protectionism—Part I. *YaleGlobal*, May 3.

Roach, S. 2004. The challenge of China and India. *Financial Times*, August 31.

Roach, S. 2006. Global investor: The hollowing ring of Davos. *Newsweek International*, February 6.

Robert Huggins Associates. 2005. *World Knowledge Competitiveness Index 2005*. Sheffield, England: Robert Huggins Associates.

Rodrik, D. 2004. Industrial policy for the twenty-first century. Unpublished paper, Harvard University, Boston, MA, September.

Rodrik, D. 2006. What's so special about China's exports? Unpublished paper, Harvard University, Boston, MA, January.

Rodrik, D., A. Subramanian, and F. Trebbi. 2004. Institutions rule: The primacy of institutions over geography and integration in economic development. *Journal of Economic Growth* 9(2): 131–165.

Rosen, D. H. 2003a. Low-tech bed, high-tech dreams. *China Economic Quarterly* (4th quarter): 20–40.

Rosen, D. H. 2003b. How China is eating Mexico's lunch. *International Economy* (spring): 22–25.

Rowley, I. 2006. Japan offers China a cold one. *BusinessWeek Online*, May 24.

Sabatier, P. 2006. No globalization, please—We are French. *YaleGlobal*, March 28.

Schramm, M., and M. Taube. 2003. Guanxi and corruption in PR China. In *Fighting Corruption in Asia: Causes, Effects and Remedies*, ed. J. Kidd and F. J. Richter. Hackensack, NJ: World Scientific, 271–296.

Scott, W. R. 1995. *Institutions and Organizations*. Thousand Oaks, CA: Sage.

Shafaeddin, S. M. 2004. Is China's accession to WTO threatening exports of developing countries? *China Economic Review* 15: 109–144.

Shaoguang, W., and H. Angang, eds. 1999. *The Political Economy of Uneven Development: The Case of China*. Armonk, NY: M. E. Sharpe.

Shenkar, O. 2005. *The Chinese Century: The Rising Chinese Economy and Its Impact on the Global Economy, the Balance of Power and Your Job*. Upper Saddle River, NJ: Wharton School Publishing.

Sheshabalya, A. 2005. *Rising Elephant: The Growing Clash with India over White-Collar Jobs and Its Challenge to America and the World*. Monroe, ME: Common Courage Press.

Singh, L. 2006. *Innovations, High-Tech Trade and Industrial Development: Theory, Evidence and Policy*. United Nations University UNU –WIDER Research Paper No 2006/27.

Sinha, J. 2005a. Checking India's vital signs. *McKinsey Quarterly 2005 Special Edition: Fulfilling India's Promise*, 16–25.

Sinha, J. 2005b. Global champions from emerging markets. *McKinsey Quarterly*, no. 2, 27–35.

Sinha, Suveen K. 2006. The global small car hub. *Business Standard New Dehli*. Rediff.com, January 13.

Smyth, R., O. K. Tam, M. Warner, and C. J. Zhu. 2005. *China's Business Reforms: Institutional Challenges in a Globalized Economy*. London: Routledge Curzon.

Srivastava, S., and R. Sen. 2004. Competing for global FDI: Opportunities and challenges for the Indian economy. *South East Asia Economic Journal* 5(2): 233–260.

Steinfeld, E. S. 2004. China's shallow integration: Networked production and the new challenges for late industrialization. *World Development* 32(11): 1971–1987.

Stewart, H. 2006. Is this the end of globalization? *Guardian*, March 10.

Sull, D. N. 2005. *Made in China: What Western Managers Can Learn from Trailblazing Chinese Entrepreneurs*. Boston, MA: Harvard Business School Press.

Sutter, R. 1999. Introduction and key findings. In *China's Future: Implications for U.S. Interests*, ed. Central Intelligence Agency. Washington, DC: Central Intelligence Agency, September.

Szczesny, J. 2005. GM to increase purchases from Asian parts suppliers. *Agence France-Presse*, August 16.

Tamamoto, M. 2006. Japanese discovery of democracy. *Japan Institute of International Affairs*, Tokyo, May 10.

Tanzi, V. 1998. Corruption around the world: Causes, consequences, scope and cures. *IMF Staff Papers* 45(4): 559–594.

Tetrault, J., M. Taoufiki, and A. O. Tazi-Riffi. 2005. Morocco's offshoring advantage. *McKinsey Quarterly*, no 4: 10–13.

Thery, E. 1901. *The Yellow Peril*. Paris: Felix Juven.

Time. 2005. Why eBay must win in China. *Time*, Global Business section, September 27–30.

Transparency International. 2005. *Corruption Perceptions Index 2005*. Berlin: Transparency International.

Twining, D. 2005. China's rise threatens to divide Asia, not unite it. *Financial Times*, August 22.

UNCTAD (United Nations Conference on Trade and Development). 2004. *Prospects for Foreign Direct Investment and the Strategies of Transnational Corporation 2004–2007*. Geneva and New York: United Nations.

UNCTAD (United Nations Conference on Trade and Development). 2005. *World Investment Report 2005: Transnational Corporations and the Internationalization of R&D*. Geneva and New York: United Nations.

UNDP (United Nations Development Program). 2005. *2005 China Human Development Report: Development with Equity*. Beijing: United Nations Development Program.

Van Den Bulcke, D., H. Zhang, and X. Li. 1999. Interactions between the business environment and corporate strategic positioning of firms in the pharmaceutical industry: A study of the entry and expansion path of MNEs in China. *Management International Review* 39(4): 353–377.

Vickers, J., and G. Yarrow. 1991. Economic perspectives on privatization. *Journal of Economic Perspectives* 5(2): 111–132.

Von Keller, E., and W. Zhou. 2003. *From Middle Kingdom to Global Market: Expansion Strategies and Success Factors for China's Emerging Multinationals*. Shanghai: Roland Berger Consultants.

Von Morgenstern, I. B. 2006. How foreign companies can compete in China's high-tech market. *McKinsey Quarterly Online*, January.

Walcott, S. 2003. *Chinese Science and Technology Industrial Parks*. Aldershot: Ashgate.

Watts, J. 2006. China vows to create a "new socialist countryside" for millions of farmers. *Guardian*, UK, February 22.

Watts, J. 2006. *Guardian*, UK, November 4.

Weber, A. 2005. Managing the reality of offshore assembly. *Assembly Magazine*, March 1.

Whyte, M. K. 2000. Chinese social trends: Stability or chaos. In *Is China Unstable?* ed. D. Shambaugh. Armonk, NY: M. E. Sharpe.

Williamson, J. 2000. What should the World Bank think about the Washington consensus? *World Bank Research Observer* 15(2): 251–264.

Wilson, D., and R. Purushothaman. 2003. Dreaming with BRICs: The path to 2050. Goldman Sachs Global Economics Paper No. 99, Goldman Sachs, New York.

Wilson, D., R. Purushothaman, and T. Fiotakis. 2004. The BRICs and global markets: Crude, cars and capital. Goldman Sachs Global Economics Paper No. 118, Goldman Sachs, New York.

Woetzel, J. R. 2004a. A guide to doing business in China. *McKinsey Quarterly 2004 Special Edition: What Global Executives Think*, 37–45.

Woetzel, J. R. 2004b. China: The best of all possible models. *McKinsey Quarterly 2004 Special Edition: China Today*, 114–117.

Wolf, C. Jr., K. C. Yeh, B. Zycher, N. Eberstandt, and S-H. Lee. 2003. *Fault Lines in China's Economic Terrain*. Santa Monica, CA: Rand.

World Bank. 1997a. *China 2020: Development Challenges in the New Century*. Washington, DC: IBRD/World Bank, September.

World Bank. 1997b. *Helping Countries Combat Corruption: The Role of the World Bank*. Washington, DC: World Bank.

World Bank. 2002. *World Development Report 2002: Building Institutions for Markets*. Washington, DC: World Bank.

World Bank. 2004. *Doing Business in 2004: Understanding Regulation*. Washington, DC: World Bank.

World Bank. 2005. *International Migration, Remittances and the Brain Drain*. Washington, DC: Development Research Group, World Bank.

Wu, F. 2005. *Corporate China Goes Global*. Unpublished paper, National University of Singapore, September.

Wu, F., and P. K. Keong. 2003. Foreign direct investment to China and Southeast Asia: Has ASEAN been losing out? *Journal of Asian Business* 19(1): 89–105.

Wu, H. X. 2001. China's comparative labor productivity performance in manufacturing 1952-1997. *China Economic Review* 12: 162–189.

Xue, B., and P. Enderwick. 2005. Economic transition and management skills: The case of China. In *Business and Management Education in China: Transition, Pedagogy and Training*, ed. A. Ilon and J. McIntrye. London: World Scientific Books, 21–46.

Yahuda, M. 2002. China and regional cooperation. In *China's Place in Global Geopolitics*, ed. K. E. Brodsgaard and B. Heurlin. London: Routledge Curzon, 102–113.

Yan, Y. 1996. The culture of Guanxi in a North China village. *China Journal* 35: 1–25.

Yao, S. 1997. Industrialization and spatial income inequality in rural China, 1986–92. *Economics of Transition* 5(1): 97–112.

Young, D., and A. Riera. 2006. Seize golden opportunity of rapid globalization. *Baltimore Sun*, March 3.

Yu, V. 2005. Institute fears unrest as wealth gap widens. *Bangkok Post*, August 23.

Zaheer, S. 1995. Overcoming the liability of foreignness. *Academy of Management Journal* 38(2): 341–363.

Zakaria, F. 2005. Does the future belong to China? *Newsweek*, May 9.

Zakaria, F. 2006a. India rising. *Newsweek*, March 6.

Zakaria, F. 2006b. How long will America lead the world? *Newsweek*, June 26.

Zhang, Z., A. Liu, and S. Yao. 2001. Convergence of China's regional incomes: 1952–1997. *China Economic Review* 12(2–3): 243–258.

Zhao, S. 2005. Changing structure of Chinese enterprises and human resource management practices in China. In *China's Business Reforms: Institutional Challenges in a Global Economy*, ed. R. Smyth, O. K. Tam, M. Warner, and C. Zhu. London: Routledge Curzon.

Zhou, Y., and S. Lall. 2005. The impact of China's FDI surge on FDI in South-East Asia: Panel data analysis for 1986–2001. *Transnational Corporations* 14(1): 41–65.

Index